# POTTERY AND SOCIAL LIFE IN MEDIEVAL ENGLAND

## TOWARDS A RELATIONAL APPROACH

*Ben Jervis*

OXBOW | books
Oxford & Philadelphia

First published in 2014. Reprinted as a paperback in the United Kingdom in 2023 by
OXBOW BOOKS
The Old Music Hall, 106-108 Cowley Road, Oxford, OX4 1JE

and in the United States by
OXBOW BOOKS
1950 Lawrence Road, Havertown, PA 19083

Paperback Edition ISBN 979-8-88857-058-6
Digital Edition: ISBN 978-1-78297-660-8

A CIP record for this book is available from the British Library

Library of Congress Cataloging-in-Publication Data

Jervis, Ben.
  Pottery and social life in medieval England : towards a relational approach / Ben Jervis.
     pages cm
  Includes bibliographical references.
  ISBN 978-1-78297-659-2
  1.  Pottery, Medieval--England--Social aspects. 2.  Archaeology, Medieval--England. 3.  Material culture--England--History--To 1500. 4.  England--Antiquities.  I. Title.
  DA175.J47 2014
  942.03--dc23
                                    2014019084

Printed in the United Kingdom by CMP Digital Print Solutions

For a complete list of Oxbow titles, please contact:

UNITED KINGDOM
Oxbow Books
Telephone (0)1226 734350
Email: oxbow@oxbowbooks.com
www.oxbowbooks.com

UNITED STATES OF AMERICA
Oxbow Books
Telephone (610) 853-9131, Fax (610) 853-9146
Email: queries@casemateacademic.com
www.casemateacademic.com/oxbow

Oxbow Books is part of the Casemate Group

*Front cover:* Saintonge Polychrome Ware jug (Image: Ben Jervis)
*Back cover:* German Stoneware (© Victoria and Albert Museum, London)

# CONTENTS

# PREFACE

It has been clear to me since my first interaction with medieval pottery, as an undergraduate on the Bishopstone Valley Research project, that there is great potential to be unlocked in through its study. Throughout my undergraduate and postgraduate careers I set out to explore this potential, seeking to go beyond asking questions about the pottery itself, to consider how pottery might be used to better understand the medieval period. In setting out to achieve this goal I have been lucky enough to draw upon a wide range of experiences, not least having the opportunity to see pottery in new light during a 3 month graduate attachment to the British Institute in East Africa, where I was exposed for the first time to the potential of ceramic usewear analysis, from the input of Andy Jones, my prehistorian PhD supervisor and the opportunity to immerse myself in the pottery of medieval Southampton, provided by an Institute for Archaeologists workplace bursary.

From all of these experiences one thing became clear, that we have the techniques available to use pottery as a tool to understand medieval society, beyond being a chronological marker and an indicator of certain economic activities, but that a framework is needed to bridge the divide between method and interpretation. In hindsight, the seeds of a relational approach presented in this book developed in my undergraduate ceramic classes where I was taught by Carl Knappett, one of the leading proponents of many of the ideas discussed here, but really developed, through my doctoral research as I sought to articulate and connect the information I had gleaned from the analysis of the large medieval pottery assemblage from Southampton.

All of this research was being undertaken at a time when artefact studies were becoming increasingly marginalised in archaeological practice, particularly in the commercial sector. It was as a reaction to this marginalisation that I decided to produce this volume, to demonstrate how, rather than being a dull, marginal and specialist subject, that pottery studies can play a central role in our understanding of medieval social life, a fact which has been picked up by specialists working with other forms of material culture who, together, form a varied but positive expansion of medieval material culture studies.

The case studies presented in this volume are the result of a varied body of work, undertaken over a long period of time. I am grateful for the guidance, supervision, advice and access provided by a number of individuals over that time, as well as for funding from several sources which has allowed me to undertake this work. My masters research, which forms an element of chapter 5 was supported by a grant from the Arts and Humanities Research Council, who also supported my doctoral research, which underpins much of this volume, and particularly case studies on the Norman Conquest presented in chapter 4 and waste management, presented in chapters 5 and 6. Work on medieval inventories, discussed in chapter 3, was generously supported by the Society for Economic History and The Newton Trust. None of this work would have been possible without the support of my MA supervisor, Dr David Williams, my PhD supervisor, Dr Andrew Jones and the support of Prof Howard Williams, Dr Chris Briggs and Dr Naomi Sykes. Much of the Southampton data was collected during my time working on a work placement at Southampton Museum, funded by the Institute for Archaeologists. I would like to extend thanks to Kate Geary and Andrea Bradley at IfA for their support whilst on this placement, and also to Victoria Bryant for her work in setting it up. Much of my research would have been impossible without the assistance of my colleagues at Southampton Museum, who willingly shared their time and knowledge whilst I was working there, and continued to provide access to collections after completion of my placement, in particular thanks are due to Sian Iles, Karen Wardley and Gill Woolrich, as well as Dr Rob Symonds at Chichester Museum.

It is inevitable, given the length of time it has taken to put this book together, that I have drawn influences and ideas from discussion with a number of colleagues, not least through participation in the Early Medieval Archaeology Student Symposium and events organised by the Medieval Pottery Research Group. In particular I would like to thank Paul Blinkhorn and Chris Cumberpatch for inviting me to present at TAG in Liverpool, a paper through which I was able to develop some case studies presented in chapters 3 and 4, Dr James Morris, Prof David Hinton, Prof Hugh Thomas, Dr Lesley MacFayden, Dr Leonie Hicks, Alison Kyle, Andrew Sage, Alice Forward, Dr Kirsten Jarrett, Pieterjan Deckers, Dr Elaine Morris, Maureen Mellor, Lorraine Mepham, Mark Hall, Dr Andy Seaman, Prof Harold Mytum, Prof David Peacock, Reuben Thorpe, Prof Mark Gardiner, Prof John Arnold, Dr Gabor Thomas, Luke Barber, Dr Chris Loveluck, Prof Roberta Gilchrist, Dr Alison Gascoigne, Simon Pearcey, Lee Broderick, Eleanor Williams, and Ruth Nugent, and all of those who commented on my research at the stimulating Archaeology After Interpretation workshop in 2012.

Finally I would like to thank all of those who have made this book possible, particularly Clare Litt at Oxbow for her forbearance, the anonymous peer reviewer for their comments, my parents for their moral and financial support, my colleagues at Berkshire Archaeology and English Heritage, particularly Fiona MacDonald and Dr Jane Sidell, for their flexibility Helen for her patience as I locked myself away writing, and last, but by no means least, Duncan Brown – who has been a constant source of support and inspiration and without whose guidance and encouragement I would probably be something boring like a lawyer.

# 1

# THE EMERGENT DISCIPLINE.
# POTTERY AND MEDIEVAL ARCHAEOLOGY

The aim of this book is to explore the potential of relational interpretive frameworks within the field of medieval archaeology and to demonstrate how the application of such frameworks can draw material culture (specifically pottery) into the centre of discourse, not only in the study of medieval archaeology, but within the wider field of medieval studies. This first chapter is intended to summarise the development of medieval archaeology as a discipline and the role of ceramic studies within it, therefore detailing the context from which the studies presented here have emerged. Amongst the archaeological discipline as a whole medieval archaeology is popularly perceived as being a-theoretical (McClain 2012, 132). In the last 15–20 years increasing engagement with social theory and participation in events such as the Theoretical Archaeology Group conference has helped to improve the wider disciplines' perception of the relevance of medieval archaeology. To call medieval archaeology a-theoretical is inaccurate however, it is an interpretive discipline and as such all conclusions have a theoretical framework behind them (Johnson 2010, 6). The problem is, instead, that medieval archaeologists are not always explicit about their framework (Johnson 1988, 116) and that the demands of the discipline, particularly an uneasy relationship with history, mean that our interpretative challenges are different to those faced by our prehistorian colleagues (see also McClain 2012). In this chapter I will track the development of ceramic studies in medieval archaeology alongside the prevailing interpretive trends, to explain the circumstances out of which the studies in this book emerged and how I intend that this work will further advance the interpretive study of medieval material culture more generally.

The study of medieval material culture has, in some ways, advanced greatly in the last two decades, with the publication of increasingly interpretive studies of objects (*e.g.* Cumberpatch 1997; Hall 2011; Hall 2012; Naum 2011; Smith 2009a; Martin 2012). The characterisation and description of objects remains a core concern. Whilst a necessity to some degree, I will argue that the focus on characterisation is the result of the large quantities of material excavated from medieval sites, conservatism in approaches grounded in the history of medieval archaeology and the marginalisation of both artefact studies and archaeological theory within medieval archaeology. The importance of medieval objects has long been acknowledged, Pitt-Rivers (1890, 13–14) for example argued that in some cases 'they afford the only evidence available' to understand the period and that the 'subject has not been much studied'. In order to promote the study of artefacts, Pitt-Rivers made their description a central part of his report on excavations at King John's House (Wiltshire). Since then a wealth of literature has been published on finds of all types.

Pottery is both marginal and central within medieval archaeology. On the one hand ceramic sequences underpin much of our chronological understanding of the period, distributions of ceramic products reveal trading patterns and studies of residuality can influence our understanding of the formation of archaeological deposits. On the other, the role of pottery in medieval society has not been convincingly assessed. It has been shown to be functional and of low economic value and therefore an unimportant part of medieval society. As knowledge has developed, ceramic studies have been increasingly marginalised, often forming appendices to excavation reports, being brought in as supporting evidence, rather than being considered in the answering of broad research questions (Blinkhorn and Cumberpatch 2012). It is not my intention in this study to furnish pottery with a status that it never had in the medieval period. It is however, my intention to demonstrate that studies of pottery, and material culture in general, should not be marginalised, as these objects were instigated in the creation of social contexts, identities and landscapes in the medieval period, in mediating experiences of everyday life, in exactly the same way as the buildings, historical sources and spaces, the study of which appear to lead the agenda of the field. Despite Pitt-Rivers' acknowledgement of the importance of medieval objects, this centrality has not been followed through.

## Pottery and Medieval Archaeology: Antiquarians, Characterisation and Developer-led Excavation

For most of medieval archaeology's history as a discipline an empirical, 'common-sense' approach to interpretation has prevailed (Rahtz 1983, 13; McClain 2012, 134). This is, in no small part, due to the pressures of rescue excavations in towns, which have been focussed on recovering as much information as possible to a tight schedule, leading to the need to process large quantities of material with limited time available for more interpretive work. A principle concern was, and still is, the gathering of data and knowledge to underpin a relatively new and insecure discipline (Austin 1990, 24; Gerrard 2003, 132). The focus has necessarily been on characterisation and understanding the production of vessels, an area of interest which has its roots in the interests of antiquarians in the early part of the 19th century. In this first section I will outline how ceramic studies developed within the emerging discipline of medieval archaeology and consider how the development of a specialist community and the recovery of large quantities of ceramics from excavations, whilst generating a great deal of knowledge, has led to ceramic studies (and material culture studies more generally) to be marginalised within medieval archaeology.

The antiquarian interest in pottery can be related to the arts and craft movement of the late 19th and early 20th centuries (Gerrard 2003, 59). The interest of these individuals relates primarily to the study of pottery as a craft object. The first publication of medieval pottery is a piece in *Archaeologia*, published in 1779, although there are occasional mentions in the minutes of The Society of Antiquaries throughout the 18th century (Hurst 1991a, 8). It was not until the mid-19th century that antiquarian finds of medieval pottery were regularly recorded (Hurst 1991a, 7). Cooking vessels are barely mentioned, indeed the unchanging and unattractive nature of these vessels was commonly cited as a problem in this area and many of these vessels were mistaken as being Roman (Gerrard 2003, 83). It was generally the jugs and exotic vessels which were the focus of attention. Chaffers' (1850) work on the history of English pottery sums up contemporary attitudes by questioning the prevailing opinion that vessels are individual art pieces, a point not fully appreciated by archaeologists until the 1940s (Hurst 1991a, 18–19). With the exception of Chaffers' insights, pottery was barely examined archaeologically until after World War 2. An exception was Myres' (1969; 1977) research, much of which was undertaken in the inter-war years. Combining the distributions of pottery of different type and date, Myres set out to use pottery to understand the settlement of south-eastern England, using data from 19th century cemetery excavations and continental parallels. Although explicitly culture-historical, in the sense that the distribution of pots is directly related to the distribution of peoples, this study is of key importance, both in exploring the interpretive potential of medieval pottery but also in pioneering the use of techniques, such as distribution maps, which are still part of the ceramicists' repertoire today.

It is no coincidence that several of the founding fathers of medieval archaeology developed interests in medieval pottery. Visionary individuals such as John Hurst and Gerald Dunning saw the value of pottery both as a dating tool, but also as a means to understand trading patterns and technological developments. Characterisation is a key element of their work, with these and other scholars such as Barton, Jope and Myres, not only producing summaries of pottery types produced in Britain but also in France (*e.g.* Hurst 1974; Barton 1974), Iberia (Hurst 1978) and Italy (Hurst 1991b). Nowhere is the value of this characterisation and synthesis clearer than in the 1959 synthesis of Anglo-Saxon pottery (Tischler, Myres, Hurst and Dunning 1959) which not only synthesised the current knowledge of Anglo-Saxon pottery types and their dating, but placed this knowledge into an international context. This body of work was clearly an important contribution to ceramic studies, forming the building blocks for all future work on medieval ceramics and putting into place the chronological sequences which underpin our understanding of medieval archaeology. In the 1950s–70s short summaries, based on material from excavations or museum collections, were regularly published in *Medieval Archaeology* (the journal of the Society for Medieval Archaeology, first published in 1967) (*e.g.* Barton 1966a; Barton 1977; Hurst 1978), as well as publications such as *The Archaeological Journal* (*e.g.* Barton 1966b) and numerous regional publications (*e.g.* Jope 1947; Hurst 1981). The questions discussed in such pieces were generally straightforward; where and when was pottery made, and where was it traded to? The addressing of such questions provided a baseline characterisation against which stratigraphic sequences could be calibrated and which fitted well with the empiricist, common sense paradigm of the time (see Moorhouse (1986), Davey (1988) and Brown (1988a) for critiques). The foundation of the Medieval Pottery Research Group (MPRG) in 1975 was an important moment in the development of ceramic studies. The journal *Medieval Ceramics* became the place where the majority of this work came to be published. The MPRG and this journal allowed specialists to exchange knowledge and findings through a developing community of specialists. Yet these positives can be weighed up against negatives. Papers on pottery became less common in journals such as *Medieval Archaeology*, removing ceramic studies from wider discourse; with specialisation came marginalisation. I wish to divert here to briefly consider the process of research and knowledge creation. Law (2004, 38) argues that 'realities' in research are formed by past research and these findings come to be distributed through future research. Against this insight it is easy to see how ceramic studies came to be marginalised. The move to specialist publication, coupled with the large backlogs from excavation projects which, when published, out of necessity, largely take the form of catalogues (see below), meant that people did not engage widely with the emerging literature on ceramic studies, with their knowledge (and perceptions of the value of pottery) emerging through pieces published more widely, particularly in journals such as *Medieval Archaeology* (Figure 1.1). Therefore, as these pieces fell in number so people's awareness of the diversity and value of pottery diminished. In order for ceramic studies to regain their place at the heart of medieval archaeology, alongside the study of buildings for instance, it is vital that ceramic archaeologists seek out high impact venues for publication and that these publications are appropriate for a broad readership. The emergence of specialists has undoubtedly been a positive move, but these specialists must remain medieval archaeologists first and pottery specialists second for the value of their work to be fully realised.

It was not only the emergence of specialist knowledge and skills which marginalised the study of pottery. In many cases it has taken several decades to characterise and synthesise the massive quantities of material recovered from urban excavations. The effect has been that pottery information has simply not been available for those writing syntheses of the medieval period, or that it was necessary to rely on a small number of, typically localised and sometimes outdated, sources of information. The majority of pottery is discussed in excavation reports or in synthetic volumes on pottery from specific settlements or regions. Necessarily these act as a catalogue of finds, which are then generally used to phase sites and discuss particular features. Many reports do include room for detailed discussion of the trade in pottery. This pressure on space in excavation reports meant that the full interpretive potential of pottery could not be realised in print. The need to publish vast quantities of material, alongside critical interpretation, led to the emergence of dedicated finds volumes, but the funding required to process assemblages often meant that these volumes were slow to emerge. Whilst

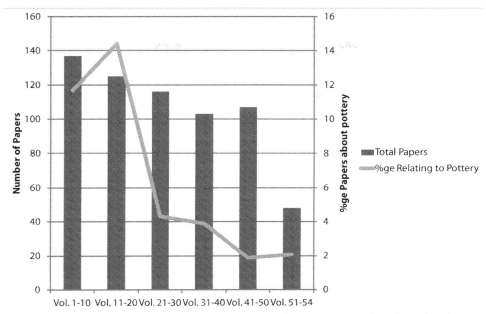

*Figure 1.1. Graph showing a decline in the quantity of papers concerned with medieval pottery published in the journal Medieval Archaeology. Notice the sharp decline between volumes 21–30, corresponding with the launch of the specialist journal Medieval Ceramics.*

valuable sources of information, the separation of artefact studies from site narratives furthered the marginalisation of ceramic studies in the writing of site narratives. In some cases the pottery has been published prior to excavation reports which have never seen print (*e.g.* Brown 2002), meaning that the ceramics cannot be considered in context. The most detailed volumes are those synthesising the ceramic evidence from a large sample of sites, such as Allan's (1984) work on Exeter (Devon) and Brown's (2002) on Southampton (Hampshire).

Underpinning much of this work was the work of Alan Vince and his colleagues in London, where dated sequences of pottery, largely from the waterfront, provided a framework which could be extrapolated widely, thanks in particular to the presence of regional and international imported products (see Vince 1985; Pearce *et al.* 1985; Pearce and Vince 1988 and the development of this work *e.g.* Blackmore and Pearce 2010). Perhaps the biggest legacy of the London project however was the opportunities provided to train archaeologists who then became the specialists responsible for the characterisation, analysis and synthesis of assemblages across the country.

Several of these large synthetic studies allowed space for interpretation. Allan, for example, was able to use ceramic evidence alongside historical documents to create a picture of Exeter's development as a port through the early middle ages, as well as discussing the function of imported wares (Allan 1984, 15–18). Trade within England is also considered, linking the movement of East Midlands and Yorkshire wares to the coal trade (*ibid*, 30), whilst demonstrating that it was those highly decorated wares, not produced locally, which were the main types of traded pottery.

The marginalisation of finds studies is by no means a universal trend and several recent projects have embraced the value of finds evidence in understanding the development and character of communities in the past. An example of such a study is Cotter's (2006) work on the pottery from Town Wall Street, Dover (Kent). Cotter considers the movement of pottery beyond trade, using a quantitative approach, which allows the isolation of pottery types which were probably moved through trade and those moved through other mechanisms. He suggests Norfolk pottery reached the site along east coast fishing routes, for example. Rather than buying and selling pottery for commerce the broken pots were simply rubbish related to this activity, with fishermen buying pots for use on their boats and discarding them once they broke (*ibid*, 410–11). Documentary evidence is also used to highlight the role piracy may have had in bringing rarer pottery to the site (*ibid*, 408). Similarly, the multi-volume report on excavations at the Anglo-Saxon site of Flixborough (Lincolnshire) includes a volume (Loveluck and Evans 2009) dedicated to the thematic synthesis of all strands of evidence, returning artefacts to the interpretative process.

A general shift from characterisation to interpretation can be seen to be occurring in the general literature on medieval material culture. Importantly the literature has seen the coverage of a broader range of topics. Whilst production, characterisation and exchange remain important, since 1990 there has been an increase in studies of pottery consumption (*e.g.* Brown 1997; Blinkhorn 1999) and particularly the application of new interpretive frameworks to medieval artefacts. The development in the 1990s of journals dealing primarily with material culture have also seen interpretive pieces published, particularly in the last decade, which are at the cutting edge of archaeological interpretation and of value not only to medieval archaeologists but also to scholars dealing with the material culture of all periods (Hall 2011; Jervis 2011; Naum 2011). By doing so, objects are shifting back into the centre of medieval archaeology, which can only lead to the development of a more balanced and realistic understanding of the past. I have briefly argued that the large quantity of material present (and by implication the funding required to process and publish this material), coupled with the development of specialist knowledge had the effect of marginalising ceramic studies within archaeological discourse, despite the building up of a large bank of knowledge of great value to our understanding of the medieval period. In the remainder of this chapter I will explore approaches to medieval pottery alongside theoretical developments in the field, before, in chapter 2, sketching a new way forward, in which artefact studies are drawn back into the centre of medieval studies.

## Beyond Dots on Maps: Science and The 'New' Medieval Archaeology

Through the 1970s the theoretical tide in archaeology as a whole was changing.

Drawing on the work of Binford (1968) and Clarke (1968) in particular, a processual paradigm, grounded in scientific method and drawing upon systems theory, swept through prehistoric archaeology. This was stimulated by similar developments in 'the new geography' and within 'the new history', although primarily for the post-medieval period, where the necessary data was most abundant (Bintliff 1986, 10–12). A major component of this movement was the development of new scientific techniques, many of which were adopted by medieval archaeologists. These include the emergence of zooarchaeology and ceramic petrology (Gerrard 2003, 159), the application of which put in place the foundations for the application of developing techniques such as GC-MS residue analysis (see Jervis in press a for a review) and ICP-MS chemical analysis for provenancing pottery in the last two decades. Although medieval archaeology remained largely descriptive and empirical, these techniques have allowed for further interpretation, as well as ever more detailed description and characterisation (Vince 2005, 232).

During the late 1970s and early 1980s, work being undertaken at The University of Southampton under the guidance of Prof David Peacock led the way in the application of these techniques to medieval pottery. Three studies in particular demonstrate the value of considering petrological data in interpretive perspective. Vince's (1977) study of pottery in the west country and Streeton's (1981) study of later medieval pottery in later medieval Sussex both focussed on examining the scale of production and exchange networks, with Streeton in particular utilising the methodologies of processual archaeologists, including thessian polygons, to interpret the mechanisms behind the distribution of wares. Richard Hodges (1982) presented the most theoretically developed study however, integrating petrological data into a consideration of early medieval trade networks and urbanism which was firmly rooted within the interpretive framework of the new archaeology, demonstrating the potential which lay within the interpretation of petrological data within a broader context. Despite these notable early studies however, a developed theoretical or interpretive framework has largely been lacking, meaning that the potential of such techniques has not been fully realised. Petrology, along with chemical analysis, has largely been utilised to characterise types, being utilised to answer specific research questions within the sub-discipline of ceramic studies (see for example the studies reviewed by Vince (2005)).

Still today the results are often marginalised in appendices to site reports or specialist journals, often only being quoted as supporting statements within a broader narrative. For example, in a recent study of Shelly Sandy Ware from London (Blackmore and Pearce 2010) petrological information is presented within a broader discussion of fabric, but is only included within the wider discussion to give a more detailed description of raw materials and to differentiate sub-types, rather than being integrated into a broader discussion of the social and economic dynamics of resource procurement. Yet these techniques provide a wealth of information about the interactions between people, their surroundings, ceramic vessels and foodstuffs, which when brought together can animate the past. Techniques such as organic residue analysis bring together foodstuffs and the material culture of food processing, allowing us to investigate cooking practices, provisioning strategies and cuisine in some detail, rather than focussing only on dietary reconstruction (see for example Blinkhorn's (2012) analysis of residues in Anglo-Saxon Ipswich Ware). Petrological analysis does not only provide us with data to reconstruct how pots moved, but provides a direct link between ceramic vessels and the spaces in which the resources were gathered and the pots were produced (see chapter 5). To get the most from these techniques it is imperative that results are synthesised and interpreted, rather than simply presented and discussed in empirical terms. If ceramic studies are divorced from archaeological discourse, these approaches are divorced by a further degree, yet, if fully integrated, they can provide bridges between different scales and classes of evidence, allowing us to go beyond reconstruction and characterisation to study process, action and effect. The work of Alan Vince (see http://archaeologydataservice. ac.uk/archives/view/alanvince_eh_2010/) in particular has produced a huge archive of data from the undertaking of programmes of thin-section and chemical analysis as part of post-excavation projects. This is a valuable resource and one in which much potential for further study and interpretation resides. Thanks to the influence of the new archaeology upon archaeological methodology we have the tools at our disposal to make ceramic studies a key component of medieval studies, what has been lacking however are explicit interpretive frameworks in which to deploy these tools.

The effect of a focus on data collection and empirical study had further implications for finds studies. This focus, coupled with the fast pace of, particularly urban, development in the late 1970s and early 1980s led to a focus on fieldwork and the recovery of large and unwieldy assemblages of material. The relentless process of excavation was coupled with a relatively slow process of post-excavation work, as specialist knowledge and skills developed. The focus on excavation and recovery further contributed to the marginalisation of artefact studies, with the impetus being on recovery rather than interpretation. By the 1980s this practice started to be questioned. Gathering data was all well and good, but what was the next phase? There was a feeling amongst the next generation of practitioners that:

> 'medieval archaeology is in danger of becoming fossilised, its practitioners too involved with the accumulation and preservation of data to find new approaches and interpretations' (D. Brown 1988b, 95).

Several scholars argued that a subservience to history and a common-sense, empirical approach were being used as a substitute for a solid theoretical base on which archaeological data could be interpreted and contribute to the understanding of our medieval past in its own right (Arnold 1986, 36). Phillip Rahtz was amongst the first to subscribe to this view, in print at least, and was the most vocal in calling for 'a New Medieval Archaeology', arguing that rather than being subservient to documentary history, that archaeology is contributory to the writing of the whole History (with a capital h) of man. Rahtz characterises the first 25 years of medieval archaeology as being concerned with data collection and proposes that the next should be spent interpreting this data (Rahtz 1983, 13). The data, we are informed, does not speak for itself; we must hypothesise and prove or disprove our theories through targeted excavation and post-excavation analysis, the techniques for which had already been developed (*ibid*, 14). What is most striking to the modern reader (or at least this modern reader) is the implicit argument that whilst prehistorians have demonstrated how these approaches can expand our horizons, that medieval archaeologists have the large and diverse data sets required to take the lead, rather than follow other areas of the discipline (*ibid*, 15). Most of all, archaeologists were urged to interpret their data in its own right, not as a secondary strand to textual sources. This call has been misinterpreted as a call to divorce archaeology from history entirely (Driscoll 1984, 105; Arnold 1986, 36). Rahtz acknowledges in a later paper (Rahtz 1984, 110) that he could have been more explicit in his aim, merely urging archaeologists to come out of the historians shadow rather than divorce themselves completely (see below).

The effect of Rahtz's call to arms appears to have been to split the discipline. Few were taken with 'the New Medieval Archaeology' as presented. Early processual works, such as Randsborg's *The Viking Age in Denmark* (1980) were given a difficult reception as reviewers seemed uncomfortable with archaeology's attempts to stride out from its subservient position (Hodges 1983, 25). This is undoubtedly one reason that the 'new archaeology' had little impact on interpretation, one exception being Hodges' (1982) *Dark Age Economics* which drew upon a number of the key themes of 'new archaeology' including systems theory and a spatial analysis of artefact distributions to radically re-conceptualise our understanding of the early medieval economy. Furthermore the jargon and complex statistical methodologies accompanying the new archaeology was put forward as another barrier by critics (Hodges 1983, 28; Bintliff 1986, 20), yet they were happy to continue to use the historians' jargon (Austin 1990, 31–2). Perhaps most of all though, archaeologists were satisfied with the site report as a means of dissemination for their work and saw new statistical sampling techniques and working practices as undermining the aim of their work, to recover and present as much information about the past as possible (Hodges 1983, 29). The necessity of these approaches, which in some ways duplicated work undertaken in history and geography, was questioned, particularly by historians, hindering the adoption of new approaches (Austin 1990, 30–1).

The 'New Medieval Archaeology' emerged in part as a critique of the primacy of history in the interpretation of archaeological materials. As a young discipline, this relationship was a particular area of insecurity. It is a relationship which can be traced back to the earliest antiquarian approaches of the 17th century. As prehistoric archaeology aligned itself closely with disciplines such as geography and geology, historical archaeology took a different trajectory, having a primary role in illustrating and, to a lesser, extent, corroborating historical texts (Bintliff 1986, 5–6). Something of a 'disciplinary inferiority complex' (*ibid*, 8; see also Austin 1990, 10) arose amongst historical archaeologists, giving the impression that archaeological finds are somehow less useful, accurate and personal than documents. The culture-historical perspective which characterises much of the earliest (particularly early medieval) archaeology partly emerged as a means to illustrate phenomena identified in the historical record, for example Myres (1969) exhaustive work on pottery distributions demonstrated the movement of Germanic peoples through southern England, illustrating the picture given by historical sources such as Bede's Ecclesiastical History (see also Austin 1990, 16–17).

Whilst some archaeologists objected to the 'New Medieval Archaeology' because of the complex terminology and methods associated with it, some historians too were resistant, questioning the very value of medieval archaeology as an independent discipline. Peter Sawyer (1983, 44), for example, saw archaeology as 'a very expensive demonstration of the obvious'. Contrary to the sampling approach and seemingly ignorant to the scale, complexity and pressures of urban archaeology in particular, Sawyer promoted total excavation. Such an approach is geared solely at recovery and data gathering and contrasts the desire of archaeologists to set research agendas and to target research to challenging particular hypotheses. To Sawyer's credit, his call for archaeologists to ensure that projects are seen to publication still resonates. He also calls for archaeologists to play to their strengths, studying technology, the environment and reconstructing topographical features such as property boundaries, (a pursuit which he claims 'amongst the most significant and revealing signs of a community's history' (Sawyer 1983, 45)). In contrast he suggests archaeologists leave documents to historians, but that co-operation is essential. Not all historians were so resistant however, Harvey (1983) argues that archaeologists have a role to play in filling in gaps in historical knowledge and that medieval archaeologists need not only contribute to the development of our understanding of the medieval period, but also to the development of archaeology as a whole. It is perhaps in this later aim which medieval archaeologists have been least successful. Whilst from a methodological perspective medieval archaeologists have been hugely influential (for example Vince's influence in relation to the development of ceramic petrology and Barker's development of open area excavation in relation to the excavation of castle sites), the discipline remains fairly insular and static, occasionally drawing upon ideas from scholars focussing on other periods (for example Hamerow's (2006) study of early Anglo-Saxon ritual deposition which drew upon ideas developed in prehistoric archaeology), but rarely providing the impetus on which scholars of other periods feel urged to act upon (which is one aim of this book). In order to push forward both our understanding of the medieval period and to contribute to the development of archaeology as a whole, archaeologists must continue to devise and follow their own research agenda, rather than limiting research questions to those posed and validated by documentary historians (Austin 1990, 13), allowing archaeological data to pose the questions. Clearly the two disciplines of history and archaeology can be complementary and a truly interdisciplinary approach must emerge to create a balanced and full understanding of the medieval period. Steps toward such an approach are outlined in chapter 3 (in which the use of historical sources, particular in the work of Moorhouse (1978; 1983), is also reviewed).

To see the 'New Medieval Archaeology' as a failure though is unfair to the revolutionary work undertaken by a handful of scholars who dared to push the interpretive boundaries and question contemporary practice. Perhaps the biggest long-term impacts were the adoption of a more scientifically orientated discipline and attempts to place medieval objects into a systemic context. Although the major advances came at the 'high end' of archaeological science, these techniques had a broader influence, in making the study of archaeological ceramics more scientifically rigorous, for example through the adoption of quantitative approaches. Such approaches allow us to draw meaningful conclusions between assemblages, for example Brown's (1997) comparison of vessel function in several medieval households demonstrated differences between urban and rural ceramic use. Blinkhorn's (1999) study combined statistical and spatial analyses to explore differences in ceramic use across a medieval hamlet. In both of these studies quantification produces a basis to understand difference, and, like the more advanced scientific techniques discussed previously, provide a means to examine the everyday relationships people formed with pottery and to go beyond these to question broader questions regarding lifestyle, economy and social status.

Furthermore, the developments of the new archaeology encouraged some to consider pottery in new ways. Stimulated by the developments of the 'new archaeology' in the 1970s, scholars began to question the dynamics of trade and production (*e.g.* Davey and Hodges 1983). Early studies, such as those by Dunning, had been largely empirical, mapping find spots to identify movements of pottery and placing these movements into a known historical context. These new studies questioned how, why and in what quantity these vessels moved and sought to understand why changes in production, identified by early characterisations of the material, occurred. Influenced by processual archaeologists, as well as developments in geography and history, these scholars argued that pottery production should be studied in a wider socioeconomic context. For example, Verhaege (1983) argues differences in the scale of pottery production and marketing in medieval Flanders can be related to the size of settlements as different settings require different types of pots and are suited to different modes of manufacture (for example intensive manufacture is better suited to urban production). These differences are then related to wider socio-economic developments. By 1988 however only three of the 78 papers published in the journal *Medieval Ceramics* addressed theoretical issues (Davey 1988, 4). Of particular note are Orton's (1985) examination of developments in ceramic production, drawing upon theories of diffusion and Blake's (1980) consideration of the relationship between supply and demand in the pottery trade. Both are grounded, at least to some degree, within a processual approach in which pottery is considered part of a system and as such utilises it as a tool to understand past society, rather than focussing upon the nature of the material itself.

Although a short lived experiment, in hindsight the 'new archaeology' played a key role in the development of medieval archaeology and particularly in ceramic studies. From a general perspective, scholars came to be motivated in forging medieval archaeology as a discipline in its own right, acknowledging that archaeological study should focus on archaeological questions. These influences also promoted the development of scientific techniques. For pottery studies in particular the emphasis on the socio-economic context provided the means to move away from the important task of characterisation to understand the dynamics of pottery production, trade and consumption. Often history and archaeology are characterised as a marriage in which history is the dominant partner (M. Johnson 2006, 134). I prefer to use a different metaphor to define this relationship. Medieval archaeology is a young discipline, one which grew under the watchful eye of history as a parent discipline. The 'new archaeology' can be seen as a rebellious teenage phase, as it tried to stand on its own two feet and pull away from an overbearing parent. If the 1980s mark these teenage years then the development of post-processual approaches can be characterised as a discipline reaching maturity, and standing on its own interpretive feet.

## Entering the Theoretical Mainstream: Post-Processual Approaches

Much has been made of the resistance to the methods and theories promoted of the 'New Medieval Archaeology' put up by established figures. Austin (1990) puts the projects failure down to a failure to convince documentary historians of its worth. Younger scholars too were reticent to Rahtz's call however, perhaps for the simple reason that by the early 1980s a post-processual critique was already established in prehistoric archaeology. Both Driscoll (1984) and Arnold (1986) for example argue against generalising laws of human behaviour and argue that documents themselves are artefacts and that material culture can be read as text (Driscoll 1984, 107–8; Arnold 1986, 37; Austin 1990, 34–5). The critique calls on us to draw evidence together, to take a holistic approach which plays to the strengths of historical and archaeological evidence and goes beyond empirical reconstruction of trade patterns or floor plans, to explore what material culture can tell us about cultural phenomena such as cuisine, ritual behaviour and medieval ideology (Driscoll 1984, 109). In doing so we can contribute to the development of history, going beyond illustrating history and filling in the gaps in documents, to pose new questions and develop new areas of investigation (Austin 1990, 24–7). These debates had set the stage for a blossoming of interpretive approaches, by the late 1980s there was a feeling that "the subject itself is in danger of becoming bogged down in the morass of data medieval archaeology has spawned" (D. Brown 1988, 95). It is inescapable that excavations, particularly in towns, generate large quantities of data and that the development of specialists leads to the fragmentation of the discipline (Austin 1990, 14). The 1990s were however to see an expansion of both methodological and theoretical approaches which allowed us to overcome these problems, as medieval archaeology was transformed from a confused adolescence to a confident and more mature discipline.

Following research in prehistoric archaeology (*e.g.* Hodder 1982) It was determined that landscapes and buildings, as well as objects, could also be seen as texts, to be read and interpreted beyond the traditional developmental narratives archaeologists had previously employed. Re-interpreting excavations at Okehampton Park (Devon), Austin and Thomas (1990) argue that buildings were structured in such a way that they were central to bringing continuity and familiarity to peoples' lives and that more than building techniques and function can be read from their remains. Instead we can use buildings as texts which tell us about the structure of everyday life and the relationship between different elements of domesticity and subsistence, a structure that was repeated both across space (at other settlements) and time (as buildings were rebuilt). The farmyard and wider landscape too, hold clues to these patterns of everyday life, which in their 'correct' reading can betray more information than changing patterns of land ownership and agricultural techniques, as they can reveal the rhythm of life. Such bottom-up narratives, concerned with the minutiae of life, allow us to create an alternative history, one in which we can question the impact of seemingly major historical events and in which we can engage with the agency of those who are absent from the historical record.

The stimulus provided by the post-processual critique within archaeology more widely proved a catalyst for further explicitly theoretical studies to be undertaken, some of which have had impacts which extend outside of medieval archaeology. Many of these studies are reviewed in some detail in subsequent sections of this book but are not discussed in detail here. It is useful however to illustrate the variety of themes that the freedom provided by new interpretive approaches allowed to be explored. Arguably the biggest impact has been made by Gilchrist's (1994; 1999) work on gender in medieval archaeology, which demonstrated how identities could be explored outside of the traditional categories of social status or ethnicity (see chapter 4 for a review of identity studies in medieval archaeology). Gilchrist's adoption of Bourdieu's (1977) concept of *habitus* (defined as the pre-disposed structuring structures, which bring continuity, familiarity and normality to a society), explicitly utilising social theory to interpret patterning in archaeological data can be seen in other contemporary work, including Blinkhorn's (1997) discussion of pottery and identity in the Anglo-Saxon period and Giles' (2000) examination of civic identity in relation to medieval guildhalls. Of equal significance to Gilchrist's work is Johnson's (1993) discussion of vernacular architecture in Suffolk, which argues that the form of vernacular houses is reflective of shared social values, in which it is possible to explore fundamental issues of socio-cultural, as well as economic, processes of continuity and change, in which the house must be considered part of a wider landscape, which is explored through a discussion of the concept of the 'closure' of domestic and agricultural spaces in the later medieval and post-medieval periods.

Within prehistoric archaeology, landscape studies have been a major area for the development of new theoretical approaches, particularly through the adoption of phenomenological approaches. Such approaches have largely not been explored by medieval archaeologists, who have largely maintained an approach grounded in traditional landscape history (see chapter 5 for an expansion of this argument). This is not to say however that such approaches have been entirely ignored by medieval archaeologists. Corcos (2001) for example considers the landscape contexts of two Somerset churches from a phenomological perspective, seeing them as 'ritual monuments', sited and experienced within a wider landscape context. What is striking about Corcos' paper is the following on an explicitly archaeological theoretical agenda, but through the application of thought developed largely in relation to prehistoric archaeology. A key criticism of such approaches in prehistoric archaeology has been the disjuncture between past and present experiences of space. An advantage of applying such approaches to medieval case studies is the possibility to combine these archaeological approaches within a truly interdisciplinary framework, for example Harvey (2002) takes influences from phenomological studies of landscape in considering how religious hagiography and folklore played a role in generating people's understanding of the landscape through the creation of memory and associations particular to their experience, leading to "a particular history (emerging) in a specific context through the creation and utilisation of a physical setting" (Harvey 2002, 14). Here, as well as in a recent study of the landscape of Irish kingship (Gleeson 2012) we see a fundamental difference to earlier studies, with archaeology and history being combined with equal standing, rather than the archaeology merely supporting the historical agenda. Concepts of sensory experience of landscapes, spaces and artefacts have been particularly vibrant in the study of early medieval mortuary practices (*e.g.* Williams 2006), which have begun to consider the mnemonic roles of landscapes, monuments and objects, both to reconstruct mortuary practices and to understand how elements of the landscape gained significance and played a significant role in the process of commemoration and memory building (see chapter 5).

At the same time, ceramicists began to further question what pottery could offer medieval archaeology. Moorhouse (1986) ably demonstrated that pottery could be utilised in a range of ways to understand archaeological sites, with a particular focus on the reconstruction of depositional pathways and spatial analysis, highlighting how the study of pottery could be related to the use of space. Two later discussions (Davey 1988; D. Brown 1988a) highlight that pottery contributed to medieval culture and as such offers, through the application of theoretical approaches, the potential to better understand medieval society. Although slow to develop, ceramic specialists moved towards the adoption of such approaches, partly in reaction to the marginalisation of artefact studies caused through the specialisation of the discipline and working practices (Blinkhorn and Cumberpatch 1998). It is noticeable that much of this work was not undertaken in the academic sector, but rather by specialists working for commercial or local authority archaeological units, who sought to utilise their data to contribute to wider debates in medieval archaeology. Identity has been a central theme in such studies, and the application of various theoretical approaches in relation to its study are summarised in chapter 4. The first area to receive attention from a post-processual perspective was the symbolism of pottery and the relation between vessels and their contexts of use in Richards' (1987), whose study of Anglo-Saxon cremation urns. This explored the relationship between certain decorative and formal attributes and the presence of grave goods to suggest that a 'symbolic language' was present. For example, vessel size appears to reflect the age and size of the deceased, whilst further correlations occur between the presence of decorative styles and certain grave goods, with different elements reflecting varying aspects of an individual's identity (Richards 1987, 196–7), a theme taken up in several later studies (Cumberpatch 1997; Spavold 2010; Jervis in press b; see chapter 3 for further discussion).

Adoption of post-processual thought has opened up new avenues for research in ceramic studies, allowing, for example a blossoming of integrated studies of dining practices and cuisine, an area in which the symbolic nature of pottery is of particular relevance. In a Merovingian context Effros (2002; 2003) has argued that funerary feasts had an important role in cementing relationships between the living and the dead, with engagements with food and drink also mediating connections between Christian and pagan communities. The vessels in which substance used to contain and consume substances have been demonstrated, on the basis of historical evidence, to be of crucial importance in symbolising purity, with vessels being cleansed or broken if polluted (Effros 2003, 222). A later example is provided by the work of Willmott (2005) who argues that pottery and other tablewares symbolised wealth, status and taste at the Tudor table. The role of pottery within households is beginning to be considered in more depth, for example Gutierrez (2000) has argued that Mediterranean pottery in southern English contexts must be seen alongside other items as a component of a 'set of coded attributes' (*ibid*, 199). These attributes were both material (clothes, ornaments etc.) and less tangible (manners and habits). Exploring dining practices in medieval Hampshire, Jervis (2013a) has explored how similarities and differences in the use of pottery and consumption of foodstuffs mediated the development of varying forms of rural and urban identity through food practices, demonstrating how pottery studies can contribute to broader debates surrounding themes such as urbanism, which are of great relevance within medieval archaeology.

The influence of post-processual thought has not been limited to the study of pottery however. Particularly in the last decade, interpretive studies of other forms of material culture have emerged, which aim to move beyond characterisation and cataloguing to understand the relevance of objects to medieval society and, in the process, developing a sub-field of medieval material culture studies, in which objects become central to our understanding of the past, rather than being subsidiary to the perspectives provided by the study of documents, buildings, landscapes and excavated features. Studies such as those by Hall (2011; 2012) of material culture from Perth are particularly good examples, which emphasise the fluidity in the ways that objects were used and perceived by medieval people (see also chapters 2 and 3). Ideas of identity have been applied to the examination of dress accessories in both the early and later medieval periods (Effros 2004; Smith 2009b), in which these items are not common-sense reflections of people's identities, but are enrolled in the processes through which identities are created (see chapter 4), the meaning of which changes and transforms throughout their use-lives (Martin 2012). Such studies demonstrate how material culture of all kinds can be utilised to build new understanding and alternate histories, which question common-sense received wisdom and have the potential to animate multiple experiences of medieval life.

## Summary

The framework developed in this book is not considered a radical shift, but rather a stage in the evolutionary process in the development of medieval archaeology. Increasingly new interpretive approaches have provided the impetus for the development of new analytical techniques and the asking of new questions. The post-processual critique saw the blossoming of interpretive approaches to ceramic studies and within medieval archaeology in general. A range of topics were explored including identity (see chapter

4), experiences of landscape (see chapter 5) and the role of pottery and other objects as symbols (see chapter 3). Where adopted, they have provided new insights both into the nature of archaeological evidence and the contexts in which objects were used and landscapes experienced. An emerging critique is questioning some of the elements of post-processual thought, principally the emphasis on symbolism and the anthropocentric conceptualisation of 'the social'. Increasingly archaeologists have questioned the role of materials and objects on people's experience and considered that, rather than residing in artefacts as symbols, meaning is temporary and unstable, emerging through people's interactions with objects. Such a critique has two major implications, the first being that to understand artefacts in the past that we must reconstruct the ways in which people interacted with them and the effect of these interactions and secondly that our interpretations are products of our own interactions with artefacts, formed through the application of particular scientific techniques. The remainder of this book is concerned with advancing a relational approach to medieval pottery, to explore the ways in which ceramic vessels were entangled within medieval life. Chapter 2 will outline the core principles of such an approach and highlight their potential in relation to medieval archaeology.

# 2

# TOWARDS A
# RELATIONAL ARCHAEOLOGY

The theoretical perspectives which underpin this book, and which are outlined in this chapter, should not be viewed as revolutionary, but rather as an evolution of contemporary 'post-processual' approaches. There is much common ground between these and the approaches discussed in the previous chapter; a concern with the meaning of things, with the nature and importance of context and concern with agency which extends beyond environmental or anthropogenic determinism. A core criticism to have recently been levied at post-processual approaches however is that a focus on objects, landscapes and buildings as texts or symbols promotes an anthropocentric view of the world, which ignores the effect of the non-human on humans (Olsen 2010, 28). The approach outlined here presents both methodological and interpretive approaches to overcoming this concern. A number of sources have provided the inspiration behind recent developments, which can be loosely termed as relational archaeology, as they focus upon the processes through which humans and non-human form relationships and the effect of these relationships on the emergence of social contexts, identities or objects.

## Relational Approaches: Divergence and Convergence

The concept of the symbol, key to post-processual studies of material culture, is derived from Saussure (1972) and is defined loosely as a sign which has a meaning attached to it by people (Knappett 2005, 88). The meaning of words and objects is therefore arbitrary, as people inscribe meaning upon their surroundings. For post-processual archaeologists the aim was to understand these sign systems, to identify symbolic grammar in pottery decoration for example (*e.g.* Braithwaite 1982; Cumberpatch 1997). This anthropocentric approach was furthered by so called 'phenomological' approaches, which focus upon human experiences of places and things. The focus on human perception of the world, through the understanding and interpretation of things as symbols, provides a reflective view of the world, meaning that the more detailed a study becomes the more distanced the objects themselves become, leaving us with a modern individual's commentary on the objects, rather than an understanding of their role in the past (Olsen 2010, 28). A relational approach seeks to move past this problem, by empirically reconstructing courses of action, before considering the effects of these processes, for example in the constitution of objects, people and places, entities which can be considered as mutually constitutive. It can be considered to have developed out of biographical approaches, which acknowledge how the meaning of things changes through their lives, which have become prevalent in contemporary material culture studies. The key advance is to consider, not only how the perception of things change, but what the effects of the interactions which make objects meaningful are on places and identities. For example, the chaîne opératoire approach to manufacturing processes is a form of biographical approach, in which the various stages of production can be seen as reflecting varying forms of identity (Gosselain 2000; Jervis 2008). However, a relational approach would extend this perspective, to consider the effects of each stage of this process, not only on craftspeople but upon the others enrolled in this process, thus allowing an understanding to develop of the ripple of effects caused through the development of relationships between people and the material world (see Malafouris 2008).

Outside of archaeology and anthropology a number of scholars had begun to critique the differentiation between human and material worlds, arguing that this was a distinction created by a modernist view of the world. A relational approach draws upon the work of such scholars, which will be discussed in more detail below. The term 'materiality' entered the literature in the early part of the 21st century in an attempt to address the divorce of human and material. The concept of objectification, in which objects are seen as a manifestation of human action and society (see Miller 2005, 7–10), is key to the study of materiality. Rather than denying a dichotomy between objects and humans, Miller (2005, 10) argues that this dichotomy exists "in the wake… of objectification"; because people consider themselves to be using objects this dichotomy must exist in reality. This is an important move towards a relational approach, as the role of action in determining the meaning of objects is acknowledged. However, implicit in such an approach is the primacy of human agency in the definition of this meaning (see Ingold 2007). Materiality is still focussed on human action and neglects the material qualities of objects, with objects merely reflecting the social system, hovering below cultural 'human' activity, awaiting meaning to become attached to them (Ingold 2007). Simultaneously, the work of Alfred Gell (1998) was becoming increasingly influential in archaeological spheres. In particular, his conceptualisation of material agency was of importance, in allowing the effective role of objects to be considered. It is utilised, for example, by Howard Williams (2006, 141) to consider how the agency for remembrance was present within the mound 1 grave at Sutton Hoo. However, as will be discussed further below, this agency takes the form of an embedded or deferred form of human agency, which resides within objects, rather than objects developing any form of agentive properties separate from human intentionality or perception (see Jones and Boivin 2011, 341). This is, in part, due to Gell's concern with art, rather than archaeological material culture, in which the artists intended meaning can be relatively easily ascertained from the subject of study, whereas other forms of objects can perhaps be considered more complex, by virtue of the less prescribed manners in which they are drawn into action.

Archaeologists also began to critique the very notion of the symbol, drawing upon Piercian semiotics to define a more complex sign system, in which, at least in some cases, the meaning of objects could become defined in relation to courses of action (see Knappett 2005; Preucel 2008). Symbols, as arbitrary signs, became one of a suite of three sign types, the others being the index and icon, which could be read. As an index objects are defined causally or through contiguity, indicating their referent (for example in the case of a weather vane indexing wind direction) whereas as an icon an objects meaning is defined in relation to other similar objects (Knappett 2005, 91–7). In both cases meaning is not pre-determined in the sense of objects being symbols, but is understood in relation to other objects, to action and to acquired knowledge of what these signs could mean. Such an approach has acknowledged that meanings of objects are not fixed, but are defined and negotiated relationally, although the nature of the context in which these meanings are negotiated is yet to be defined.

The aim of this short introduction has been to demonstrate that for some time archaeologists have been experimenting with approaches which move the focus away from anthropocentric approaches to the past, to consider the role of objects and materials more critically. The largest body of work, and the body into which this book fits, is influenced, to varying degrees, by approaches derived in sociology, particularly the work of Actor-Network Theory scholars in the sub-field of science and technology studies, the writings of post-modern scholars such as Deleuze and Guttari and developments in other disciplines, particularly the development of 'non-representational theory' in the field of human geography. These approaches have two fundamental positions. Firstly action does not occur in a pre-existing social or cultural context, but instead action leads to the emergence of these contexts, which are fluid and unstable. Secondly, objects do not reflect these contexts (as with the concept of objectification, for example) but instead it is the relationships between people and their material surroundings which form and maintain what can be termed 'the social'. Such an approach demands us to move away from drawing conclusions based on fairly broad and undefined social explanations, towards using the study of objects to understand how a particular 'social' developed and was sustained.

Numerous terms have been used to define such an approach archaeologically, each with a subtly different focus behind them. Amongst the first to acknowledge the value of a relational approach was Schiffer (1999). His 'Material Life of Human Beings' critiques the emphasis on language and symbology in studies of human interaction. Directly emerging from his 'behavioural archaeology', a largely processual approach, and thus grounded in the empirical reconstruction of practice, Schiffer argues that life consists of unending and varied interactions amongst people and things and that in nearly all interactions humans are accompanied by artefacts (Schiffer 1999, 1–3). The emphasis of Schiffer's work is communication. He argues that studies of human interaction across the social sciences largely lack a consideration of the role of objects (Schiffer 1999, 6–8). One reason that Schiffer's work has not been widely used, at least not by European scholars, is the seemingly unending and complex jargon used in the study. However once the key points are distilled this work outlines a number of the key points of relevance to a relational archaeology; that people need artefacts to interact, that the meaning and qualities of objects emerge through these relationships and that these relationships form an unbounded network (termed a behavioural system) which emerges and changes through action. Overall, Schiffer's approach appears over-complicated and mechanistic, but is important, particularly in critiquing the language centred approaches applied to the understanding of social interaction and in considering the ways in which the properties of objects emerge relationally (see chapters 3 and 6).

A second group of relational archaeologists emerged through the publication of a group of papers under the umbrella of 'symmetrical archaeology' (see Shanks 2007). The aim of this so called symmetrical approach was to acknowledge the effect of things, both in the construction of past societies and in our understanding of these societies. These scholars identified a need to collapse the dualisms inherent in post-processual archaeology, between subject and object, meaning and referent, representation and represented and past and present, to acknowledge that these are entangled within each other rather than being defined separately (Webmoor 2007). Through study we are bound up in particular sets of relationships with objects, which determine how we come to understand the past for example, whilst the past continues to act upon us in the present (Shanks 2007, 591). Just as in the past 'the social' emerged through action; the past emerges through relationships built in the present. Furthermore, the ontological distinctions inherent in archaeological interpretation, particularly that between humans and non-humans, should not be considered to exist *a priori* (Witmore 2007), indeed numerous indigenous ontologies can be cited in which such a distinction does not exist (see the discussion of animism in chapter 3). Such a distinction emerges through action and the nature of our relationships with the material world. Rather than taking such a distinction as read we must work to understand how it comes about. Fundamentally, symmetry makes us consider how humans live with, rather than in, the world, as they become drawn into mixtures and entanglements through action. Crucially the process of undertaking such an archaeology, in which meaning emerges through interaction, is defined not as a theoretical framework, but as a methodological approach, something echoed in the work of the Actor-Network Theory scholars discussed below. Symmetrical archaeology offers a rhetoric, an impetus, to rethink the way we study artefacts and how we generate knowledge about them. It leads us to critically examine how the past acts upon us and makes us who we are, whilst also considering how our actions create our understanding and representation of archaeology. Methodologically we must rethink artefacts, to consider processes of entanglement and emergent meanings, to consider how people and objects are made together.

A major driving force behind symmetrical archaeology is the work of Actor-Network Theory (ANT) scholars, particularly Bruno Latour (Latour 1993; but see also Law 1992; Law and Hassard 1999). ANT is above all a methodological approach, in which 'the social' is seen as a network of actors (or more specifically actants) which are both human and non-human. These actors are brought together through action and therefore 'the social' emerges through action. As a methodology it can be used to reconstruct, explain and understand the social (Callon 1999, 194). The term Actor-Network Theory requires some explanation. Firstly we have established that ANT is more of a method than a theory. Network analysis has received increasing attention in archaeology (Brughmans 2010), including within medieval archaeology (Sindbæk 2007), however within the ANT literature the term has a specific definition. Rather than being a network in the sense of connected nodes through which information passes without any form of deformation, actors should be seen as a series of translations (Latour 1999, 15), associations through which meaning is in some way distorted or formed, a process which leave traces. Through the study of these traces we can reconstruct the network and thus understand 'the social'. The 'actors' within the network are mediators, transforming and transferring meaning through interactions (Latour 2005, 37). Anything and anyone can be an actor, even if only fleetingly, a realisation which leads to us reconsidering the nature of agency (see below). It is the understanding of the relationship between humans and non-humans which is the central thread which joins these approaches together. Understanding these relationships leads to a consideration of the processes of assembly and the introduction of the term assemblage. The formation of relationships can be conceptualised as a process of assembly, the bringing together of the humans and non-humans which are the building blocks of a given social context, or 'social assemblage'. But it is not just the 'social' which is an assemblage. Each actor is themselves an actor-network, formed and sustained through associations (Callon 1999, 181).

These approaches have informed a number of archaeologists who have begun to develop a range of non-representational insights to various periods, data sets and regions, most notably within prehistoric and post-medieval archaeology. From early prehistory Conneller (2011), for example, considers how the properties of materials can be considered as emergent, being defined relationally as they are drawn into social relationships, allowing them to be considered not as constraints on human action, but as fluid substances, the meaning of which develops as they are drawn into the social process. The neolithic and bronze age periods have been particularly fertile grounds for the development of such approaches. By utilising the concept of distributed personhood, Fowler (2001) considers that persons are not purely human constructions, but rather emerge through the relationships formed between bodies and their surroundings, a concept which demands us to rethink how we consider how people perceived themselves within the material world, where identity is not the result of human intentionality but becomes a process in which a person forms through a bodies connections with spaces and things. Working on the neolithic of Orkney, Jones (2002) has demonstrated the ability of such approaches to draw together positivist scientific approaches and constructivist interpretive approaches to reconstruct the biographies of ceramic vessels and explore the relationships through which persons, pots and places were mutually constituted. Similarly, by appreciating the connections between people and materials Knappett (2005; 2011) has created an archaeology of the bronze age Aegean which acknowledges the effect of material interactions in enacting the social contexts in which things, people and spaces became meaningful, countering the traditional perspective in which people operate within a social context in which they possess a primary agency, reflected in the production and use of material culture. Working within historical archaeology, Hicks (2007) explores the connected nature of gardens on both sides of the Atlantic, arguing that these are not meaningful spaces, but rather are joined through a bundle of messy connections which emerge through analysis and which transcend both scale and time, as they are enacted as objects of research focussed upon understanding how they were enacted in the past. Working within a similar period, Dolwick's (2008) study of steamship technology in North America stresses the need to include things in understanding the constitution of social contexts, and to explore how persons and their material surroundings are mutually constituted. Such approaches have clear utility within medieval archaeology. The presence of the historical record adds further richness, not to corroborate our findings, but as a further actor whose presence we can trace in the emergence of 'the social' (see chapter 3). Studies from prehistory offer a methodology in which we can consider the connectedness of things, people and places, to see social contexts not as stages for action but as constituted through it, along with people, places and objects. Studies from historical archaeology highlight the relevance to periods where a broader and more complex range of evidence is present, providing a framework in which the effect of enacting things (in the broadest sense of the term) can be understood through the reconstruction of the connections formed by courses of action.

Medieval archaeology is clearly a suitable venue for the applicability of such approaches to archaeological research to be examined and developed, and could benefit from such experimentation. The adoption of new methodologies can assist in overcoming sub-disciplinary divisions based around the scale and stuff of study, whilst interpretively it will be possible to increasingly develop plural narratives through the reconstruction of the action which created *realities*, rather than relying upon the archaeological and historical record to reflect a single *reality*. It is surprising therefore that medieval archaeologists have not embraced these ideas with the same level of enthusiasm as their prehistorian and historical archaeologist colleagues. There are, of course, exceptions. Indeed, general considerations of material agency and the fluidity and situational nature of meanings are increasingly common, although these differ from the approaches discussed above in being primarily anthropocentric, seeing for example, materials as symbols which were culturally meaningful (*e.g.* Gilchrist 2008), rather than as substances which become meaningful with a social context. Furthermore, material agency is largely considered to be secondary to human agency, and therefore the human is considered to be the primal agent in the construction, rather than emergence, of the world (*e.g.* through the application of Gell's theory of agency in the work of Williams (2011) and Martin (2012)). Principally in relation to material culture, Mark Hall (2011; 2012) has utilised the work of Latour to provide a framework to explore the fluid and emergent meanings and effects of material culture in medieval Perth, particularly in relation to patterns of devotion. In relation to the transition into the early post-medieval period in Finland Vesa-Pekka Herva and his colleagues have considered the process of becoming in relation to objects in some detail, seeing objects as affective processes rather than bounded physical entities, which were entangled with humans through action, providing a medium for continuity in what was a period of profound change, particularly through a consideration of magic and folk beliefs (Herva and Nermi 2009; Herva 2009; Herva *et al.* 2012; see also chapter 3). Thinking relationally can greatly benefit medieval archaeology in questioning the nature of meaning and the meanings of things. We can question what the effects of interactions with the material world on the identities of people, the nature of places and the perceptions of the items which we find archaeologically, whilst also providing a means to reflect upon the process of archaeological interpretation and a methodology for overcoming the fragmentation which inherent within medieval studies more widely.

Before discussing some of these concepts in more depth I briefly wish to deviate into the field of human geography to summarise the impact of relational thought on the emergence of what have been termed 'non-representational' approaches (Thrift 2008). Like relational approaches in archaeology, these approaches are concerned with interaction and practice, in relation to the varying nature of human experiences and the multiple unravelling of 'the social' Through taking such approaches geographers have worked towards the collapsing of the dichotomy between 'human' and 'physical' geography and allowing the role of the material to be considered in the creation of place (Anderson and Harrison 2010; see also chapter 5). The term non-representational has been the focus of some debate (Lorrimer 2005). As the symmetrical archaeologists have shown us, representation and represented is a dichotomy which can be challenged by relational thought. Action does not represent a world but re-presents it, as particular associations are activated (Anderson and Harrison 2010, 14). Our study of artefacts must be seen in similar terms. Artefact assemblages are not static representations of past social contexts, but through forming relationships with these objects we are able to activate them in the re-presentation of the past, enacting individual understandings of the past, which contribute to our broader knowledge, perception and understanding of the medieval world.

This summary does not claim to have been an exhaustive review of relational approaches within archaeology. It has however outlined the core principles of such an approach, primarily the conceptualisation of 'the social' as a fluid and changing bundle of associations, formed and maintained through action, rather than a pre-determined stage on which action unfolds. It is something to be explained, rather than offering an explanation. In the remainder of this chapter I wish to discuss four of these principals in further detail, before considering how such approaches can be put into practice in the study of archaeological objects.

## Topology and Multiplicity

We have established that within a relational perspective 'the social' is an assemblage of actors, which are themselves actor-networks, composed of relationships and associations, both physical and metaphysical. People, for example, are not just flesh and bones; personhood and identity are distributed through the relationships humans form with their material surroundings (see chapter 5). Because actors are themselves assemblages, the question of scale is removed from analysis. Everything, no matter how big or small, is constructed of associations and therefore "we should analyse the great in exactly the same way that we would anybody else" (Law 1992, 1). In practice this means we need to follow the relationships and associations to understand a process of assembly and the assemblage it creates, be this an object, a document, a person, an organisation, or a landscape. This thought 'localises' action, seeing everything as connected and therefore part of the fabric of 'the social'; everything acting at some moment in some place is coming from and affecting other places through the coming together of human and non-human actors. Rather than action taking place within a global 'social', everything which is connected comes to be localised, meaning that 'the social' is created through action. A further consideration is that 'the social' itself is flat. By tracing connections we work from the bottom up, seeing groups, be they a local jogging club or a major government as being formed in exactly the same way, through connections and relationships. Status is therefore not inherent within a group, nor hierarchy within 'the social', instead these groups are formed, maintained and defined through associations and relationships, through which the agency for social hierarchy and other characteristics such as wealth emerge. This is of key importance when considering the medieval period, a period known to be highly structured and in which objects have often been interpreted within a framework based around a hierarchical structure without a critical sociological consideration of how this structure emerges.

'The social' is not formed of a neat arrangement of connections. Rather, it is a messy, entangled bundle of intersecting, partial connections, in which things act in multiple ways and is formed of action in multiple places. 'The social' must be considered as a collection of worlds, formed through diverse courses of action (see below). Places, things and people form intersections where these multiple worlds collide. This is well demonstrated in the work of Mol and Law (1995, 288–90), through a discussion of three stories and the nature of the associations which connect them. The common presence between these stories, which recount experiences within a hospital, is an ultra-scan machine. However, they argue that to see these stories as simply being three stories about the same machine is overly simplistic, making assumptions about the materiality of this item, chiefly that it is the same object to all people, with a fixed meaning within a static social context. They argue that, in fact, these stories are connected by a series of partial connections, leading to the emergence of a patchwork effect, in which things are stitched together in multiple ways as the machine is enacted in multiple ways as it is entwined in varying courses of action. It can be considered a node, through which individual social realities become entangled, meaning that 'the social' is not a neat entity in which things are joined in a straight forward way, reflecting socially determined meanings, but is the opposite; a messy bundle of partial connections which is constantly in motion as these connections form, are maintained and dissolve through action.

A relational approach has the effect of allowing us to consider multiplicity and to work across scale. By following relationships and connections we can investigate the big and the small, the near and the distant, on the same terms. Rather than scale, we can work in terms of resolution or zoom, focussing in on specific connections related to a place or object, or zooming out to consider an unbounded bundle of connections to take a broader perspective. Whichever resolution we work at, we need to acknowledge that we are framing our data, but with a permeable frame, in which external actors can act upon the network as we see it and in which these actors can act outside of our frame of reference (Callon 1999, 89). It is in this way that a relational approach allows us to place objects at the centre of medieval archaeology, not by privileging them over any other type of data, but by focussing upon the relationships which bring them into being and entangled them in the making of medieval worlds.

## Movement, Trajectory and Durability

'The social' is inherently unstable. Connections are continually made and dissolved, meaning that social contexts, people and objects are fluid, with new meanings emerging and old ones dissolving. Furthermore, as discussed above, multiple meanings or worlds can emerge through partially connected courses of action. We are then not dealing with one social context, but with multiple courses of action, sets of relationships and worlds, which pose a challenge archaeologically. Objects are constantly in motion, being brought into new sets of relationships, through which their meaning is renegotiated and in which they affect the emergence of new relationships, understandings and conceptualisations of the world. By being caught in multiple courses of action objects can move down multiple trajectories, having multiple and different affects simultaneously. Meaning and agency are fluid, flowing through connections, becoming deformed by the mediatory qualities of human and non-human actors (Urry 2000; Latour 2005, 39). Archaeologists have successfully coped with the concept of movement and changing meanings through the adoption of biographical approaches (*e.g.* Williams 2003; Morris 2011; Jones 2002; Joy 2010), derived from the work of Appudari (1986) and Kopytoff (1986). These scholars argue that objects don't possess an inherent value, but that social and economic value is gained through economic exchange and therefore commoditisation is a phase in an object's life history, as it negotiates contexts in which it gains value. Biography offers a metaphor for the entwinement of people, objects and places in a transitory manner (Gosden and Marshall 1999, 169; Mytum 2010, 244). Biographies need not follow linear trajectories, as things are caught in cycles of use, in which connections can be remade (Gosden 1994, 17). To fully relate object biographies to the mobile 'social' however, the process through which meaning is formed must be understood relationally. Studying how objects are drawn into a series of multiple relationships allows us to embrace fluidity and the partial and divergent nature of the connections into which objects are brought and to consider their effect if the creation of a changing 'social' (see Jervis 2011). Several case studies in this book focus on the reconstruction and interpretation of moments in the biography of pottery, including production (chapter 5), use (chapter 4) and deposition (chapters 5 and 6).

Yet, meaning and relationships are not entirely fluid. 'The social' is infused with a degree of durability. It is here that the properties of materials play a role. The material durability of things gives them the potential for associations to last, allowing 'the social' to become durable, for as long as relationships continue to be made with an object (Law 1992, 6). Durability then is "achieved through the power exerted through entities that don't sleep and don't break down" (Latour 2005, 70). Once these associations cease to exist the object comes to stand for past associations and networks, rather than being actively engaged within them (although, of course, it can be drawn into a new network of associations). As we shall see, a medieval pot, as part of medieval life, was active in the preservation of a particular domestic network. Some objects (*e.g.* buildings) have a high level of material durability, meaning that continued engagements with them act to make 'the social' durable. Many objects are more ephemeral, as they are used episodically. Past action is indexed in use, evoking memory and, in the process, creating a network of meaning in which particular categories, or understandings, are created and maintained. For associations to be made durable they must be continually remade (see Jones 2007, 84).

Objects can outlive their connections and power can only be exerted for as long as the object is in a network where it can act (see Law and Mol 1995, 279). This need not always be the same network. By being durable, the objects of the past still act, becoming enmeshed in new associations (Witmore 2007, 557; Webmoor 2007, 571; Thrift 2008, 9). In other words, whilst indexing past associations new meaning is created, as objects are drawn into new networks of associations. Even modern objects are gatherings of achievements from various times and places (Witmore 2007, 557), demonstrating the continuous making and remaking of associations and the varying levels of material and associative durability; for example, a car consists of ancient technology (the wheel), but also new technology (electronics). Documents add a further element to this concept. Like objects, documents can be considered to need to be enacted, through enrolment in courses of action, to retain their meaning, but in doing so can become a means through which past associations are 'black-boxed', allowing them to continue to be effective long after the moment in which they dissolved (see chapter 3). 'Black-boxing' is an important concept, and refers to the way in which meanings can be made durable, for example by recording them in a text. This creates a reference which can be re-enacted in courses of action, ensuring that meanings do not to be constantly re-defined, and therefore, bringing an element of stability and continuity to fluid social assemblages. Meaning flows between contexts, as past associations are indexed in the making, or remaking, of new ones (Jones 2007, 79). It is the associations, not the object themselves, which generate meaning and, therefore, meaning can flow between objects and through contexts; it is constructed, reconstructed and made durable through links. Objects are active in constructing a context through associations and act as mediators on the same level as any actor within the network. Their material durability brings a particular set of characteristics to an assemblage, but, like any property, this must be activated through continued interaction for it to bring durability to a social assemblage.

Our networks are fluid and consist of mediators joined by connections, which can be physical or metaphysical and which gather and assemble a collective. This fluidity though is countered by the potential for durability, inherent in the physical characteristics of objects, which must be continually enacted through the maintenance of these relationships.

## Emergent Categories and Emergent Properties

Objects are social assemblages, implying that they emerge relationally and are fundamentally unstable. However, their material properties provide them with a level of durability which gives them the impression of outlasting the connections of which they are constructed. A distinction can be drawn between artefacts as objects and artefacts as things. As things they sit in the background, awaiting relationships to be formed. Once these relationships are formed they emerge as objects, with properties which are defined through these connections (Brown 2001; Knappett 2011, 175–6). This has implications both for how we think about the properties of objects but also how we categorise them. Implicit within this acknowledgement of a shift in status from thing to object is a rejection of categories of object pre-existing action. Instead, categories emerge through action (see Olsen 2010, 49) and crucially in relation to other actors. Therefore categories can cut across materials (as for example in the case of skeumorphs; see chapter 3) and a single object can simultaneously belong to multiple categories. This is in contrast to the majority of categorisation methodologies within archaeology. Where naturalistic (*e.g.* Henrickson and McDonald 1983), typological or mathematical (*e.g.* Read 2007) approaches are used, objects come to be categorised in the present, in categories which do not acknowledge the fluidity of processes of interaction with objects. Such categories emerge from our own interaction with objects, as analysts, allowing these objects to act upon us in building interpretations of the past. They fail to acknowledge the multiple ways in which objects were categorised in the past. Using such approaches the sorting of objects into some kind of logical pattern becomes both a means and an end in artefact analysis, often focussing on characteristics an object acquired in a particular stage of its biography (typically manufacture).

Early post-processual approaches, which saw categories of objects as symbols or text, are equally monolithic and static. In this scheme, categories of objects reflect the reproduction of a social context, with particular meanings residing within objects amongst populations who understand them as symbols (see, for example, Braithwaite 1982; Hodder 1982; Thomas 1991, 85). Miller (1985) developed a more subtle understanding of categorisation process through ethno-archaeological study. He argues that categories of objects form in production, but that these meanings were multiple, depending upon the ways in which people engaged with them (for example functionally, technologically or through use in religious practices). By being understood within a system of categorisation, the use of specific types of pottery in specific ways worked to re-make a particular social context. Miller's study is important because rather than vessels being categorised by the analysis of arbitrary characteristics, their identification is informed by an understanding of the relationships in which these vessels were drawn into, relationships through which categories of people (*e.g.* in relation to the caste system) were also maintained and constantly defined. The relationships formed with objects start to be of importance in understanding how they are categorised, however this is not a truly relational approach, as the vessels are placed within a narrative in which they are related to the re-production of a social context and the maintenance of pre-defined groups, rather than seeing groups of pottery and people emerging simultaneously through action. The biographical approach discussed above allows us to acknowledge that things were categorised in multiple ways through their lives and, if a range of methodological approaches are applied, we can begin to reconstruct the various interactions between people and objects. Crucially these actions must be seen as the processes through which categories of objects and people emerged and were maintained, rather than reflecting and re-producing a pre-defined social scene.

Because categories of object emerge through action, we must also see the properties of these objects as emergent. They cannot be inherent within an object because the category of object is itself emergent. That is not to say that things do not have material properties, simply that these properties do not define them as an object. Instead, the artefact and its characteristics are defined and understood relationally, through action. Schiffer (1999) distinguishes physical properties, such as the size and shape of artefacts, from what he terms 'performance characteristics'. These characteristics emerge relationally, being defined as an artefacts ability to act or perform. Within a thing these characteristics remain as a potential, it is only once a thing becomes an object, through active engagement, that this potential is realised. In simple terms, a pot has the potential to become a cooking, storage or transport vessel, but its potential to fall into any of these categories is only met through a particular pattern of use, whilst through being embedded in multiple (either parallel or subsequent) courses of action, the vessel can fall into multiple groups, shifting from being a thing to being an object in this moment of action, before returning to being a thing, awaiting further action. Other scholars too have considered the relational nature of an object's properties. In her study of palaeolithic material culture, Conneller (2011) argues for a relational ontology, in which things and materials are seen as equivalent, as mobile groups sought new materials which could be enacting in the reforming of their material world. Whilst I do not seek to impose a relational ontology upon medieval populations, such considerations are useful to think with, as they force us to challenge the extrapolation of our own perceptions onto the minds of medieval people, providing a framework in which we can question how something became meaningful in a particular place at a particular time to a particular person or community.

A further way that the emergent and relational nature of objects' properties have been conceptualised is through the idea of affordances, derived from the work of Gibson (1979) and first applied to archaeological material by Knappett (2005, 47–9). Affordances relate to the potential which lies within a thing by virtue of its material properties, but are also dependent upon relationality. For example, grass affords eating as long as there are grazing animals to eat it, as this affordance does not exist within the relationship between humans and grass (Knappett 2005, 48–9). In some cases the affordances of a thing emerge in the moment, for example a wall may afford balance if a person uses it to support themselves whilst falling. In others the recognition of affordances requires an element of learning or awareness, for example in understanding that a chair affords sitting or a letter box affords posting a letter (see Knappett 2005, 46–8). In such cases affordances require a degree of memory and knowledge, built through past interactions with a thing and cited in future action. Affordances are emergent and relational, but have durability through knowledge. This knowledge is mediated through action, not residing within a person, but being formed and remade through the maintenance of relations between people and their surroundings. In this way the affordances of an object emerge through particular sets of relationships, allowing them to vary between cultures or even between people. Affordances and properties are not defined by humans and allocated to objects, they emerge through action. This becomes even clearer when one considers the constraints that the material properties of things put on us. Action is guided by these material properties, as it may only be possible to use them in a limited number of ways, for example. The ability to act then comes to be distributed between people and the objects, the utility and meaning of objects emerging through relationships between a range of actors which come together to open up but also constrain possible courses of action.

All of these ideas lead to two key points. Firstly, objects are categorised through action. They are multiple objects, both at different times and at the same time. The transfer from thing to object is reliant upon action and can be related to Latour's distinction between intermediaries (things) and mediators (objects). Categories of objects are not stable, but fluid; objects are always in motion, moving between groups as they categorised in multiple ways. Secondly, properties (affordances or performance characteristics) do not reside within objects, but are defined, recognised and maintained relationally, meaning that the same object can afford different things to different people, within the constraints which logic and a things material properties put on action. This has a profound impact on the process of artefact analysis. The process of categorisation and cataloguing must be acknowledged as forming categories through our own relationships with archaeological objects, which may bare little or no relationship to those which formed at some point in the past. Instead, we must think about the processes or courses of action in which these object were enmeshed, allowing us to explore how different properties emerged at different times and in different places and the effect that this had upon the perception of these objects. These ideas are considered further in chapter 6.

## Agency

So far I have argued that 'the social' is formed through action and that this same action leads to the emergence of objects (from a malaise of things), each with relationally defined properties, affordances or performance characteristics. Similarly, people are defined through these same processes. Groups (or identities) can also be argued to emerge and be maintained through action, defined relationally and being both unstable and multiple. An approach to identity is advanced in chapter 4, here it suffices to demonstrate that people and objects are defined in the same way – through relationships. If properties or characteristics do not reside within things it follows that agency too is not inherent within an actor, but instead this too is formed through action. By thinking relationally, the ANT literature has successfully conflated the concepts of sociality and materiality, as people and the material world are joined through relationships and action (Law and Mol 1995, 274). Agency too must be seen in a distributed way, as being formed in the relationships between people and things. As such neither humans nor objects have agency, instead all things have the potential to produce agency, to affect a course of action.

Debates around the nature of agency have focussed on the question of material agency. It is widely acknowledged (*e.g.* Miller 2005, Jones and Boivin 2011) that this concept was first brought to the archaeologists' attention by the work of Gell (1998), who argued that objects (in this case art) acted as an index for social agency. He argued that art could not be a primary agent as it lacks intentionality. Instead, as a secondary agent, it acts as a medium for human agency, an approach which has since been transferred onto objects as seeing them as having 'embedded human agency' (including by this author; Jervis 2008; see also Gosden 2005). The term agency itself is widely attributed to Giddens (1979), who set the concept up in opposition to structure in his structuration theory, arguing that the material conditions both enable and are reproduced by social (*i.e.* human) agents. This inadvertently gives a notion of material agency, as material contexts enable the reproduction of a social structure by humans.

We can question though if objects do more than this; they have the power to act on humans, a statement explored by Jones and Boivin (2011) through a discussion of animism and fetishism. If, as ANT scholars, particularly Latour (2005), state, things and people are enfolded in one another, action and thus agency must be distributed through both, it is not possible to only see objects as secondary agents. Therefore, intentionality cannot be a property of a 'primary' agent, instead it is a property of the relationship *between* humans and things; it is distributed through the two and 'spun' as they come together (Jones and Boivin 2011, 341; Whatmore 1999, 27). In order to be able to study this redistribution of agency we need to return to the arguments over the nature of materiality and particularly the point that an objectification approach, as defined by Miller, leads to things simply reflecting the social system, rather than being active in its constitution. This re-enforces, rather than bridges, the divide between social and material (see Malafouris 2004, 53). We need an approach which combines the study of the material properties of objects with their role in social practice, they need to be both material and cultural, substance and concept (Boivin 2004; Malafouris 2004; Jones and Boivin 2011, 350). Examples could be the way that Boivin (2000) studies the remaking of structures in Rajasthan in relation to the cultural calendar, or the links between agriculture, landscape and pottery studied by Andrew Jones (2002).

A relational approach requires us to see human and material actors as equal, with intentionality distributed between them. This requires us to rethink both material and human agency and, therefore, the concept of agency itself. Latour (2005, 46) states that "an actor is what is made to act by many others". Therefore, agency is not a property of an actor but the result of action. Objects or humans do not have agency, it is produced through performance and action (Jones and Boivin 2011, 351; Witmore 2007, 552; Olsen 2007, 584; Law 2004, 134). Agency is therefore present in these associations as a potential energy until the actors begin to act, the network is mobilised and 'the social' constructed. We have constructed a model of interaction whereby actors are human and non-human, they are mediators and cause each other to act by acting themselves. It is important to emphasise that such an approach does not call for objects and humans to be seen as equivalents, or that we wish to see the world as undifferentiated, just that the two are considered together, as equals in terms of analytical attention, to allow us to study how distributed collectives negotiate the world (Witmore 2007, 547).

## Summary: The Practice of Relational Archaeology

The relational archaeology sketched out in this chapter is centred on understanding the relationships and associations between people and things. In doing so, we come to an understanding of the world as a fluid web of connections, in which meaning and agency are not inherent within people or things, but emerge through, and are sustained by, particular relationships. For medieval archaeology this has several implicactions. Firstly we must acknowledge the interconnectedness of things across evidence classes. That is not to say that we must not specialise in the study of particular classes of evidence. What we must not do though is to allow specialist study to marginalise particular types of evidence in archaeological discourse. It is the responsibility of specialists to acknowledge how their evidence is connected to other types of evidence and to explore these connections. That does not simply mean that ceramicists should understand glass or faunal remains. It means that landscape archaeologists must understand the potential for relationships between the land and objects (see chapter 5) or that architectural specialists must understand how relationships may have formed between buildings and things (see chapter 6) and be prepared to follow these connections through collaborative, interdisciplinary research. Secondly, we must develop new methodologies, and use existing ones, to reconstruct the biography of objects, landscapes and buildings. This means going beyond characterisation and phased plans or reconstructions, to explore how at different points in their lives things were drawn into particular relationships, allowing us to examine connectivity and investigate durability and effect. In many cases we have the methodologies required; we simply need to use them in a creative way. This does not mean that we need to reconstruct entire biographies, but rather we can devise ways of acknowledging and exploring fluidity when investigating objects, be it in the examination of their use, production or deposition. Finally, a truly relational medieval archaeology must be part of a truly relational field of medieval studies. We must identify links between things and documents and understand documents not as a factual roadmap, as a scaffold, for archaeological interpretation. Instead we must follow the lead of post-modernist historians in understanding the fluid meaning of texts and question how these came about and what the effect of engagement with them was

(Ermarth 1991 (1997, 48); Jordanova 2000, 109–10). A relational medieval archaeology is an interdisciplinary exercise which will require much work, but will greatly enrich our understanding of the medieval period.

Within this mould, the case studies presented in this book focus on a single category of evidence, pottery, but attempt to explore the ways in which it is connected to other sources of evidence relating to the medieval period. Chapter 3 investigates the relationships which lead to the emergence of pots and objects through examination of the relationships between pottery, documents, people and other materials, to explore the emergence of particular properties (or performance characteristics). Chapter 4 uses pottery to examine the formation and maintenance of identities, considering how tracing interactions between people and pottery lets us observe the emergence of groups, rather than seeking to identify 'known' groups within archaeological evidence. Chapter 5 focusses on the emergence of landscape, arguing that landscapes emerge through action, rather than being a stage on which it occurs, exploring how multiple landscapes emerge through resource procurement and depositional practices. Finally, chapter 6 examines pottery in motion, considering how its meaning changes in relation to other actors in particular settings. By acknowledging the medieval period as a bundle, a collection, of partially associated actors, acting upon each other, mediating, rather than transmitting, meaning and generating agency through action a relational approach will bring multiplicity and movement to archaeological analysis. The focus moves from the safe ground of 'truth' to the more interpretive arena of understanding, allowing us to consider multiple medieval experiences from various perspectives, through the following of varying courses of action. Doing so will be rewarding, not only in that it will allow us to realise the potential of our sources, but also in enriching our understanding of medieval society as vibrant and dynamic, rather than static and prescribed.

argues that the products were produced by immigrant potters, with historical evidence being used to question how and why this industry developed, with an argument that the cathedral was a patron for the immigrant potters, emerging. History then not only guided the interpretation of ceramics, but provided a wealth of additional information that can be integrated into the interpretation of ceramic assemblages. It becomes clear, when such a viewpoint emerges, that the study of historical and archaeological sources cannot be separated and must be undertaken together, without one type of evidence having primacy over the other. These sources emerged from different but inter-twined courses of action in the past and it is our role to reconstruct this action to understand how particular ceramic assemblages emerged, how these processes affected people in the past and crucially how these courses of action are connected to other courses of action. The key point here is that neither historical or archaeological scholars set the agenda, instead it is set by interactions with the sources, be they written or material, as we are forced to question how particular phenomena came about and what the effect of these processes was.

Although medieval archaeologists have, undoubtedly, been successful in the last 30 years at pulling away from the shadow of history and pursuing their own research agendas (see chapter 1), it is noticeable that there have been few explicit attempts to further define, understand and engage with the disciplinary interface between history and archaeology (McClain 2012, 136). Whilst history has continued to provide context, be it framing the monasteries investigated by Gilchrist (1994) or the guildhalls examined by Giles (2000), or providing clear episodes of peasant resistance against which dress accessories can be examined (Smith 2009b), the opportunity to examine the interconnectedness of archaeological objects and written sources has largely been missed. Similarly historians have utilised historical and archaeological sources, for example to build up an understanding of the role of silk in Anglo-Saxon England (Fleming 2007), yet such studies typically utilise these two strands in a descriptive manner. Such text-aided archaeologies (or archaeology-aided histories) use sources selectively, rather than exploring how documents and things occupied, and were effective within, the same material contexts (Moreland 2006, 137).

Following Wicker (1999, 169), approaches can be considered to be cross-disciplinary (combining historical and archaeological sources to reach a common goal) or multi-disciplinary (using historical and archaeological sources separately to address similar questions), but rarely truly interdisciplinary (using an innovative, integrated approach to solve problems using the materials of multiple disciplines). With this in mind, it is worth considering how a relational approach may assist in the development of truly interdisciplinary approaches. Both archaeological objects and historical documents can be considered the product of relationships, between people and their surroundings, both in the physical sense but also in terms of the processes through which the developed and maintained (and continue to develop and maintain) meaning (Moreland 2006). Both sets of evidence also affect future relationships, both in our understanding of the past, but also in the lives of past populations (for example rules may impact behaviour and social relationships). Like objects, documents must have the potential to act and develop agency through interactions. Texts are things which become objects through relations. In one sense texts such as rules and charters have an inherent durability. They are constantly engaged with and enacted, although not necessarily in a physical sense. They continue to act as part of a collective. Yet the words themselves are not inherently meaningful and we must acknowledge that documents are defined and understood relationally. Therefore they cannot be taken at face value. Instead we must consider how they came to be activated in different ways, as they became entwined in multiple courses of action. A relational approach therefore allows us to consider that documentary sources do not have primacy over archaeological sources, but rather that both act at the same level, although their properties mean that they act in different ways. I am not arguing that texts should be treated as archaeological objects, as their unique character means they demand specialist study. We must however acknowledge that neither texts nor objects have fixed meanings or inherent agency. Both have the potential to inform our understanding of the past through interaction and both acted in the past. What we must understand is the courses of action in which both were entwined, the ways that they were connected and that meaning emerged, rather than seeing texts or things as direct reflections of how things were.

Relational archaeology and particularly a conceptualisation of distributed agency offers great potential for developing truly interdisciplinary approaches to the medieval period, in which we are defined as medievalists first and archaeologists or historians second. In doing so, by following relationships and associations, tracing the emergence of agency through these relationships, we can move to a multi-faceted, dynamic and fluid understanding of the medieval period, rather than re-producing a monolithic cannon of knowledge by seeing objects and texts as reflections of fact, in which 'research' acts to reify received wisdom. In this section I explore how such a perspective can lead to a more truly interdisciplinary approach within medieval studies as a whole. In doing so it is first necessary to problematize the relationship between material culture and text (Moreland 2006, 138), before presenting a relational approach and exploring this through the case study of medieval inventories.

## Material Culture as Text and Documents as Material Culture

A key concept within early post-processual approaches to material culture was the assertion that material culture could be read as text and that elements of an object, such as form and decoration, relate to a symbolic grammar (Shanks and Tilley 1992, 132; Holten 1997, 184). The decoration of pottery for example did not only deliver a specific cultural message, but by being read and understood, played a role in the re-making of a particular social context (Braithwaite 1982; Thomas 1991, 85; see also Driscoll 1984, 107–8; Austin and Thomas 1990). The fundamental basis is that the archaeological record is meaningfully constituted, and therefore that the meaning behind it can be deciphered through analysis (Tabaczynski 1993, 7). Further approaches enrolled the concept of the metaphor into the interpretation of material culture. Objects became a mode of representation, standing for concepts or structures in a non-literal way, linking the concrete and the abstract and providing means by which groups become linked through a shared reading and understanding of their surroundings (Tilley 1999). As symbols, objects can only be 'read' or understood within their context and therefore this concept, that objects can be read and achieve multiple meanings, underpinned the post-processual critique of global systems, and promoted the emergence of a contextually situated archaeology. More recent approaches have approached the concept through the use of Piercian semiotics, considering how, whilst objects may be symbols (requiring meaning to form and be re-made as cultural knowledge through repeated use), they may also act as an index or icon, forms of sign which can be more widely understood and interpreted, being understood relationally, rather than having fixed, arbitrary and culturally specific meanings (see chapter 2). By considering that objects become meaningful through association, the concept that artefacts are the same as texts, which carry messages to be decoded by situating them within a context, becomes unstitched. Rather the focus shifts to understanding how objects are enrolled in the emergence of meaning; neither archaeological contexts or texts are meaningfully constituted, rather meaning emerges *through* their formation and subsequent enrolment in courses of action, be that scientific analysis or subsequent use of a document, thing or building.

Conceptualising material culture as a text to be read therefore poses a fundamental problem. Such an approach relies upon there being a meaning inscribed within something which can then be read. I have argued that this is not the case, as meaning is not carried by things, but emerges through engagement with them. The problem is, at a simple level, a taxonomic one. Documents and things occupy the same material spaces and are entangled in the same courses of action. Therefore rather than treating material culture (in the archaeological sense) as text, we should consider that texts are one category of material culture (Andrén 1998, 145–6; Moreland 2006, 139). Therefore, just as objects play a role in constituting identities or social contexts, so too are documents enrolled in these processes; agency is spun through the production and use of documents and therefore they do not amount to passive reflections of how things were, but rather contributed to making them that way (Driscoll 1988, 167; Moreland 2006, 142). Such an approach finds a parallel in the approach to reconciling history and archaeology taken by Leone (1988), in which the two sources are studied in a reflexive manner, in which the effects of documents can be seen in the material record, whilst through experiencing the landscape in particular ways the meaning of the text comes into focus. Whilst documents may only relate specifically to one portion of a society (the literate) (Driscoll 1988, 168), by being caught up in effective courses of action the effect of documents were rippled outwards, impacting upon those who could not read, for example by restricting behaviour through the enforcement of rules or charters (Moreland 2006, 144). Therefore, just as objects cannot be considered reflections of a context, but were enrolled in its maintenance and formation (chapter 2), so documents, as material culture, performed in a similar way (Andrén 1998, 155).

The meaning of both texts and objects is relational; both have biographies and are caught up in flows of action (Hodder 1994, 394). Although an explicitly expressive form of material culture, texts are just one end of the spectrum of material manifestations of human life, interactions with which effect the ways in which we perceive ourselves in relation to our surroundings, contribute to memory building and to the emergence and maintenance of the entangled individual realities which comprise the broader 'social'. By seeing text at the same taxonomic level as other artefacts, considering them to have formed, developed meaning and caused effect both in the same way, and through mutual entanglement, it becomes possible to reconcile the interdisciplinary schism between history and archaeology, to explore the inter-relationships between texts and documents in an interdisciplinary manner, rather than use them to corroborate each other in a cross-disciplinary manner, or consider them separately in a multi-disciplinary manner.

## A Relational Perspective on the Nature of Documents

Following the concepts outlined in chapter 2, we can consider that texts are assembled, as the coming together of people, the material culture of writing and, presumably, some other connections which form the subject matter at hand. But what actually are these documents, and what do they do? Unsurprisingly, documents have not been considered in any depth by relational archaeologists, largely because the majority are concerned with prehistory (although see Knappett 2008). We must therefore turn to other disciplines to consider how documents may be considered in relational perspective, and specifically to Latour's (2010) *The Making of Law*, an ethnographic study of French administrative law, which is firmly rooted within Actor-Network Theory.

Latour's work considers the various documents which are both formed through legal action (for example judgements), but also those pre-existing documents, such as maps or newspaper cuttings, which become enrolled in these actions, by taking their place in case files. Whilst these documents play specific roles in the ongoing making and re-making of law (defined as a bundle of referential associations which is constantly in motion, being re-defined through the enacting of legal courses of action (Latour 2010, 106)), none are inherently legal. Rather these documents *become* legal through being enrolled in courses of action (Latour 2010, 2007). Therefore any document can become legal (Latour 2010, 101), with its character as a legal document being re-formed through its continued enrolment in legal action. This is most visible in those documents formed through legal action, which serve to 'black-box' legal decisions (recording them so that they can be re-enacted in future action, without the need to reach the decisions again; see definition of this concept in chapter 2), infusing a durability which means, that although continually being reformed, the law and the courses of action behind it are largely consistent. These are powerful texts, upon which the agency to remake the law is reliant, as without them it cannot be spun (Latour 2010, 163). In other words, the law is not remade by human agency, nor is human agency deferred onto or enshrined within documents. Rather, these documents must be present and enacted to reform the citational network of the law, and by extension, effect continuity in 'the social' (Latour 2010, 160). The first point then relates to the meaning of documents, which can be extended to that of any object. That is that documents are not inherently meaningful. Even though the words don't change, they must be written or read (engaged with) to cause effect and, furthermore, they become meaningful as particular forms of document, with particular effects, by being enacted through enrolment in specific (in this case legal) courses of action. This is well summed up by Latour (2010, 223):

> "we find ourselves in a textual universe which has the double peculiarity of being so close to the reality that it can take its place, and yet unintelligible without an ongoing work of interpretation".

Documents then, are meaningless if not continually re-enacted, and are deceptive in providing the historian with a substitute for a past 'social', but one which is only meaningful if the courses of action in which these documents were enrolled are understood. Secondly, if these courses of action change, then new meanings can develop, leading to the enacting of the document having varying effect (Latour 2010, 163). Like non-documentary objects then, the meaning of documents emerges as they become enacted through enrolment in courses of action. They can serve to infuse durability into action, and thus 'the social' (Law and Mol 1995, 279), but only for as long as they are enacted. Furthermore, it can be considered that documents are key to the transformation of an artefact from a nameless, meaningless 'thing' to a meaningful, named 'object', as the objects role is black-boxed in written form, and its meaning re-enacted through the enrolment of the document in action, even in the absence of the object at stake (Knappett 2008, 145). Documents like other objects become meaningful through action, they are caught in tangled courses of action in which they are enrolled with people and things, and therefore are crucial to our understanding of the forming and re-forming of these social contexts.

A second area to consider is the form which documents take. We have already seen that any document can be enacted as a legal document, but, just as with an object, the form of a document is influenced by other connections. An example of this is the differences apparent in the style adopted by authors of academic texts and of informal correspondences. Here it can be considered that the author is being drawn into a network of associations not only with their writing materials and subject matter, but also their future audience, with the agency behind the document being formed through the coming together of this bundle of heterogeneous and dispersed actors (Latour 2010, 205). The web of associations from which the agency (or motivation) to produce a specific document are therefore materialised (or black-boxed) in the form it takes. Medieval wills, for example, display an increasing concern with the inheritance of material possessions (Cohn 2012, 990), indexing contemporary attitudes and materialising the motivations behind the formation of this document. Yet by being produced and enacted, the document also has effects, making this attitude durable as it is enacted in the distribution of goods after death.

Finally, we can consider the effects of documents. These are clearly far reaching. By being enrolled in legal courses of action, with people, they are effective in the emergence and maintenance of the identities of legal practitioners (Latour 2010, 126), but also extend beyond the courtroom, by documenting and black boxing what is and isn't acceptable within a society (see also Moreland 2006, 144). Furthermore, although the documents are not the law, they play a role in legal decision making, black-boxing opinions and past decisions and thus constraining the courses of action a judge can take in determining a case (Latour 2010, 192).

What then, are the implications of this work for thinking about the relationships between documents and objects? Firstly, we can consider that whilst the material properties of each are fixed, by being enrolled together in courses of action, in terms of meaning and effect they are mutually constitutive. Secondly, whilst both infuse durability into 'the social', documents do this in a specific way, which may include black-boxing values (see below) or attitudes to the material trappings of life, which are reformed through the enacting of the document. Finally, both are effective, as they are caught up in the spinning of agency and unfolding and re-formation of 'the social'. In the remainder of this section these ideas will be applied to a specific form of medieval document, household inventories, through an exploration of the relationships between these documents and pottery.

*Introducing Inventories*

A number of documents are at the disposal of the archaeologist or historian seeking references to pottery. As discussed above however, the majority have been used to complement archaeological material, rather than examine the dynamic relationship between these two forms of material culture. In particular the discrepancies between the historical and archaeological record have been highlighted, with it being demonstrated that taken in isolation both the historical and archaeological records can be considered incomplete, and, therefore, misleading (Beddel 2000, 226). An exception within medieval archaeology is Brown's (1998) study of Southampton's port books, which highlights the customable values of pottery imported into Southampton and begins to consider the implications of these in relation to understanding contemporary attitudes to pottery. A similar approach can be seen in Courtney's (1997, 103–4) discussion of ideas of consumption in relation to ceramics, in which documents and pottery are taken together to consider spending habits and the role of ceramics as a commodity within medieval society. Whereas other approaches may be considered cross-disciplinary, such approaches move more towards an interdisciplinary perspective, in which the dynamics between the making of documents and the meaning of things is considered.

Medieval archaeologists have rarely considered the evidence provided by inventories, although historians studying them have engaged in cross-disciplinary research (Field 1965; Dyer 1998 169–75; Briggs in press). This is in contrast to American historical archaeology, where sophisticated studies of probate inventories, produced for estate and tax purposes, have provided a great deal of insight into contemporary value systems and perceptions of material culture (see Beddel 2000 for a review). Such studies move towards a more interdisciplinary consideration of the inventory, exploring the formation processes behind them (see M. Brown 1988) and the ways in which they were enrolled in the making and re-forming of these value systems and systems of meaning. It is clear that there are discrepancies between the historical and archaeological record. Archaeologists recover the wooden and metal vessels used alongside the ubiquitous ceramics comparatively rarely; creating a misleading picture of past consumption patterns (Beddel 2000, 226). Inventories too are incomplete, being produced to a set of written (but lost) or unwritten rules about what it was appropriate to include within these lists, and to what level of detail (Beddel 2000, 228), meaning, therefore, that they were never intended to be complete. Whilst some items are therefore more likely to appear within inventories than in the archaeological record, due to processes of recycling, re-use or decay, but others may only appear in the archaeological record, by virtue of the processes through which the inventories emerged.

Whilst the conclusions reached through the study of documents dating to the early modern period cannot be directly extrapolated back to the Middle Ages, a number of points are potentially of use to us in considering medieval documents. The first of these is that these documents provide insights into taxonomic systems, identifying what features of these items were of importance to the compilers of these documents, be it form, function, colour or source (see Beaudry 1988). Secondly, the monetary valuations attached to these items also provide us with a relative hierarchy of materials and forms, which may reflect market value, although it should be considered that, like the estimations of customable values found in medieval port books, these figures may represent more of an index of value than the going rate. Thirdly, and most importantly for the study which follows, the inclusion and omission of objects from these documents is telling. The ways in which objects are grouped, rather than discussed individually, or indeed omitted from inventories altogether, suggests the cataloguing of such mundane, commonplace and low value items was tedious (indeed some documents even state this), does not mean these items were meaningless, but rather that the perception of them was such that their presence was taken for granted, or seen as un-noteworthy (Hodge 2006, 9). Even where inventories create the illusion of detail in relation to cheaper items such as ceramics, comparison with the archaeological record suggests some forms were afforded more attention than others in the compilation of inventories (Beddel 2000, 234). Creating a simple correlation between monetary value and the attention paid to them in inventories is however simplistic and over-reliant on modern pre-conceptions of the relative value of things (see Hodge 2006). Different communities developed different systems of value. This is well demonstrated, for example, by the occurrence of pewter, an item comparatively rarely recovered archaeologically, in North American historic period probate inventories. Evidence suggests, for example, that these items were preferred over imported ceramics in poorer households, despite their higher cost, due to their durability and the fact that vessels could be recast, a material property which underpins their occurrence in inventories, even in broken form (Martin 1989, 19). Rather we need to consider the processes through which the document emerged as material culture and the interactions between people and material culture which underpinned its emergence. Furthermore, by considering the effect of these processes we can build an understanding of the agentive role of these documents, as they effected the durability of these systems of value.

Most simply the process of inventorying can be considered one of translation, in which objects become words and the meaning of the object in question comes to be distributed through this process (Hodge 2006, 2). Therefore, rather than the words standing for a value, they were enrolled in the process through which that value, which can be considered an emergent property of things, was made durable. As documents were made and enacted through the process of valuation, they served to black-box the system and remake it through subsequent courses of action. Furthermore, these documents index varying 'appreciation trajectories' (Hodge 2006, 4), as the relationships into which objects were drawn (and therefore the resultant meanings and values emerging from these interactions) varied through time. For example, in relation to 18th century inventories from the north-eastern USA, Beddel (2000, 238) concludes that although the primary reason behind the omission of ceramics from inventories is their low monetary worth, the reasons behind this are not simple. As these lists were produced for probate purposes, they only contained items of sufficient value to be the subject of a dispute. However, the recording and omission of ceramics is not uniform across these inventories. It is noted that in wealthier households ceramics were more likely to be noted, potentially because there were higher quantities present, meaning that they could not be ignored (Beddel 2000, 239). Because of both of these issues, inventories perhaps present the homes of the poorer as sparser in material terms than they were in reality, and than is suggested in the archaeological record. Furthermore, in these households it is likely that coloured ceramics may have played a very different role than in wealthy homes, allowing the infusion of colour, decoration and symbolism into the home in a manner appropriate to the household's means (Beddel 2000, 244), with the meaning and worth of these vessels emerging through a very different set of human-material relationships to those in the wealthier households, in which the ceramics are more prevalent in the inventory record (see also Martin 1989, 22). Inventories are complex documents, formed through varying social processes, in which objects came to be valued relationally, being the result of a particular set of processes and having the effect of reifying, or black-boxing, varying systems of value.

With these considerations in mind, we can move towards an examination of the relationships formed with pottery through the formation and enacting of inventories in medieval England. Two recent studies have considered these documents in historical perspective. Briggs (in press) has examined the evidence provided by rural peasant inventories, found in manorial rolls of the 14th–16th centuries, produced on occasions when it was the lord's right to seize the goods belonging to a peasant tenant. Three such occasions are identified; on conviction of a felony, on death intestate and on a peasant fleeing the manor. In particular, Briggs is concerned with the motivations behind the compilation of these documents and the nature of the items which are included and omitted. It is clear that these lists are incomplete. Pottery, the most ubiquitous artefact from medieval rural excavations, is all but absent and it appears that village appraisers worked to a particular system of value in the compilation of these documents, albeit a system which appears to have varied both regionally and temporally. The concept of differential systems of value is also considered by Goldberg (2008) in a consideration of inventories from urban and rural contexts. Goldberg identifies clear differences in the spending habits of urban and rural populations, with the former spending more on goods associated with comfort, such as cushions, and objects of status (silver spoons), whilst rural populations invested more heavily in utensils and tools. This, he argues, is more related to varying lifestyles and concerns than fundamental differences in wealth. Goldberg's study demonstrates that objects became meaningful in different ways to urban and rural communities and, by extension, that they were enrolled in very different processes of social assembly, which both spun and maintained the agency for varying social realities of medieval life to occur.

## Enacting Documents: Pottery and Inventories

Having established a framework through which to examine the relationships between documents and objects, and outlined some of the core issues associated with the study of inventories, we can now move to examine the relationship between pottery and these documents in medieval England. Two sets of documents will be considered, the first are the peasant inventories examined by Briggs (in press) and the second are a collection of later medieval probate inventories from Southampton.

It is immediately apparent that pottery is excluded from the processes of inventorying undertaken on rural manors. In order to examine the relationship between these documents and the material record a survey of material culture from 17 rural excavations in the same area was undertaken (Figure 3.1). As is to be expected, pottery dominated the artefact assemblages from these sites, generally taking the form of locally or regionally produced jars, bowls and jugs (Table 3.1). From the fourteen inventories considered in Briggs' study only two contain references to pottery; one is mentioned individually and valued at 1d and the other is part of a list of vessels in wood, earthenware and metal. Statistically, wooden vessels are most common, although the majority come from a single inventory. The only vessels to be present across a wide range of inventories are those of

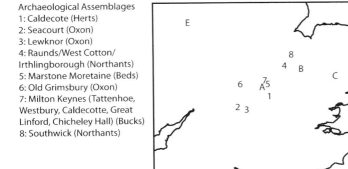

Archaeological Assemblages
1: Caldecote (Herts)
2: Seacourt (Oxon)
3: Lewknor (Oxon)
4: Raunds/West Cotton/
Irthlingborough (Northants)
5: Marstone Moretaine (Beds)
6: Old Grimsbury (Oxon)
7: Milton Keynes (Tattenhoe,
Westbury, Caldecotte, Great
Linford, Chicheley Hall) (Bucks)
8: Southwick (Northants)

Inventories
A: Thornborough/
Great Horwood (Bucks)
B: Barton/Oakington/
Willingham/Sutton/
Cottenham (Cambs)
C: Walsham le Willows
(Suffolk)
D: Bunwell/Horsham St Faith/
Coltishall (Norfolk)
E: Ruyton (Shropshire)

*Figure 3.1. Map showing locations associated with the archaeological assemblages and peasant inventories under discussion. Note that sites in close proximity have been grouped together for clarity. Drawing: Ben Jervis.*

*Table 3.1: Quantification of pottery from the rural sites studied by form. Note that data was not available for all sites. (SC: Sherd Count, EVE: Estimated vessel equivalent, VC: Vessel count).*

| Site Name | Jar | | | Jug | | | Bowl/Dish | | | Other | | |
|---|---|---|---|---|---|---|---|---|---|---|---|---|
| | SC | EVE | VC | SC | EVE | VC | SC | EVE | VC | SC | EVE | VC |
| Caldecotte (Bucks) | | | 61 | | | 5 | | | 19 | | | |
| Lime Street, Irthlingborough | | 11 | | | 4 | | | 3 | | | 0 | |
| Loughton | 905 | | | 102 | | | 255 | | | 13 | | |
| Old Grimsbury, Banbury | | | 58 | | | 10 | | | 17 | | | 5 |
| Westbury, Milton Keynes | 47 | | | 27 | | | 24 | | | 2 | | |

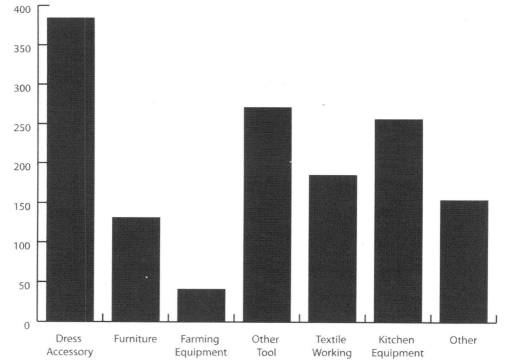

*Figure 3.2. Quantification of non-ceramic artefacts from the rural assemblages studied. Drawing: Ben Jervis. (y axis: number of objects).*

bronze or copper alloy, items which are comparatively rare in the archaeological record, with only 49 being recovered from the 17 sites considered (see also Egan 2005, 198; 201) (Figures 3.2 and 3.3). In interpreting this information it is important to consider the formation processes behind these two sources of data. Whereas the inventories record the items present within a single snapshot of time, the archaeological record accumulates over many years, if not decades. Metal vessels are likely to be recycled as scrap, whereas wooden vessels could be burnt as fuel. Ceramics have their own issues.

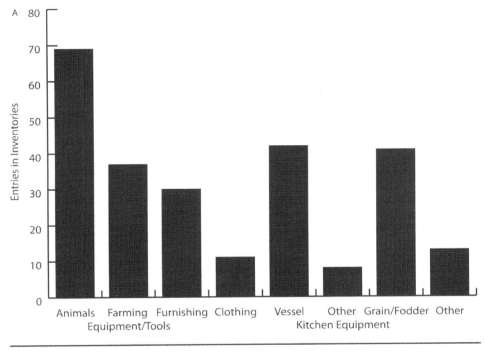

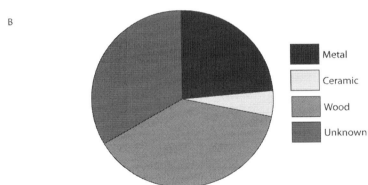

*Figure 3.3. A) Quantification of items appearing in peasant inventories studied by Briggs. B) Quantification of vessels appearing in peasant inventories studied by Briggs, categorised by material (N=42). Drawing: Ben Jervis.*

They have a comparatively short use life in relation to metal vessels, meaning that many ceramic pots may be used within the life of a single metal vessel, whilst their material properties mean that they are the best preserved of any vessels used in the medieval home. However, comparative evidence suggests that pottery was present in significant quantities within the peasant home. At Dinna Clerks (Devon) a peasant house burnt down, resulting in the pottery used being preserved *in situ*. Here 12 vessels, mostly taking the form of locally produced jars were present (Beresford 1979). Therefore, whilst time depth does exaggerate the quantity of pottery used, it remains true that ceramic vessels can be expected to have been present within the homes being surveyed in significant quantities. Similarly, on the basis of the inventories, when time depth is considered, metal vessels are considerably under-represented in the archaeological record.

It would be reasonable to conclude that pottery was not recorded within inventories because of its inherently low value. However, to do so would be to ignore the emergent and relational nature of value, and to see the document as a simple reflection of a fixed medieval value system, rather than an object formed, enacted and enrolled in the making and re-making of such systems. We have already seen through the examples highlighted above, and elsewhere in this book, that the meaning and value of pottery is fluid, with it being perceived in different ways by, and being effective upon the experiences of, different communities in varying ways. Furthermore, meaning can be maintained through repeated action, or, by cuing memory, can sediment within a thing. The documents therefore record a particular value, which emerged through a particular course of action, which was effective upon and affected by the formation and maintenance of external relationships, which spilled over to impact upon the ways in which people related to their material surroundings; as demonstrated, for example, by Cohn's (2012) examination of the recording of material culture in wills and changing patterns of inheritance in later medieval Italy (see above).

Just as Latour (2010) demonstrated that documents are not the law, but play a specific role in its formation and re-formation, so inventories are not value systems, but rather are enrolled in the process of things being enacted as valuable objects. They serve to black-box past evaluations, providing points of reference which can be enacted through future processes of inventorying, or the use of the inventories in the division of assets. These documents then do not reflect medieval attitudes to pottery. Rather, the act of inventorying created a context, in which these documents were enacted as references and things became objects of worth, a process which cannot be divorced from the biographies of these things, through which they intermittently formed and re-formed as meaningful and valuable objects in ways which affect the trajectories of action in which they can be enrolled. As Hodge (2006) argues, it is the act of inscribing, of translating the value of an object into written form, which maintains its worth. A central component of a relational approach is a consideration that meaning and value emerges in the moment through action. Documents play a specific role, not simply recording the value achieved through a particular process, but also, by being enrolled in the process through which value emerges, are entangled within the spinning of the agency for this particular value to be reached. We can conclude therefore, that these documents are effective, as they are enrolled in the re-making of value systems, and therefore do not simply reflect attitudes to material culture within a social context, but were active in the re-forming of those attitudes and in the emergence and maintenance of the medieval 'social'.

Further insight into this process can perhaps be provided through a brief consideration of later medieval probate inventories. A large number of inventories relating to individuals from Southampton have been published and record the presence of a considerable breadth of material culture, including household linens, furniture and kitchen equipment (Roberts and Parker 1992). In contrast to the earlier inventories, records of kitchen equipment do seem to include lower value items such as cooking pots, although in many cases the material of these vessels is not recorded. The most detailed records relate to 'plate', high value silver or pewter ware, which acquired its value through rarity and through its use in forms of conspicuous consumption acquired a particular social value (Roberts and Parker 1992, xxxii–xxxiv). A contrast can be drawn between these and the earlier peasant inventories in the way in which lower value items are recorded. Whereas these objects were not recorded (and therefore can be considered to not have been enacted as objects of value) in the formation of peasant inventories, here a hierarchy of value can be detected, based upon the detail in which an item is recorded (see also Beddel 2000; Hodge 2006). A case in point is the recording of Rhenish stoneware jugs or bottles. Typically these are not recorded in detail, however through modification, the addition of a silver lid (Figure 3.4), these vessels acquired further value and this is reflected in the enhanced records for these items within the inventories. Through paying reference to the ways in which these objects have previously been recorded, it can perhaps be seen that these inventories were enrolled in the emergence of thresholds of value, determining which items were worthy of an enhanced record and which fall into a malaise of background 'thing-ness'. It can perhaps be argued that it is through attention to detail, rather than attention to the presence or absence of the object that value was 'black-boxed' in these documents. Further analysis of these documents will undoubtedly prove rewarding, in elucidating further the varying formation processes behind them and the variety of ways in which things came to be valued. What this second example demonstrates however, through its differences in relation to the peasant inventories, is that these documents, whilst both the result of processes of inventorying, were the products of very different courses of action, which were situated in different wider webs of interaction. Whilst the end result of both processes was for objects to emerge as valuable, the ways in which the value achieved and sedimented through previous action was translated through this process varied.

*Summary: Pottery and Documents*
Traditionally documentary history has been seen as having little to offer the ceramic archaeologist. However, by reconsidering the relationship between pottery and documents it becomes apparent that at particular stages of an items biography, they were drawn into effective relationships, in which pots came to be enacted as objects of worth, value and meaning. A truly interdisciplinary medieval archaeology must engage with such moments of interaction, to understand the dynamic relationship between these forms of material culture, rather than see the documents as a simple fossilisation of medieval attitudes towards varying forms of object. Clearly the case study presented here represents an early stage of work, but one which shows the potential of such an

*Figure 3.4. (left) 16th Century Stoneware elaborate baartman jug with pewter lid. © Victoria and Albert Museum, London.*

*Figure 3.5. (below) Inscribed medieval jugs from A) Coventry, B) Canon's Ashby and C) Abthorpe Abthorpe. Redrawn from Dunning 1967 and Dunning 1974. Not to scale.*

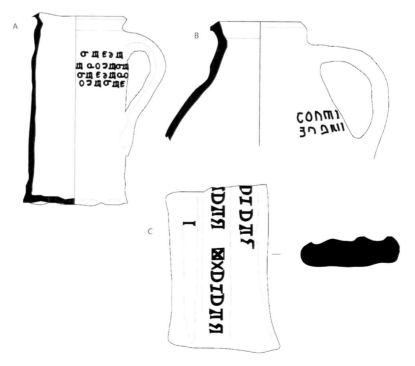

*Figure 3.6. (right) Saintonge Polychrome Ware.*
*Photograph: Ben Jervis.*

*Figure 3.7. (below) Examples of A) Ceramic*
*and B) Metal Cauldrons from London. After*
*Blackmore and Pearce 2010 and Egan 2010..*

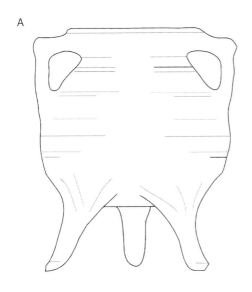

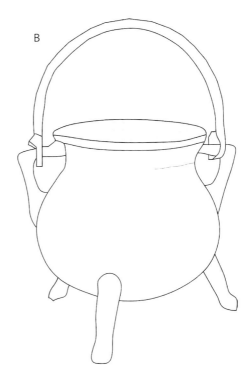

approach. More generally, a relational approach has huge potential for addressing the age old divide between history and archaeology, by providing a methodology in which diverse sources can be considered as formed and entangled with each other, being mutually constitutive in the creation of meaning and value, through action. Such an approach is reliant on a biographical framework, in which meaning and value are seen as emergent in relation both to texts and material things, and in which the dynamism of their emergent qualities can be elucidated through a focus on moments of entanglement, such as the creation of an inventory.

## A Kind of Magic: Text as Decoration

Whilst the representation of pottery in texts allows us to question how pottery became meaningful, the decoration of pottery can be taken as contextually, if not inherently, meaningful. Yet, just as in the previous case study, meaning is emergent and must develop through practice. The aim of this section is to explore how decoration became meaningful through the study of three vessels from the Midlands, which exhibit an unusual form of decoration, that of writing.

The study of pottery decoration is less developed than that of fabric and form, but is of no less interpretive value. Indeed, early studies utilised decoration as a means to investigate elements of identity (Myres 1969; see chapter 4) and the spread of technology (Hurst 1969). Over the last 30 years more theoretically developed approaches have emerged. These largely draw upon the insights of post-processual scholars who examined decoration from an ethnographic perspective. Such approaches consider decoration to be a means of communication, re-producing messages between members of social groups and highlighting differences between them, with evidence suggesting that decoration was particular important at moments when identities or the social order became ambiguous, for example in times of transition (Braithwaite 1982; Sterner 1989). Such approaches are built on assumption that decoration is in some way culturally meaningful and, therefore, by studying pottery within its social context we may be able to unravel its meaning and its significance to past populations.

Within medieval archaeology two studies are of particular note. Richards' (1987) examination of Anglo-Saxon cremation urns concluded that the decorative motifs, along with their position on a pot and the size of a vessel, communicated information about the age, gender and social status of the interned individual, being structured by a symbolic 'grammar' which was comprehendible amongst Anglo-Saxon communities. Working in the later medieval period, Cumberpatch (1997; 2006) has drawn upon the archaeological application of phenomological thought to interpret the decoration of medieval pottery. He argues that the material properties of pottery, including their colour, played a role in the reproduction of medieval *habitus* and that binary oppositions between elements such as colour (bright versus dull) or texture (fine versus coarse) relate to other oppositions which underpin the social order (for example between high and low status, male and female or production and consumption) (Cumberpatch 1997). Such an approach finds parallels within studies of medieval architecture in particular, for example in the relationships Gilchrist (1999) identifies between gendered and public/private spaces through the application of the concept of *habitus*. The binary oppositions utilised by Cumberpatch are problematic, as they themselves can be defined in a subjective manner, and are inherently relational, meaning that for them to be used, we must understand how such categorisations were reached in the past, by understanding the courses of action through which they were defined, rather than utilising the concept of *habitus* to identify oppositions which may have been universally understood within a culture. Developing this work, Cumberpatch (2006) focussed on a particular type of decorated pottery, jugs featuring anthropomorphic decoration, typically in the form of a bearded face. Placed into their context of use, believed to be communal drinking, Cumberpatch argues that this decoration explicitly relates to the expression of masculine identities, drawing upon contemporary attitudes towards facial hair in particular, and suggests that these vessels may even be associated with rites of passage, such as wedding feasts. In both cases decoration is seen as communicating a meaning to its audience, which can be comprehended to some degree once the pot is analysed within its social context. As will be discussed below however, such an approach suggests that decoration is symbolic; that it has a culturally defined meaning attached to it, and therefore fails to address the plurality of ways that decoration may have been understood and the various ways in which it may have affected its viewer.

The notion that decoration is 'meaning bearing' appears to be of particular relevance to the pottery under discussion in this case study. The case study focusses upon three jugs previously examined and published by Gerald Dunning (1967; 1974) (Figure 3.5). All were recovered from the Midlands and belong to the late medieval (14th–15th century) 'Midlands Purple Ware' group. The vessels are all jugs and are further related by the presence of lettering on their body. The first example was found at Abthorpe (Northamptonshire) and features the letters RACICX[X] stamped onto its handle. A second example, from Hertford Street in Coventry, is inscribed with a continuous band of letters reading MEAMQODMQ. A third example was found at the medieval village of Canons Asbhy (Northamptonshire) and is inscribed CONMMQEIDM (Dunning 1974). In all cases the text is in lombardic script, which finds parallels on contemporary seals and floor tiles. Although the letters do not spell words, Dunning (1967, 236) considers that these letters are in some way meaningful, and are not simply the result of illiterate potters drawing inspiration from inscribed floor tiles, which they may also have been involved in producing. In all three cases, Dunning suggests that the letters carry some form of religious meaning. The Abthorpe example, it is suggested, may relate to the cult of St. Osburga, who died in 1016. It is suggested that the letters may, in fact, be Roman numerals reading RA (ratum) MX (1010), relating the inscription to a saint of local significance (Osburga is connected to the monastery at Coventry) and finding parallels in floor tiles produced and used locally. A different interpretation is put forward for the Coventry jug, with its repeated sequence of letters. This motif, it is suggested, is a formula, perhaps for a prayer or chant, which may have been intended to protect the user against poison, or exorcise the water it contained. Such a device is also found on a contemporary pot from Spilsby (Lincolnshire), as well as on contemporary floor tiles, produced for ecclesiastical contexts. A similar interpretation is put forward for the vessel from Canons Ashby. The exact context in which these vessels is unknown, however Dunning cites continental examples, where similar vessels have been found in association with house foundations, a phenomena which will be discussed further below. Importantly, these vessels demonstrate that ceramics were part of a wider socio-material phenomenon in which inscribed objects in a variety of materials, including wood (Janne Harjula pers. comm.) and metal (Hall 2011) could develop magical qualities.

That these vessels may have carried some religious significance is further supported by the iconography found on some Cistercian Ware vessels, produced in the late medieval and early post-medieval periods in the Midlands, and a derivative of the Midlands Purple Ware type. A study by Spavold (2010) has identified a variety of motifs which have religious significance on vessels produced at Ticknall in Derbyshire, including IHS motifs (similar to those found on contemporary maiolica produced in Italy and the Netherlands), as well as depictions of fish, suns and ears of wheat, which can be paralleled in other media, including church architecture. This iconography declines after the Dissolution, supporting the interpretation that it carries Christian significance, and Spavold considers that these vessels relate to their users desire to express their beliefs and devotion throughout the course of daily life, and in particular through eating and drinking. It is debatable whether images and text are equivalent. Whereas images may be characterised as a mnemonic device, or a subtle way to create citational relationships between secular and ecclesiastical spaces, text could be read aloud, enrolled in practices through which the meaning of an object may fundamentally change.

In the previous case study it was argued that texts do not carry meaning, but rather they are enacted as meaningful through enrolment in courses of action. Such an assertion can be extrapolated to imagery and iconography depicted on pottery too. Therefore, it should be considered that whilst carrying Christian iconography, it was through being enacted through use that this decoration became meaningful and retained its meaning and power within medieval society. This is particularly the case for those vessels inscribed with text, which were perhaps enacted through the reciting of chants or prayers through ritualised (as in a repeated pattern of behaviour, rather than a proxy for religious behaviour) activity. A recent study (Williams and Nugent 2012) has begun to consider the decoration of Anglo-Saxon cremation urns from a similar perspective. It is argued that the decoration on these vessels is not meaningful in the sense that they provide a metaphor for the body inside, but rather that they developed animistic properties, demanding people to interact with them in particular ways by guiding tactile and ocular experiences, with openings and depictions of eyes offering a means for the dead to observe the living. These pots therefore had an effect upon those who interacted with them, becoming meaningful through experience and developing agentive properties, rather than being passive transmitters of meaning; in Latour's (2005) terms they switch from being intermediaries to mediators.

*Decoration as Mediator: Beyond Representation*

In order to discuss the agentive properties of ceramic decoration we first need to return to the work of Alfred Gell (1998), discussed briefly in the previous chapter. Gell's work on art and agency has been hugely influential within archaeological studies of material culture, and provided the possibility, for the first time, that inanimate things could have some form of agency. Gell defines agency a causal force and therefore equates it to being a property of an agent possessing intentionality. As such, Gell's approach to agency is still anthropocentric, in that material agency is a form of secondary, or deferred, human agency. Gell's approach is, however, distinctive in its rejection of the textual analogy of art. Rather than being structured by symbolic grammar to be read, Gell considers art to consist of indexical and iconographic signs, rather than symbols. Therefore, art indexes the agency of its creator (which may be the artist, but equally their patron), providing a medium through which they can effect the viewer remotely, and consists of depictions, or icons, which at one level are widely meaningful, but become 'abducted' in specific cultural contexts to stand for a wider range of associations. Rather than consisting of arbitrary symbols therefore, art is meaningful because it depicts things, however these depictions may affect the viewer in different ways, depending upon their cultural background. Our inscribed pots are subtly different, in that they feature text rather than images. Text is a symbolic sign, in that language is largely defined arbitrarily (Knappett 2005, 90). However, a similar conceptualisation of agency can be considered here, in that the text indexes the actions of the potter and effects culturally knowledgeable actors in particular ways.

Although Gell's approach considers agency and therefore moves from seeing art as a purely communicative media, to being an effective one, a relational approach to ceramic decoration forces us to go further. Firstly, Gell's approach relies upon the presence of 'culture' as a container for action. Within a relational approach, in which 'the social' does not pre-exist action, but rather forms and re-forms through it, things cannot be socially or culturally meaningful at an explanatory level, rather they become meaningful, as they and culture are mutually constituted through threads of action. Secondly, for Gell agency is a property of a human actor, which can be deferred onto an object or artwork. Clearly this is at odds with the relational conceptualisation of agency outlined in the previous chapter, in which agency emerges through processes of social assembly, rather than being a permanent property of any one actor. The agency for these depictions to become meaningful is therefore generated as people form associations with them, as part of a wider web of social relationships. Images do not 'mean', neither do they 'do' in the prescribed manner implied by the concept of deferred agency. In order to address the agentive power of decoration it is necessary to revise the questions we ask. Rather than focussing on what an image is or means, which limits the answers we can give, we need to be concerned with how it effects and operates (Sjostrand 2012, 170). Gell's perspective begins to draw us down this route, but a sustained application of non-representational perspectives allows us to explore the role of decoration and images in further depth.

Firstly, by taking such an approach, we are able to acknowledge that images can operate in unexpected ways, as they are entangled in social courses of action they interfere with the world, as the agency for them to have elicit effects is formed (Back Daniellson *et al.* 2012, 4–5; Fahlander 2012, 98). Secondly, because 'the social' is constantly forming and re-forming, images cannot have a fixed meaning. Rather the same image or pot can be enacted in multiple ways, as it forms a nodal point in a patchwork of action (Law and Mol 1995, 289) Rather than residing within an image, meaning is formed through the 'doing' of art, the image is always in a state of becoming as it is more than the physical depiction, just as people can be considered to extend beyond the flesh of the body (see the discussion of relational personhood in chapter 4) (Alberti 2012, 13–15; Fahlander 2012). This is not to deny that once they become meaningful that images cannot retain their meaning as they are re-enacted through enrolment in continued courses of action, but rather that this meaning is fluid and must be underpinned by action, rather than existing outside of it. Furthermore, particular elements of meaning can be 'black-boxed' through documents. Medieval colour symbolism, for example, relates closely to humeral theory and religious thought (Woolgar 2007, 156–7). Therefore, as documents and images or objects were enrolled in dispersed, but connected, courses of action the ways in which an image or thing could become meaningful were limited, until these processes changed.

Decoration can be considered to extend beyond the pot, becoming meaningful in a variety of ways, depending upon the associations which were formed with it through action. This is well illustrated by a study of Saintonge Polychrome Ware (Jervis in press b), a highly decorated form of pottery produced in south-western France (Figure 3.6). Elements of the decoration of these vessels find parallels in contemporary proto-maiolica from Italy and Spain (although the Saintonge vessels are lead glazed) and can be considered to fit into a Mediterranean style, even though specific motifs, forms and elements of technology vary between and within these areas. The agency behind the emergence of this type has been considered elsewhere, but it is worth briefly reflecting upon the ways in which these pots, and specifically their decoration, were entangled in different processes of becoming in varying contexts of use; the home of a wealthy burgess in the cosmopolitan port of Southampton and a castle on the Welsh marches. In Southampton it is suggested that the vessels were drawn into relationships with other bright, lustrous vessels, including pottery from the Mediterranean, as well as a pewter dish and glass vessels (Platt and Coleman-Smith 1975), and was enrolled in the emergence and maintenance of a cosmopolitan aesthetic, through which the householder could build a cosmopolitan identity. The lustre of these vessels corresponds with contemporary attitudes to colour and light ('black-boxed' in religious writings and other texts), in which objects were considered to transmit light, equating lustrous objects with virtue and, by extension, contributing to the image which the household wished to portray. At Sully Castle in Glamorganshire (Dowdell 1990) the decoration of these vessels can be considered to have been enacted in a different way. These vessels were taken out of the milieu of mercantile life (in this case in the port of Bristol), being re-distributed to what was an outpost of English lordship in the colonised south of Wales. These objects, with their link to English dominance in Gascony, as well as their biography in which they were sourced from an English port, suggests that they may have been enacted in use as tools in the maintenance of English identity, even though they were produced in France. The iconography, birds and shields, which can be considered to have developed lordly associations (through the hierarchical restrictions placed on activities such as hunting and knighthood) and therefore, the use of these vessels was active in re-enforcing lordly identity through the enrolment of these images in visual activities such as formal dining. Therefore, the colour and iconography of these vessels do more than demonstrate cultural links with the Mediterranean, but rather they contributed to the development of particular aesthetics and identities, having varying effects as they came to be enrolled in different courses of action.

A relational approach allows us to explore the potency and power of artefacts and images, to consider their effect on people, allowing them to be mediators rather than intermediaries in social networks. So far, and for the majority of this book, a relational approach has been used as an interpretive framework, rather than attempting to impose a relational ontology upon medieval society. The work of Williams and Nugent (2012) does raise the possibility however that the divide between people and things may not have been as rigid as we might believe, at least in a pre-Christian funerary context, by suggesting that, for the living, cremation urns had animistic qualities through which the dead could be perceived as interacting with the living. Drawing upon recent work on religious objects in later medieval archaeology, the concept of animism can perhaps be extended to the inscribed vessels under discussion here.

Animism can be defined as an ontology in which non-humans have the capacity to possess the qualities of personhood – to be and act like a person (Brown and Walker 2008, 297; Nieves Zedeno 2009, 410). The concept of animacy has long been related to anachronistic world views, however in recent scholarship it has changed from being a generalised belief in an 'animating' spirit or soul, to being a form of relational ontology (Alberti and Marshall 2009, 345). Indeed the equation of animacy with a form of belief hinders its application, as it sets up a dichotomy between sacred and profane, or ritual and mundane in which things are set in opposition to spiritually animated things (Groleau 2009, 398). Rather than being a property of *things* however, animism is the property of the social *relationships* between humans and non-humans. As such, animism should not be considered as an interpretation or explanation of an object, but rather it is a process, in which the power of objects emerges. Animism is not equivalent to agency, but is rather a very specific way in which an artefact is perceived, which allows it to be enacted as a powerful (Groleau 2009, 399; Nieves Zedeno 2009, 410). Rather than reflecting a worldview built on animism therefore, the identification of this process in the archaeological record provides an insight into the ways in which worlds were made; the processes of becoming through which things, places and people were constituted through action, with practice serving to stabilise the instability of 'the social' and the fluidity of meaning (Alberti and Marshall 2009, 350–3). Such an approach allows us to consider the ways in which the three inscribed vessels under discussion did more than represent Christian belief, but were enacted through action in which they can be considered to have acted in an animistic manner.

*Enacting Decoration: Pottery, Devotion and Magic*

The varying effects and fluid meaning of iconography identifiable to use as in some way 'religious' is well illustrated by recent analysis of cross marked pottery from slave contexts in North America. Fennel (2003) suggests that the cross motif found inscribed onto Colono Ware (a type of pottery produced and used by slaves) was not universally meaningful, but acted as an icon of spirituality, becoming meaningful to different groups as it was enrolled in spiritual courses of action. Rather than representing a particular system of belief, the cross developed meaning as it was enacted as a symbol of individual devotion and identity, but also through action through which a new group emerged, with the cross becoming a symbol of group identity, devotion and resistance as it was used in this context by a diverse group, joined through the slave trade (Fennel 2003, 24). The cross was not inherently meaningful, but was identified as a religious symbol, its ubiquity and simplicity allowing it to be translated through being enrolled in the emergence of multiple social realities. This example demonstrates that symbols of devotion do not reflect belief, but rather provide a medium through which devotion can be improvised and practiced (Cochrane 2012, 136). Through being enrolled in repeated, ritualised action they develop a durable meaning and are enrolled in the re-becoming of people as believers and members of a religious group.

Studies of artefacts from later medieval and early post-medieval contexts have started to address this concept of translation, in particular by breaking down barriers between sacred and profane spaces by showing how religious practice permeated domestic life (Hall 2011). In particular, this has been achieved through considering the magical and potentially animistic qualities of objects, which emerged through their engagement in devotional (or spiritual) practices both in mortuary (Gilchrist 2008) and domestic contexts (Herva 2009). Mark Hall (2011) has identified a number of objects amongst the artefact assemblage from medieval Perth which can be related to the cult of saints. These items vary in character, from those with clear, direct relationships to particular saints (such as pilgrim badges and ampulae) to more mundane objects which have developed religious associations through their biographies, for example, coins which seem to have been deliberately placed as foundation deposits (see also Hall 2012). The presence of these objects within a domestic context demonstrates how ritualised behaviour (defined as a purposeful and rational set of actions within an individual or group's worldview (Hall 2011, 81)) associated with devotion and the cult of saints was not limited to ecclesiastical contexts, but infused daily life. Objects with clear links to particular saints were utilised in a variety of ways, through which they retained meaning outside of their contexts of acquisition. Inscribed spangles, for example, created a sensory medium through which an individual could explicitly demonstrate their wearers' outlook (Hall 2011, 91), whilst ampulae appear to have been deliberately deposited in a crushed state. It is suggested (Hall 2011, 91) that the deliberate breakage and deposition of these objects was a ritual, designed to harness the magical and protective power of either the vessel or its contents. These magical associations can perhaps support a suggestion that throughout their biographies these objects acquired animistic, protective properties, which were enacted through their enrolment in particular ritualised activities. Further objects, such as a bronze age arrowhead recovered from a foundation deposit, may also have been related to some magical and protective quality, perhaps a desire to protect a house from fire, supported by the medieval understanding of these objects as elf shot, and in the context of Perth made particularly meaningful through the depiction of such items on the altar of St John's Kirk (Hall 2011, 94).

Further evidence for domestic objects becoming enrolled in processes of animism come from recent studies of material culture in later medieval and early post medieval Tornio, Finland (Herva 2009; Hervan and Nurmi 2009). Considering the biography of utilitarian objects (pottery and clay pipes), Herva (2009, 391–2) considers that through continued use these items became meaningful to their users, demonstrated, for example through evidence for repair, recycling and marking. By being integrated into the earth through processes of deposition it is suggested that the properties which emerged through the lives of these objects were infused into the ground which, within the context of folk belief (which in fact related to a specific way of 'being in the world' rather than being an abstract fallacy) the animate qualities of these objects were transferred into the wider landscape. The placement of foundation deposits in houses furthers this argument (Herva 2009, 394), as rather than being inhabited by spirits, houses could themselves be seen as animate, with the process of placing foundation deposits serving to mediate the relationship between human and non-human 'persons' within this particular social reality.

In both Perth and Tornio we see that objects were enacted as animistic by being enrolled within courses of action in which they became meaningful and were perceived to have a protective effect on their social context. Such perceptions of object can be related to folk magic. Gilchrist (2008, 120) has argued that medieval archaeologists have been reluctant to discuss magic, equating it to pre-Christian beliefs and thus setting it in opposition to organised religion. The church, however can be shown to have absorbed folk practices, such as the use of charms, and indeed through the development of the cult of saints and of relics in particular, created their own magical items (Jolly 2002, 7). Certain objects came to be understood to have natural power (Gilchrist 2008, 123), equating perhaps to a concept of animism, which was enacted through its enrolment in rituals designed to harness their protective qualities (Gilchrist 2008, 137). Man-made objects too were enacted. Talismans, for example, carried text similar to those found on the pots under discussion, which again can be considered to have been enrolled within rituals related to healing or protection (Gilchrist 2008, 125–8; Murray Jones 2007, 100). Like the houses in Tornio, the spirits can be considered not to have resided within these objects, as they became animate themselves as they were enrolled within processes of social assembly through the undertaking of ritual, devotional behaviour.

These studies provide a context in which we can consider the role of the writing inscribed onto the three pots described above. Religious activity incorporated magical practices and practices of devotion extended beyond the church to permeate all areas of everyday life. Through these practices objects could become animate, as they were enacted as such through these processes – through these relationships they came to afford protection. It is unfortunate that all three vessels were not recovered from well stratified contexts and therefore that the exact nature of the action in which this text became meaningful cannot be fully grasped. All three however are clearly from domestic contexts and the parallel drawn by Dunning (1967) for the burial of inscribed pots in the Netherlands correlates well both with the evidence for the burial of objects in both Perth and Tornio (see also Merrifield 1987, 118). The formula of the text strongly suggests that these pots depict prayer formulae or charms, designed to be read out and engaged with. This process can be considered to have quite literally breathed life into the pot, enacting it through practice as an effective entity, their power perhaps being made durable through rituals associated with consumption activity, in which the pots were re-animated, or through the memory of a process of burial, in which the pot lived on as an animate entity, protecting the structure under which it was buried. Reading and interacting with the pot did not summon the spirits as such, but rather enacted the pot as an animate being.

If we follow Dunning's interpretation that these inscriptions are in some way related to religious or magical practice, it is necessary to briefly consider the context from which these vessels emerged and, through use, constituted. In later medieval Europe there was a firm, but poorly defined, division between the concepts of superstition (into which fell elements of malevolent magic, but also any form of practice which could be seen to rely upon interaction with 'demons') and Christian religion. Indeed, the place at which this divide was drawn appears to be contextually and regionally specific (Jolly 2002, 25; Bailey 2006, 7; 13; Kamerick 2008, 30). Furthermore, magic can be considered an unstable form of practice, in which, because of its rational grounding in the contemporary mind, may not have been appreciated as such by those practicing it (Bailey 2006, 2) and indeed, in some cases the church, rather than condemning those practicing magic, considered them to be ignorant rather than deliberately subversive (Kamerick 2008, 31). Superstitious practices, a term which I use broadly to describe practices in which supernatural forces were enrolled, and not in a pejorative sense, were undertaken across medieval society from before the conversion period and largely blurred into religious practice, as the church absorbed folk practices and the names of saints or of Jesus or God were invoked in these practices (Jolly 2002, 13). In the 14th and 15th centuries however the idea of witchcraft can be shown to have emerged, as the product of a large scale re-mapping of the social landscape of medieval Europe. Large scale social impacts; the result of the Black Death, warfare and financial collapse at the Europe wide scale joined with more local changes to make this period particularly unstable (Peters 2002, 225–6), making people increasingly aware of the malevolent forces which may underlie some of these less desirable developments. The rise of lay literacy also contributed to this process, as the publication of 'self-help' books formalised magical practice and provided the potential for these documents to be set in opposition to religious texts, especially in the context of developing concepts of heresy (Jolly 2002, 23). More fundamentally, the development of necromancy primarily associated with elite households, increased exposure to magic and awareness of its potentially harmful consequences (Bailey 2001, 966). Through religious writing in particular folk magic and necromancy gradually came to be amalgamated as malevolent forms of magic, which were set in opposition to Christian practice, being explained by the forming of a pact between practitioners and the devil (Bailey 2001, 984). A fear of witchcraft, fostered by the church, can be seen to be the result of a wide reaching bundle of changing associations, which impacted upon how people were able to practice devotion and interact with the world around them.

It is against this background of unrest that the pots under discussion can be considered as protective objects. There is no evidence to suggest that these vessels were used for the practicing of malevolent magic. They can, perhaps, be taken as evidence of the blurred boundary between magical practice and Christian practice, particularly if the Abthorpe vessel is indeed related to the cult of Saint Osburga and the other two vessels mimic the use of lettering on church floor tiles, as Dunning suggests. These vessels, within a situation of unease, can be considered to have been enrolled as protective talismans, activity which may have been perceived by the church as witchcraft, but by those performing these practices as an acceptable form of personal religious practice. In considering how these vessels came to be enacted as protective objects, we must consider medieval concepts of animism. A range of objects were utilised as magical items, but they only came to be animated through their enrolment in practices, which were largely reliant on the performance of charms, spells or prayers, indeed medieval magic was built upon a common assumption that used correctly, words were effective (Jolly 2002, 35–6). Although these spoken devices can be divided into different forms (such as prayers, blessings and adjurations), there is considerable overlap between them, as sections of prayers were inserted into adjurations (which may also have abducted narratives from religious texts, including the lives of saints) (Kieckhefer 1990, 70–2). Following Dunning, I argue that the text on these vessels relates to such an oral performance, or perhaps in some cases an inner monologue or the memory of an earlier performance, through which, I suggest, these vessels came to be perceived as animated as protective talismans.

Although the vessels are out of context, by considering the text it is possible to explore how they may have been drawn into a process of animism. Talismans are defined as manmade objects which feature text, the enrolment of which in action unlocked the power of the object and animated it as a protective entity (Murray Jones 2007, 92–3; Jolly 2002, 41; Kieckhefer 1990, 77). The empowerment of these objects through their enrolment in ritualised action, principally the reciting of charms, gave them a protective power, perhaps best illustrated through the evocation of the names of saints in such rituals, which generated a form of 'non-authenticated relic' (Jolly 2002, 46), in the same ways as items such as pilgrim badges may have become sacralised during visits to shrines or religious places (Murray Jones 2007, 100–101). The text on these items could be unintelligible, as it is on the pottery, as it equates more to a formula, or 'stage directions', related to the performance through which these items become animated (Olsan 1992, 122; Jolly 2002, 40). Indeed the [X] mark may be a direction to make the sign of the cross during the ritual performance (Kieckhefer 1990, 73). The efficacy of these vessels depends upon their role in these practices. If the pots were buried they may only have been enacted once, through the performance of burial (such as the placing of a foundation deposit), whilst if they were related to exorcism or protection through consumption they may have had to be re-enacted through every use (Jolly 2002, 42; Murray Jones 2007, 104). As an aside, it is important to consider that literacy was not widespread in the period (although lay literacy was higher than in earlier periods), and prayers and charms were often recited from memory, rather than from text (Swanson 2006, 137). Therefore, these vessels may be indicative of special cases of inscribed vessels (in which the words garnished them with extra power), but relate to a broader, and archaeologically invisible, set of ritual practices, in which similar charms were performed without recourse to writing on the vessel. Such performance is likely to have been private and the result of a specific need, perhaps medicinal (if the vessels were designed to hold medicine), or some broader form of protection within a context of heightened suspicion and fear (Olsan 1992, 136).

Against this background it is now possible to revisit the specific vessels under discussion. If Dunning is correct in relating the Abthorpe vessel to the cult of Saint Osburga then it can be situated within a localised web of associations in which it became meaningful through enrolment in an oral tradition of story telling, a tradition which 'black-boxed' the relevance of the inscription, serving to harness and maintain Osburga's power within the local community. Adjurations typically abduct narratives and therefore the story of Saint Osburga is likely to have played a specific role in the animating of this vessel, perhaps seeing it become enacted as a powerful 'non-authenticated relic'. This processes of sacralisation spun the agency for the pot to be considered animate and effective, a process which became meaningful through its association with the processes of sacralisation undertaken as part of pilgrimage, in the delivering of the sacrament and in interaction with saint's relics. The veneration of local saints contributed to a geographic patchwork of patterns of devotion in the Middle Ages (McHardy 2006, 97) and given the relevance of the saint in local religious practice, this may be an instance where the boundary between local superstition and religious practice was blurred through private devotion utilising what may have been perceived by outsiders as superstitious magic, but by the people performing the rituals as personal devotion, occupying a position of ambiguity over the level of acceptability of such practice (Bailey 2008, 125).

The other two vessels, with their cyclical inscriptions, must be interpreted within a broader network of inscribed material culture. In the 15th century a cult of the holy name developed, in which the name of Jesus, often in the abbreviated 'IHS' form appeared on vessels in a range of media, including pottery, textiles, church architecture (including tiles) and metalware (Blake *et al.* 2003). Included within this corpus are Midlands Purple Ware and Cistercian Ware vessels exhibiting the 'IHS' motif (Blake *et al.* 2003, 182; Spavold 2010). There is a degree of ambiguity as to the extent to which such inscriptions were enacted for their religious power, or whether they functioned more as fashion pieces, as they became increasingly utilised within a broad range of domestic material culture (Blake *et al.* 2003, 186). These vessels therefore fit into an ambiguous class of inscribed material culture, in which text could be activated for devotional or magical means, but in which the text could also lie passively and harmless, as the user was not aware of, or chose not to recognise, their power. Within a context in which witchcraft and magic were increasingly condemned, pottery may have become a suitable medium for the subtle placement of charms or prayer formulas, in which they could blur into a mileu of inscribed 'thingness', but could be activated and animated by being drawn into specific courses of ritualised action. The format of the text finds parallels with contemporary church tiles, in which the readers' eye is drawn to interact with the text in a particular way (what might be termed a 'sightway' after Williams and Nugent 2012, 191). Whilst in the case of tiles this most likely led to them being read through an inner monologue, given the regulated context in which people came into contact with them, the formula on the pot guided action and likely led to the verbal reciting of a prayer or charm. In both cases the meaning was enacted through comprehension. As out of context objects these pots appear to be curiosities. However, within their material context they can be seen as caught up in referential bundle of associations, through which they found meaning through their association with other forms of inscribed material culture, which developed religious power through their enrolment in religious practices. These included inscribed elements of church architecture, but also inscribed personal items such as pilgrim badges or ampullae. The implications of immersion in this network were twofold. Firstly, they provided a network of associations in which the text could be legitimately perceived as religious, through its association with church spaces and secondly, it provided a mask in which the power of these items was not visible to outsiders who were not drawn into the ritualised action through which these items became powerful.

A further intriguing link can be found between these vessels and Books of Hours, prayer books utilised by all sections of society, but which varied in their form and elaboration in line with their owners' wealth (Duffy 2006). These items, like the vessels, were drawn into devotional practice, through the recital of prayers. Yet these books do not appear to have developed an animistic quality, the power was situated in the moment of recital. Crucially the prayers included within these books included protective devices, for example those designed to prevent a house burning down (Duffy 2006, 161), emphasising the blurring between acceptable prayer and magical charms or spells, in which objects, such as these pots, may have been enacted as protective talismans. Central to this difference may be the nature of pots as vessels, which could perhaps contain demons, either following exorcism (as traps) or prior to exorcism (resulting in the poisoning of the contents, for example). Whilst a fear of demons was perhaps considered appropriate, invoking Christ and the saints in the performance of folk rituals which directly engage demons can be considered subversive, marking a clear and important distinction between the ways in which these different types of objects were enrolled in private devotion to bring about protection.

The interpretation of these three vessels is limited by the absence of detailed context. By situating them within the wider world of later medieval religion and magic it is possible however to consider the effect of their decoration as it was activated through ritualised practice. By being drawn into particular social relationships – with people and texts in particular, these vessels developed specific 'performance characteristics' or affordances, in which they were understood to have developed some form of animistic, protective quality. The agency behind their emergence can be considered far reaching. Paradoxically they appear to be a product of increased fear of witchcraft and magic, perhaps as lay people sought to protect themselves from malevolent magic through forms of ritualised action which were ambiguous, relating in part to existing folk superstitions, but with the content, for example through the evocation of Saint Osburgha, being firmly grounded in local religious practice. The situational nature of these vessels is well demonstrated by the disappearance of religious iconography on Cistercian ware (Spavold 2010) and a wider disappearance of symbols and fetishized words and letters following the Reformation (Tarlow 2003, 110). Identifying these inscriptions as charms or spells, or seeking to fully understand them, limits our understanding of these vessels, a fact understood by Dunning who sought to create a context in which the meaning of the text could be understood. Rather than being an intermediary transmitter of information, this text was activated as a mediator, having an effect upon individual experience and social realities, and by extension on 'the social' itself. Through participation in magical practice new ways of relational thinking could develop, which allowed the conventions of life to be questioned and reconfigured through engaging with the supernatural (Klaasen 2012, 33) and offering a point through which, at a personal scale, an individual could relate to a larger network of belief, particularly by offering a meaningful way to cope with chance-driven events.

A consideration of magic offers an opportunity to explore a medieval form of relational ontology, in which objects were able to be enacted through processes of animism. The introduction of the concept of animism forces us to re-consider our own ontological background and consider that of medieval people (Alberti and Bray 2009, 338), allowing us to question how these vessels were entangled in the formation of a 'social' in which things could seemingly develop protective qualities and in which the mediatory power of the text could only be released through the development of associations with other forms of material culture and textual and oral traditions. More generally, such an approach allows us to consider what decoration did, rather than what it depicts and represents, providing a further means to unlock the plurality of experiences and social realities of medieval life.

## Is This Pottery? Thinking about Skeuomorphs

So far we have considered how pottery became meaningful through text and how one element of it, decoration, developed meaning through its enrolment in distinctive patterns of use. In the final section of this chapter I wish to explore the relationship between pottery/clay and other materials, through a discussion of the concept of skeuomorphs. Archaeologists have long recognised the concept of the skeuomorph, defined as an object which imitates or mimics one typically produced in another material, either in terms of form or appearance (Fahlander 2008, 70). Traditionally, these have been interpreted within a relatively monolithic framework, associated with modern conceptualisations of technological process, either providing a medium for prestige items to be copied in a lower status material, or providing a means through which new materials could be incorporated into an existing repertoire of forms (*e.g.* beaker pottery exhibiting decoration mimicking basketry) (Frieman 2010, 34). Studies of skeuomorphism have demonstrated however, that the phenomena is considerably more complex, particularly through considering their mediatory role in times of change or upheaval.

In particular, the role of skeuomorphs in colonial contexts has been considered in some depth. Harrison (2003) discusses knapped points from Australia, produced from bottle glass rather than the traditional flint. Considering knapped glass assemblages, Harrison is able to contrast informal retouched glass, used as *ad hoc* tools, with finely knapped points, which imitate traditional aboriginal forms which ceased to be produced some 1500 years prior to European contact. Harrison considers that the process of knapping a material introduced by a colonising population provided a means through which distant social memory could be evoked, with the process of skeuomorphism providing a means through which the new could be translated into the traditional, subverting the new material by making it meaningful in new ways, whilst also re-instituting a version of older meanings. Howey (2011) observes a similar phenomenon in North America, where a ceramic vessel has been identified which imitates the form of European copper kettles, which were imported into the region in vast quantities, and found their way to Native American groups who had not had any direct contact with European settlers or traders. Like the knapped points from Australia, the ceramic kettle is seen as a mimetic object, the production and use of which provided a means for the population to take control of a changing world (Howey 2011, 351). The ceramic kettle is particularly interesting because it is a miniature object, which demanded people take notice of it and interact with it in specific ways, directing the effect that the object could have on its user by directing them down specific pathways of association and citation (Howey 2011, 353).

Knappett (2002) has highlighted two forms of skeuomorph. The first is indexical in nature, with production methods mimicking or copying those used to produce objects in another material. An example of such an indexical skeuomorph are ceramic vessels from bronze age Hungary, which mimic the production of metal vessels (Sofaer 2006). The second are iconic skeuomoporhs, which resemble another object, but share little with it other than form and/or appearance. Examples of this type are ceramic cups from the bronze age Aegean which mimic silver vessels. Knappett (2002, 111) argues that these are more than a means through which communities can emulate the upper strata of society through using objects which are in some way similar to more prestigious items. Rather, these items abduct the meaning of these items, which might be taken as an index of an elite group, thus allowing it to not only be related through its form, but also by enabling individuals to participate in patterns of use and alter their own sense of identity or personhood, so that they weren't simply copying a group they became them, in their own mind at least.

Skeuomorphs are more than simple copies. They can be considered to be a set of phenomena (Hurcombe 2008, 102), translations of objects into different media, through which objects and materials can enter alternative processes of becoming, either abducting the meaning of another thing (as in the case of the Minoan cups) or being enacted as something different (as with the knapped glass and ceramic kettle). Further complexity to the concept is added by Conneller's (2011) study of materials in early prehistory. Examining the emergence of new materials in the archaeological record, Conneller (2011, 104) argues that the properties of materials emerge within the contexts of technological interactions. In other words, before clay could be used to produce vessels, it was not viewed as a suitable material. Rather, clay's utility as a material emerged through technological interactions, as its malleability was harnessed as the need for new forms of material culture emerged in the neolithic (see also chapter 6). Conneller's approach differs from traditional approaches by privileging material over form, arguing that elements of sameness were identified between materials, allowing their properties to emerge relationally as equivalents, for example as anatomically modern humans moved across Europe they adopted new materials for bead manufacture, which shared similarities with the lustrous shells used for these purposes in coastal areas, but which were not available further inland. Fossil shells are the closest likeness (Conneller 2011, 112), but alternatives such as bright stones or teeth, which share similarities of lustre and form with shells were also utilised (Conneller 2011, 113). These materials had similar effect to shells, and in some cases skeuomorphic representations of shells were produced from materials such as ivory and stone (*ibid*). Such imitation also opened up means for the transfer of techniques between materials (what Knappett has identified as indexical skeuomorphs) (Conneller 2011, 115). We can consider therefore, that the material properties of things are important and distinguish them, but this does not prevent materials from developing the capability to stand for, or become, another.

There are few studies of skeuomorphism in medieval material culture, but the concept has been pursued most effectively within the field of early medieval stone sculpture studies from Anglo-Saxon, Irish and Scottish contexts. It is widely acknowledged that similar motifs are present on stone sculpture to those found on contemporary metalwork and in manuscript illuminations (*e.g.* Henderson 1987, 64–5). It can be suggested that this is simply the result of craftsmen finding inspiration in other objects. The cross-media relationships identified in stone sculpture across medieval Britain may have further significance that displaying artistic influences. Given the landscape context of such monuments, they can perhaps be considered to be high status objects, commissioned by discerning patrons who were concerned with creating a particular aesthetic by creating situations in which objects and manuscripts could act together (Hall *et al.* 2005, 312). It can also be considered that the adoption of insular motifs in new media related to Christianity served to mediate processes of transition surrounding conversion. Such an argument has also been pursued by Ó Carragáin (2007) in relation to the copying of wooden churches in stone in early medieval Ireland a process, which coupled with the re-use of stone from earlier structures, served to mediate continuity and build links with 'the age of saints' in a period of profound political change in the 9th–11th centuries. A yet more complex argument regarding the significance of skeuomorphism is presented by Hawkes (2003) in her analysis of The Sandbach Crosses, a pair of extant stone cross shafts of Anglo-Saxon date in the town of Sandbach, Cheshire. Hawkes (2003, 11) identifies that iconography is present which is also found in other media but presents several readings of the monuments to explore the significance of these relationships. By considering how the monument can be read, Hawkes could be considered to be taking a relational approach, in which the monument comes to be enacted in different ways to different readers (see also Jones 2004 on the meaning of stone monuments in contemporary Scotland). Whilst similarities between stone monuments, metalwork and manuscripts can be considered simple iconographic skeuomorphs, it is perhaps more rewarding to consider them as indexical ones. The motifs make the monuments into a kind of public text, understood by a Christian population not only as a symbol of belief to the outside world, but as an object enrolled in communal practices of belief. This indexical relationship is furthered when one considers that the monuments are likely to have been brightly coloured and decorated with paint and metal. Pellets on the stone can be considered to imitate metal nails, creating an iconographic link with metal crosses used in church contexts, but also an indexical link as these monumental crosses were perhaps enacted in communal acts of devotion (Hawkes 2003, 27). Therefore, through being enacted through practice, stone crosses became meaningful as texts and as metal objects, blurring the distinctions between materials as they developed similar, relational, performance characteristics, but playing to the material strengths of stone (its availability, durability and malleability) to transcend scale, from portable to monumental. A similar phenomenon has been noted by Rynne (1998) in relation to the earliest 'Celtic' high crosses in Ireland, which are often considered skeuomorphs of earlier, potentially portable, wooden examples.

The example of stone sculpture, as well as Conneller's (2011) analysis of prehistoric material culture, demonstrates how new relationships between people and things led to processes of translation and transformation, in this case of decorative motifs but also of form. The properties of things emerged relationally, through the development and transfer of technologies, motifs and forms one material could become another, by transforming substances into objects and translating materials into other media. Stone crosses can be considered to have become metal, by aping elements of metal technology in their decoration, through their bright colours and motifs. Therefore, they came to act as a monumental form of the portable crosses used in church worship and drew the capacity to become meaningful from this citational relationship. Therefore, whilst the physical properties of materials can constrain action, their attributes also afford the emergence of new properties, or 'performance characteristics' to use the language of Schiffer (1999), through which they become meaningful in new ways.

The concept of skeuomorphs therefore brings into question our own way of thinking about materials. How relevant are the clear divisions drawn through archaeological practice for understanding past societies? The colonial examples discussed above demonstrate how new materials (bottle glass) can develop properties akin to those of familiar materials (flint), whilst familiar materials (clay) can be used to make sense of new forms (kettles). Textual evidence proves to some degree that the categories of material which we use in archaeological practice (ceramic, wood, bronze *etc.*) were relevant to some degree in the medieval period (see for example, the discussion of inventories above). But text cannot capture the full subtleties of the material world, and certain elements of pottery, chiefly form and decoration, hint at referential relationships between materials, in which these clear distinctions may be blurred, as some things try to be others and the properties of pottery and clay emerged through technologies of production and use.

### *The Intersection of Form and Material: Pottery and Metalware in Medieval London*

Throughout the thirteenth century there are some major developments in the pottery of London. Around the turn of the century potters began to diversify, experimenting with the production of ceramic cauldrons which imitate metal equivalents (Blackmore and Pearce 2010, 238), but which did not become a major ceramic form until around a century later (Figure 3.7). Potters also began to produce more complex jug forms and aquaminales which find equivalence in metal forms, whilst they also drew inspiration from highly decorated ceramics, for example through copying Rouen-type Ware jugs in London-type Ware (Pearce *et al.* 1985). These developments have largely been interpreted as the result of iconic skeumorphism, that is the copying of a form in one media into another (*e.g.* Pearce *et al.* 1985, 126), with the driving factor seeming to be social emulation – allowing the lower classes to copy the cooking and consumption practices of urban elites. Such an interpretation has a number of issues. Firstly, it is built upon a modern perspective on the value of materials. As we have seen through the study of inventories, metalware was available to peasant households and therefore is equally likely to have been available to lower status town dwellers, although probably not the poorest members of urban society. Furthermore, as the example of pewter in 17th century America demonstrated, consumer choices are not always straightforward, and the durability and recycling value of metalware may have appealed over the disposability of cheap pottery. Secondly, by seeing ceramics simply as a lower status media ignores their material properties, chiefly the ability to create highly decorated and colourful vessels, which could not easily be achieved in metalware, and may have played a role in the negotiation of identities even at the high status table (see chapter 4). Finally, it assumes that social emulation was both desirable and possible in medieval society. Smith, in her (2009b) study of peasant dress accessories argues that such emulation was in fact a form of resistance in the strictly hierarchical medieval society and that on the whole the social structure stifled ambition to progress up the social ladder. As will be discussed in chapter 4, ceramic vessels need not be representative of low social status, but rather their use allowed the negotiation of increasingly complex sets of social relationships and the development of more varied identities through serving. Therefore, just as in the case of the Minoan silver cups discussed my Knappett, the aping of metal forms in pottery need not reflect social emulation, but rather developed from a need to negotiate these relationships and their use served to permit the development and maintenance of new forms of identity through serving activity.

The emulation conclusion is also predicated on an assumption that the ceramic and metal vessels are equivalent; that a simple iconographic relationship exists between the two. Whilst in general terms these vessels may afford similar activities, their material properties limit or direct the form that these activities can take. In his ethnoarchaeological work in the Phillipenes, Skibo (2013, 53–4) noted that for particular functions ceramic vessels were used, even though households had enough metal vessels to fulfil these functions. Rice was cooked in metal pots, as these heated quickly, whereas vegetables and meat, which required a slower simmer, were cooked in ceramic pots. With this in mind we can question whether a simple iconographic relationship between metal and ceramic is appropriate. Clearly vessels emerged with similar formal characteristics, but very different material ones, meaning that although they looked the same and emerged together, they potentially fulfilled different roles within the home. These materials came to be understood through the technology of cooking, with similarities and differences being embraced through consistency of form. The question which must be posed therefore is are these vessels the same, or are they different?

In order to consider this point we can focus on cooking vessels (cauldrons). Within London copper alloy vessels appear to have been imported into from the mid 13th century, principally from Germany, although vessels produced in England were also in use (Egan 2010, 158). The size of these cauldrons varies from diameters of 160–380mm, showing, that as with pottery, there is considerable variation in vessel size and, presumably therefore, of function. Contemporary depictions show these vessels used in a variety of ways, and being present in a range of sizes, with some being used as primary cooking pots and others being utilised in a process of 'double boiling', whereby a pot or pots are suspended within a cauldron of boiling liquid (Margesson 1993, 90). Much of the published pottery from London does not come from domestic contexts, but rather was recovered from dumps of material used to reclaim land along the Thames, and therefore it is not possible to discuss the distribution of these ceramic and metal forms throughout the city in any great detail (Vince 1985, 26–7). It is noticeable that ceramic versions of metal vessels do not emerge at this relatively early date in all medieval towns. In Southampton, for example, jar forms persist in the late 15th or early 16th century, although ceramic tripod cauldrons were imported from the Low Countries in small quantities (Brown 2002), whilst in Norwich similar vessels are not produced until the 15th–16th centuries, their introduction considered to be the result of continental influences (Jennings 1981, 61). It is likely therefore that the introduction of these forms, in both ceramic and metalware, vary regionally, with simpler suspended cauldrons (more akin to the traditional ceramic jar/cooking pot) perhaps persisting in some areas for longer.

We can consider therefore that, in London at least, the agency for these forms emerged at around the same time, and, rather than one medium simply copying the other, that these emerged as part of a broader shift in cooking practice. A number of factors can be considered to have contributed to their emergence in London. The first of these is trade and contact with Germany and the Low Countries. Ceramic cauldrons had been produced in Dutch Redware since the early 13th century (Baart 1994, 20) and these vessels, as well as their metal equivalents are known to have been imported into London by the 14th century (Vince 1985, 52; Egan 2010, 158). The availability

# 4

# EMERGENT PEOPLE:
# POTTERY AND IDENTITY

Since Roberta Gilchrist (1994, 9) wrote "the absence of theory in later medieval archaeology may be explained by the limited purpose which it has been set by those who practise archaeology" there has been a massive expansion in archaeological research grounded in elements of social theory, through which identity has been a common and ever present theme (Gilchrist 2009, 338; McClain 2012, 132). Gradually a positivist stance within medieval archaeology has been supplemented by a wide spectrum of approaches (McClain 2012, 133), which can only thicken and enrich our understanding of the medieval period. Pottery in particular has been examined in new ways, allowing it to be seen as more than an indicator of ethnicity or status, but as enrolled in some way in the process of identity formation or re-creation. This chapter maps out a possible next step in understanding the role of pottery in the emergence, as opposed to the formation, of identities and particularly the multiple effects which its use has upon the identities of people who come into contact with it. In order to do so it is necessary to briefly consider the relationships between practice and identity, pottery and identity and identity and medieval archaeology.

It has been established, largely through influences drawn from the work of the sociologist Pierre Bourdieu (1977), that there is an association between identity formation and practice. Practice offers a medium through which to experience the world and can be reconstructed from the archaeological record, meaning that it has provided a lens through which archaeologists have considered past identities (*e.g.* Jones 1997, 90). However, whilst some studies utilise practice as a mechanism to explore the fluidity of identity (*e.g.* Dellino Musgrave 2005), for others it has replaced the object as a passive symbol or signifier of identity. In considering the development of identity studies within Roman archaeology, Pitts (2007) has critiqued the approaches taken by scholars working with a range of forms of evidence and examining a variety of forms of identity. He identified a pre-occupation with issues of ethnicity, perhaps related to the need to assess the extent and character of 'Romanisation' (Pitts 2007, 695–6) but also a growth in the study of areas of identity such as gender, which is mirrored, as we shall see, in studies of medieval archaeology. Pitts makes two key points in regard to the study of identity which are of relevance here. The first of these is that the idea of identity is rarely adequately theorised or defined (Pitts 2007, 699), with the potential result of it being a meaningless term, inserted into discourse because it is fashionable. Secondly, whilst acknowledging that identities are formed and maintained through practice, we must be careful not to simply take practice as a replacement for objects in standing for identities (Pitts 2007, 701). Doing so would simply lead to a more elaborate version of culture-historical approaches which focus on the presence of particular artefacts or combinations of artefacts. The aim of the opening part of this chapter is therefore to examine the extent to which medieval archaeologists have been successful in addressing these issues in identity studies. The second part will define identity within a relational framework and explore this concept through the use of two extended case studies.

## Pottery, Identity and Medieval Archaeology

Examinations of medieval identity have a long association with ceramic studies, largely due to the work of J.N.L. Myres (1969; 1977). His research into the relationship between pottery styles and early medieval migrations underpinned a culture historical approach within Anglo-Saxon archaeology which persisted for several decades and the vestiges of which can, arguably, still be seen in modern approaches to the period. Further to establishing that pottery can provide information about the identities of the people who made, moved and used it however, Myres' work was innovative in its use of distribution plots and the synthesis of material from modern and antiquarian excavations, using these data to build and develop his interpretation.

It was not until the 1990s however that identity once again became a key theme in medieval pottery studies. An important exception was Richards' (1987) study of the form and decoration of Anglo-Saxon cremation urns, which argues that these attributes form an underlying symbolic association with elements of the deceased's identity (particularly age and gender) (see chapter 3). This work has been elaborated upon by Gareth Perry (forthcoming), who has demonstrated a potential relationship between the pre-burial use of these vessels in brewing and the role played by individuals at different life stages in this process. The 1970s and 80s, as we have already seen, were largely a time of synthesis, although within these works space could occasionally be found to consider the identity of the users, for example in Allan's (1984) study of Exeter the correlation between social status as derived from historical documents and imported pottery is explored.

Moving then to contemporary studies, we can return to those two issues posed by Pitts; is identity clearly defined as a concept and how does the concept of practice contribute to our understanding of past identities? The first study to explicitly address the relationship between pottery, practice and identity is Blinkhorn's (1997) examination of Anglo-Saxon pottery and identity, which offers a critique of contemporary approaches to ceramic analysis and focuses primarily upon the production and distribution of ceramics. Blinkhorn's concept of identity is built upon the basis of anthropological work, particularly Hodder's (1979) examination of Baringo pottery, which demonstrates how differences in processes of pottery manufacture relate to group identities. Blinkhorn (1997, 124) argues that differences in pottery were overt cultural statements about group identity, demonstrating this, for example, through a discussion of the zoned distribution of pottery types at sites in the midlands. Blinkhorn's stated aim is to tease meaning from a form of pottery which is largely considered homogeneous to the untrained eye and to move beyond a simple correlation between decoration and ethnic groups. In defining identity therefore Blinkhorn is partially successful, in that his concept of group identity is built upon ethnographic parallels and therefore has a sound theoretical basis. However, through the study of tempering and forming practices these groups are essentially the product of archaeological analysis and therefore the meaning of these observations in interpretive terms are unclear. It seems that practice has become a different means of establishing the presence of groups which potentially cross-cut those ethnic groups identified by Myres and therefore the traces of particular forms of practice are seen as standing for a group. Analysis of this study demonstrates that whilst ceramic analysis provides a window into practice, we need to understand the dynamics of identity formation as they occurred through these practices, otherwise we run the risk of identifying nebulous and undefined groups.

Despite the limitations of Blinkhorn's study it is undeniable that it had both direct and indirect impact on the ways in which people began to think about medieval pottery from the mid 1990s. Davey's (2000) study of Manx early medieval pottery was undertaken against a backdrop of the role of archaeology in the negotiation of contemporary Manx identity. Using the evidence derived from manufacturing techniques, and particularly resource procurement, Davey argues that these vessels are a hybrid cultural phenomena, drawing upon local interpretations of Danish and Irish influences and are therefore a materialisation of a Manx identity, built upon particularly Manx ways of doing. Davey therefore sets out with a clear research question based around the issue of identity; did pottery play a role in the definition of a Manx identity in the medieval period? By drawing on evidence of manufacturing practices he argues that it does, particularly by demonstrating the influences present at different stages in the manufacturing process. This study therefore considers practice more as process and as such is able to consider the effect of each stage in identity formation. Practice here does not become a simple reflection of identity, but central to the way in which it is negotiated. A similar approach has been taken by Jervis (2008), who, drawing upon ethnographic work into pottery production and scales of identity formation (Gosselain 2000) argues that the process of pottery manufacture led to the formation of multiple forms of identity, for example through engagement with the wider community in the landscape through resource procurement and with family members through the development of potting skill. In both cases the breaking down of practice into discrete stages, for example through the adoption of the chaîne opératoire approach to ceramic production, in which each stage is seen as embedded within a wider social system, has allowed a picture of dynamic identity formation, rather than passive identity reflection, to be explored.

Pottery production does not exist in isolation and several recent studies have focussed upon broader issues of ceramic production, distribution, use and their relationship to identity. Naum's study of Baltic Ware in medieval Denmark is one such example. Here the concept of identity is rooted within studies of colonialism and migration and is combined with the study of practice to explore the relationship between politics, identity and the use and manufacture of pottery. Baltic Ware is now understood to relate to the movement of people into Denmark in the early medieval period (Naum 2011, 96), but rather than standing for an immigrant group, Naum's study explores the ways in which its production and use played a role in identity formation. Naum (2011, 109–10) argues that pottery manufacture was a way in which immigrants could 're-make' places in their new surroundings, with frequent encounters with the material mitigating feelings of displacement and unfamiliarity. Therefore pottery production found new meaning for this immigrant community, being more than a product of habitual practice, but being reminders, bound up within processes of memory work and therefore of identity retention, both through the replication of experience and the passing on of skill and knowledge to subsequent generations (Naum 2011, 110). Here practice is a process, in which identities are formed and re-formed as people experience the material world and seek to replicate their environment and identity can be considered a product of this process, be it an intended consequence or an un-intended or sub-conscious by-product. The study is of particular significance because it offers a re-interpretation of material which has traditionally been studied within a representational and culture-historical paradigm.

A similarly insightful study is that by Kyle (2012) into the repair of Soutterain Ware vessels in early medieval Ireland. Soutterain Ware pottery is found in Northern Ireland prior to the Anglo-Norman conquest and numerous examples of vessel repair are known and this activity is considered by Kyle to be grounded in the *habitus* of early medieval communities (Kyle 2012, 86). Having identified this activity at sites outside of the core Souterrain Ware distribution, Kyle contends that this activity is the result of people moving to new locations and undertaking familiar practices, simultaneously re-enforcing elements of their personal identity at the domestic scale (Kyle 2012, 87). Indeed, the presence of repaired Souterrain Ware and Scandinavian building practices at the site of Inishkea North is considered to be indicative of the emergence of hybrid identities, through the mixing of two groups, each enacting elements of their *habitus* in domestic life (Kyle 2012, 88). Furthermore, evidence of repair on post-Conquest Everted Rim Ware, produced in the same way as previous Souterrain Ware vessels, but with a form more akin to Anglo-Norman vessels, can be taken as further elements of cultural mixing and continuity of, potentially resistant, identities in Anglo-Norman Ireland, rather than this change in form representing imposition of Anglo-Norman pottery traditions as has previously been argued (Kyle 2012, 88–9). Therefore by focussing on practices, in this case repair, Kyle, like Naum, has shown that vessels do not stand for groups, but rather that their identities are formed and reformed through habitual engagements with domestic material culture.

A final example demonstrating how ceramicists have successfully explored the relationship between pottery, practice and identity can be found in the work of Vroom (2011). Like Pitts (2007), Vroom identifies the need to critically assess the concept of identity itself, in particular considering that the same objects can develop multiple meanings to different social groups and therefore the role of pottery in identity formation is fluid and contextual, an important observation which will be expanded upon later in this chapter (Vroom 2011, 409–10). Focussing initially on the decoration of pottery, Vroom argues that the mixing of Islamic technology (the use of tin glaze) and Frankish motifs (soldiers) on Crusader period pottery from the eastern Mediterranean is indicative of cultural mixing, with these vessels being part of a process of acculturation, rather than standing for established and defined hybrid identities (Vroom 2011, 411). By seeing decoration as practice and acknowledging the fluidity both of identity and the meaning of vessels, this study adds further depth to our understanding of the relationship between pottery and identity by beginning to consider the effect of practice on the infusion of a social context with its character, rather than being a simple reflection of cultural mixing. Vroom advances to examine changes in dining practices through an analysis of vessel shapes alongside a consideration of dietary data and artistic representations of dining, with, again, the practice of eating contributing to a process of acculturation, rather than standing for monolithic and clearly defined, tangible changes in identity (Vroom 2011, 425–6).

The final three studies all demonstrate that if we consider practice as the process through which identity forms, rather than standing for existing identities, then the relationship between practice, identity and ceramics is a useful one to advance. It is interesting to note however that all three papers draw upon different, although related, conceptualisations of what identity is, serving to demonstrate both the vibrancy of identity studies, but also the complex nature of the concept, therefore amplifying Pitts' (2007) point that a clear, theoretically grounded, definition of the term is required as the basis of any study of past identities. A relational approach allows us to focus on the role of practice in constituting the processes of social assembly and disassembly and therefore to consider the effects of action on the emergence of varying identities, for example by marginalising some and elevating others. To consider the role of pottery in identity formation in isolation is clearly restrictive however. The relationship between pottery, people and other things and spaces in constituting practice and therefore identities should not be ignored. These relationships are well demonstrated by Guttierez's (2000) study of Mediterranean pottery in Wessex, which argues that pottery must be seen alongside other objects but also patterns of use (such as manners) in the construction of cosmopolitan identities and negotiation of social position through displays of wealth. By being bound up in contextually located practice Mediterranean pottery developed a distinctive value in medieval Wessex and that, by extension, it played a particular role in identity building in this area, both within immigrant and high status communities. It is in the understanding of these relationships and comings together that a relational approach to identity formation can further thicken our understanding of the processes of identity formation and the roles which pottery and objects played within them.

So far it has been demonstrated that purely archaeological studies of pottery, practice and identity have moved beyond seeing either artefacts or the practices behind their formation as simply standing for groups. Rather a range of approaches have been adopted to examine the effect of 'doing' on senses of identity, be that in the production, use, decoration or repair of pottery. A further area for consideration however is the relationship between pottery and groups well attested to in historical documents. So far we have dealt with somewhat nebulous groups such as immigrant Slavs in Denmark or Viking settlers on the Isle of Man. What though of groups who have clearly attested corporate identities within the historical record? An example of such a group is the Hansa, a group built largely on an economic footing, but which developed, according to evidence provided by history, archaeology, art and architecture, a Hanseatic culture which spread throughout the North Sea area in the later middle ages (Gaimster 2007, 410). Gaimster (2007) argues that the spread of ceramics, particularly German stoneware and stove tiles, contributed to the formation of a homogeneous urban culture throughout the Hanseatic zone, in which mercantile, urban communities set trends in cultures of consumption. Evidence of resistance to this culture at the fringes of the Hanseatic world is offered through the example of Novgorod, where these ceramics failed to take hold, other than within immigrant or mercantile communities. In Novgorod therefore the Hanseatic 'package' can be seen as relating to a form of use practices which contributed to the construction of a form of ethnic identity (Gaimster 2007, 419), which was actively resisted though the continuity of practice within Novgorod. This study presents something of a contrast to those discussed above. On the one hand, artefacts are seen as standing for the Hansa, their culture and sphere of influence. However, by situating the spread of this culture within its social and particularly, economic context, ceramics are transformed into a medium through which corporate identity was formed and expressed, as is most in evidence in Novgorod. Such a contextualised relationship between historically attested groups and pottery production and use is put forward by Brown (2003) in his examination of pottery tradition in Anglo-Saxon England. The relationship between historically attested groups and ceramics remains, it seems, a more challenging area to explore in a theoretically informed manner. The primacy of the documentary evidence sends us in search of a signature for a group, to determine whether they are visible in the archaeological record. Whilst interdisciplinary study has allowed a consideration of the role of ceramics in the creation of these groups, it could be considered that their results in terms of understanding the dynamics of identity formation are less rich than those put forward in the archaeologically led studies outlined above. Clearly this is a challenge which remains to be fully addressed by archaeologists and relational approaches to the study of historical and archaeological sources, such as those outlined in the previous chapter, could help to address these issues, by thinking about how these identities were formed through the coming together of a range of things, documents and people in particular spaces and times. In doing so it would finally be possible to move away from hunting for archaeological signatures for historically attested groups, to gaining a clearer understanding of the dynamics of group formation, a process which Actor-Network Theory in particular is well equipped to examine (see Latour 2005, 27).

## Identity and the Middle Ages

For the medieval archaeologist, identity studies can be argued to have two core roots; the examination of the archaeology of 'known' groups, derived from historical sources, as with the discussion of the Hansa above (see also Hinton 2009) and the study of ethnicity, particularly in relation to the early medieval period. Clearly there is overlap between these areas and there has been particular concern in many areas with identifying the archaeological signatures of defined ethnic groups. Within both medieval archaeology and history however the focus on ethnicity has given way to broader studies of identity, based around, for example, issues of gender, age, social status and collective identity through the establishment of social memory. It is important to examine some of the perspectives raised by these studies in order to contextualise both the preceding examination of the relationship between ceramics and identity and also the establishment of a relational approach to identity which follows.

Given the importance of ethnicity, both to medieval archaeology but also to the first case study outlined in this chapter, we can take this concept as our starting point. The culture historical paradigm of associating objects with particular ethnic groups is engrained within archaeological practice, however in some areas it is more residual than others (*e.g.* Jones 1997, 13; see also Curta 2007 for contemporary debates within the archaeology of Germany and the Balkans). The identification of named groups has resulted in the archaeological conceptualisation of ethnicity as monothetic, with a focus on type artefacts, rather than the more ubiquitous types which cross cut social boundaries, furthering the cause of culture history and, through the mapping of their distribution, creating a picture of cultural uniformity which, arguably, never existed and in which small groups gradually coalesced into familiar groupings such as 'the English' (Curta 2007, 163; Effros 2004, 165; Theuws 2009, 290; Moreland 2000, 29). The use of ethnic labels within historical documents cannot however be taken as a direct and factual representation of the presence of identified or identifiable groups within medieval society. As we saw in the previous chapter, documents are written with agendas and the use of specific terminology can be considered to be calculated and deliberate or ambiguous in the minds of the majority of a community (Hadley 2002, 47; Theuws 2009, 291). Furthermore, references to ethnic or other social groups within documents such as law codes did not simply reflect an identity, but rather may have acted to reify it, through adherence to particular rules, which came to be a central component of an individual or groups identity (Hadley 2002, 52–3; Abrams 2012, 21). Similarly in the manufacture or use of material culture ethnic identities were not reflected, but rather social relationships were formed, through which new forms of social identity could emerge (Hadley 2002, 64–9; Thomas 2012, 508–9).

It is important to consider what is meant by ethnicity. In contemporary circles it is largely considered as a social construction, one which is separate to any biological trait, but a form of identity that it may be possible to be born with (Curta 2007, 166), or perhaps more accurately, be born into (see Jones 1997, 57). As constructed identities, entry and membership of ethnic groups are negotiated, in part through the

use of material culture in specific ways, linking identity, *habitus* and objects so that
ethnicity is constructed through ways of doing, not simply of having or displaying
particular artefacts (Curta 2007, 177). Indeed, Bartlett (2001, 53) argues that medieval
conceptions of race, nationhood and ethnicity were closely embedded within each other,
with communities being distinguished by customs (that is ways of doing, rather than
ownership of particular possessions) and language rather than physical features such
as skin colour or skull shape. In the early medieval world at least, it can be shown that
ethnicity was a means by which communities were separated, as is demonstrated, for
example, by the numerous references to groups in texts such as Bede's *Ecclesiastical
History of the English Church and People*. Therefore, the distribution of artefacts may
create a false image of culturally homogeneous ethnic groupings, particularly through
the study of grave goods, which have formed a central component of ethnicity studies
within medieval archaeology. Rather than seeing the presence of certain dress accessories
as simple markers of ethnicity for example, a full range of factors must be considered
behind their patterning, including local customs, gift-exchange, trade and the location
of workshops (Effros 2004, 166). Therefore differences which are truly regional have
been misperceived as ethnic due to a fixed and pre-determined understanding of the
meaning of material culture as an ethnic marker.

Adopting ideas of diaspora, in opposition to rigid issues of identity, Abrams (2012)
considers that social practice created collective memory and a common culture within
North Sea and Atlantic Europe in the Viking Age. By adopting such an approach objects
do not become simple ethnic markers, but rather become enrolled in mediating personal
and collective experiences of continuity and change, which generate with them a sense of
collective identity which could, perhaps, be considered sub-ethnic, in that elements of a
Scandinavian identity was maintained but was manipulated through localised processes
of hybridisation, resistance and expression. Furthermore, ethnicity is not a constant, but
becomes expressed in different ways at certain times, with groups potentially dissolving
or new ones forming, with times of tension being particularly important moments for
the display of group solidarity (Curta 2007, 183; Bartlett 2001, 51; Theuws 2009).
There are however cases where archaeologists are able to identify ethnic differences
which appear to have existed within the minds of medieval communities. An example
is Gerrard's study of Islamic and Christian communities in medieval Aragon, where it
can be shown through the integrated study of multiple forms of material culture that
ethnic and racial divides existed within the community. In particular the segregation
of fields and cemeteries (Gerrard 1999, 147–8) reflects these divisions, which became
further exacerbated as the Templars re-organised the space, marginalising Islamic
communities. However these differences are based primarily on custom, on ways of
doing, although they are further amplified and exacerbated through the enforcing of
formal regulations (Gerrard 1999, 155). What is key to this approach to ethnicity
however is not that the presence of these groups, known from historical documents, is
identified in the archaeological record, but rather that integrated archaeological study
allows the examination of the dynamics of social relationships through which ethnic
differences were maintained through differences in practice, which were also impacted

through relationships of status and power. Here then ethnicity is not reflected in the archaeological record, but rather its construction can be mapped as the politicisation of culture (Curta 2007, 166), which cut across multiple media.

Whilst ethnicity is given an elevated status within archaeological identity studies, largely due to the culture historical roots of the discipline, critiques levied at monolithic identities and fixed and limited ethnic interpretations of material culture, have resulted in the examination of other forms of socially constructed identity, in particular gender and status, which, although often studied in isolation, vary along with, and not in opposition to, ethnicity (Jones 1997, 84; Curta 2007, 176; Theuws 2009, Halsall 2004, 19). In particular a focus on dress accessories, such as brooches, has led to a consideration of ethnicity which rests on modern gender stereotypes; chiefly that women were passive transmitters of ethnicity, rather than focussing upon how these items were bound up in the formation of gendered identities (Effros 2004, 167). When considered together, medieval archaeologists can be shown to have come to appreciate the fluidity of ethnicity and particularly the ways in which different forms of ethnic identity are negotiated in particular contexts (see also Jones 1997, 117). Through this brief resumé of ethnicity studies in medieval archaeology we can see a trajectory emerging from a wholly representational interpretation of material culture to a more relational one, in which identities are negotiated through interactions with material culture. The emphasis has shifted from objects showing which identities were present, to being a means to understand the means through which they were constructed, an activity which may have chiefly occurred at particular times, for example in times of tension. An explicitly relational approach can therefore further this agenda, by considering the effects of these interactions not only in relation to the emergence of ethnic, but also of other, interconnected forms of identity, as we shall see through a discussion of identity around the time of the Norman Conquest (below). Indeed compartmentalised ideas of specific forms of identity may even give way to an understanding of humans as multi-faceted, with cross cutting and connected modes of identification characterising their sense of self.

Foremost amongst these other facets of identity to have been considered by medieval archaeologists, and indeed by scholars of the medieval period more generally, is gender. Like ethnicity, gender can be considered a constructed, or performed, identity, emphasising social, rather than biological difference between men and women (Gilchrist 1994, 2; Halsall 2004, 18–19). The area of gender archaeology, as well of studies of gender in other areas of medieval studies, has blossomed, from a feminist critique to a fully established component of modern interpretive archaeology, which has stretched beyond acknowledging the presence of women to examining medieval ideas of gender and the ways in which these identities and ideas were formed through the use of space, material culture and text (Gilchrist 1994, 3). In the context of early medieval Europe, Effros (2004, 175) has argued that the simple relationship between gender and material culture which has prevailed in earlier studies is based upon a number of gender assumptions, not least the power of women's individual agency was somehow stifled. In particular, progress has been such that studies have moved beyond simple binary oppositions between male and female, to appreciate the vibrancy of forms of gendered identity which may have existed in the past (Gilchrist 1994, 7–8). Primarily, gender has been interpreted as a form of *habitus*, with gendered identities being formed and re-made through engrained social practices within the logic and structure of medieval society more generally, for example being re-enforced through the way in which architecture structures experiences of space (Gilchrist 1994, 16).

Key to addressing multiple forms of gendered identity is the exploration of its relationship to other forms of identity, such as ethnicity. For example, engagement in religious practice created varying forms of femininity within medieval society, whilst the difference in the perception of men and women in society more generally meant that gendered forms of religious identity, which may have cut across religious boundaries also occurred. (Baumgarten 2008, 215–6). From these observations two key points can be taken. Firstly, gendered identity can be seen as associated with other forms to create various forms of masculinity or femininity and, secondly, one's gender, in association with other forms of identity, could be an active form of identity, which both limited and made accessible courses of action and therefore experiences of the world (see also Halsall 1996, 22). By emphasising one form of identity over the other, archaeologists have failed to address the full symbolic function of artefacts and the practices surrounding their use, for example by privileging the construction of ethnic identity over the construction of gendered identity in the study of early medieval grave goods (Effros 2004, 179). What is key, argues Effros, to understanding these objects is that their meaning was fluid, and, whilst they could be used to construct ethnic identities in particular contexts, they could also be used to follow or subvert conventional gendered identities or, indeed form gendered forms of ethnicity (Effros 2004, 183). Within the same time period, Halsall (2004, 26–27) has argued that in order to maintain a particular form of elite masculinity and therefore legitimacy to power following the fall of the Roman Empire that objects were utilised in new ways, for example through the establishment of furnished burial traditions. The collapse of the imperial system, within which the ideas of gender and processes of gendered identity formation were to be found, led to the re-negotiation of gendered identities in relation to new power structures and expressions of ethnicity (Halsall 2004, 33–4). The variation in responses to the fall of Rome in relation to the use of artefacts to express gender, as well as other facets of individual and group identity, demonstrates well both the situational nature of identity, but also the ways in which objects could be abducted into the process of identity formation, allowing them to develop new meaning in relation to their user(s) or bearer.

There has been particular interest in the expression and construction of gendered identities through burial in Anglo-Saxon England. Hadley (2004, 301) suggests that gender was "erratically determined and variously expressed" highlighting both the fluid and situational nature of gendered identity. These studies have emphasised not only the role of gender in burial, but also the relation of gender, not just to social status and ethnicity, but also stages of the lifecourse. Focussing on graves dating to the transition from the Roman to Anglo-Saxon periods, Gowland (2007, 59) identifies fluctuations in the grave goods present in relation to stages of the lifecourse, arguing that a gendered identity appears to emerge between the ages of 7–12, whilst the presence of Roman objects is taken not as a symbol of ethnicity or cultural continuity but, rather, due to their prevalence in relation to particular age ranges are considered to relate to other, undefined, elements of social identity (Gowland 2007, 62–3; see also Eckhardt and Williams 2003). Similarly within the early Anglo-Saxon period, Stoodley (2000) demonstrates age and gender based patterning in grave goods, arguing that burial was a process through which systems of social organisation relating to the lifecycle could be explicitly enacted through burial. In relation to women, Stoodley (2000, 465–6) considers there to be a link between burial rite and age stages developed around physical maturity and a wider concept of motherhood, with different packages of grave goods accompanying older women, who had passed the child bearing stage of their lives. In contrast, men appear to have passed through a single threshold, relating to the development of the weapon burial rite, which, whilst not necessarily indicating the adoption of a warrior lifestyle, sees increasing association with symbols of masculinity and power (Stoodley 2000, 467; see also Härke 1990). Considering late Anglo-Saxon and Viking age stone sculpture in England, Hadley (2004, 321) considers inscribed text and motifs not to relate to the identity of an individual, but rather to an extended familial identity related to processes of cultural assimilation (see above); processes which did not just enact status relationships but also brought into existence marriages, families and therefore negotiations of gendered identities. The primarily masculine iconography on these sculptures is however take to indicate a stressing of masculinity in what was a time of political and social stress (Hadley 2004, 323).

It is telling that much of the archaeological literature concerned with gender mostly relates to burial archaeology, largely in relation to the early medieval period, where a clear link can be drawn between the individual's biological sex and the forms of material culture with which they were, or perhaps more accurately, became, associated through the practice of furnished burial rites. In several cases however gender has been demonstrated to relate to other elements of identity, largely status or ethnicity, with a particular relationship occurring between gender and age categories. In considering Pitts' criticism of identity in Roman archaeology it can be considered that neither of his points is wholly salient in relation to the cases outlined above. Gender is clearly considered a form of constructed identity, a process in which material culture in particular has been particularly entangled. Practice therefore is not reflecting gender identities in these instances, but rather the process of burial saw the materialisation of concepts of gender and the construction of gendered identities in relation to particular social circumstances. Indeed, the most ground breaking work on gender and the archaeology of the 'living' is Gilchrist's (1994) examination of female religious houses where a clear link can again be drawn between biological sex and the occupation of space. Gilchrist considers gender to be a culturally significant categorisation of sex. Her study of female religious houses examines how identities of femininity were created through the occupation and experience of space. Crucially, she argues that female religious experiences were different from male ones, for example in relation to the degree of self sufficiency of houses (Gilchrist 1994, 91), but also that the architecture of these places was influenced by and served to maintain contemporary ideas of femininity. In particular similarities are drawn between the architecture of these houses and that of gentry houses and associated parish churches, with it being argued that within the architecture is represented the *habitus* of the medieval gentry woman (Gilchrist 1994, 168). By occupying these spaces therefore contemporary attitudes to femininity were enacted, however, due to patterns of patronage and the nature of the women living in these houses, these gendered identities had a class component too them them too. A key element here is the active role of space in the formation of gendered identities, however the approach taken is fundamentally at odds with the approach to identity which will be proposed here as it is reliant on the presence of *habitus* and therefore of a formation of gendered identities within a pre-existing social context.

One criticism levelled at Gilchrist's work is that whilst links are drawn between class and gender, the plurality of gendered identities achieved within these institutions is not fully explored (Gero 1996, 127). In her critique Gero uses the word 'relational' several times, highlighting that multiple forms of gendered identities may emerge in these houses, both due to the varying backgrounds of the inhabitants and the varying ways in which they experienced monastic space. A more general parallel can be drawn here with Cubbit's (2000) examination of the relationship between adherence to monastic rules and the formation of identity and memory. Rather than seeing adherence to the rule as homogenising religious identity and experience of monastic life, Cubbit suggests monasteries were experienced in a multitude of ways depending upon the actions performed in these spaces. Therefore whilst at one level a communal identity may emerge (Cubbit 2000, 273) within a monastery or more widely within an order, individual senses of identity within these spaces were highly variable (Cubbit 2000, 261). In both cases however identities can be seen as forming through experiences of space, with space and non-human elements such as rules acting upon the ways in which groups formed, individuals perceived themselves and were perceived by others. By moving away from a focus on burial evidence we can consider the ways in which experiences were fundamental to the living identities of individuals, rather than simply created as a means to re-enforce social norms or legitimise rights to property or power.

It is not only in relation to monasticism that the active role of space has been considered in relation to identity. Considering the guildhalls of medieval York, Giles (2000) has similarly argued for a relationship between the *habitus* of medieval populations and the architecture of these public spaces. In particular parallels between public and domestic space are examined (Giles 2000, 59–60), with it being argued that the use of space reflected and re-enforced power relationships, both within the structure and in the wider landscape (Giles 2000, 62). Rather than being constructed to a symbolic grammar, these buildings are taken as evidence of the *habitus* which structured the formation and maintenance of social identity (Giles 2000, 67). This study, like Gilchrist's, is reliant on the presence of a pre-existing social context, of which *habitus* is a part. Therefore, although far reaching in its considerations of elements of identity (for example discussing civic identity and power relations), the effect of space is considered from a primarily anthropocentric perspective. The effects of these structures are constrained by *habitus*, excluding the potential for unintended or unusual effects to occur.

The study of guild identities and civic identities more generally, particularly in medieval Flanders, has been a fruitful area of recent historical research however. In these studies performance is given greater weight, for example of feasting (Crombie 2011) or gift giving (Damen 2007), opening the possibility of a more dynamic understanding of the processes through which identities form and the effects of performative action on the ways people perceive themselves, are perceived and form into groups, an insight which is of relevance to the second case study in this chapter, concerned with the performance of dining in medieval castles. In particular it has been considered that towns are contested spaces (Boone 2002; Attreed 2002), understood in different ways, leading to multiple and multi-faceted conceptualisations of urban identity developing. Saunders (2000, 228) considers the laying out of towns as an expression of lordly identity, yet living in these spaces caused new social relations to form, leading to the emergence of particular forms of urban identity (Saunders 2000, 231). The emergence of varying forms of urban identity is demonstrated well through a consideration of seals from medieval London (McEwan 2005) in which the motifs, when placed into context, can be shown to demonstrate a move towards a corporate sense of identity on the part of wealthy Londoners, shifting away from an association with seigniorial elites following the granting of autonomous rule to the city in 1191. Here objects which stand very clearly for the identity of an individual (see also Bedos Rezak 2000) were manipulated to demonstrate the emergence of a particular sense of civic group identity, demonstrating how the contestation of power over urban space transcended scales, from the monumental (the laying out of towns) to the personal and minute.

The subject of power relations has also considered in relation to medieval villages, both through a consideration of space (Saunders 1990; 2000) and material culture (Smith 2009a; Smith 2009b). Saunders (1990) promotes a top-down approach to power relations in the countryside, considering the laying out of field systems and the planning of settlements as an expression of dominance over the peasantry (Saunders 1990, 194). This was not a simple reflection of lordly power, but rather the creation of bounded spaces in which this power could be exerted and re-enforced, in order to maintain a dominant class position (Saunders 1990, 192; Saunders 2000, 221). Such a top down approach fails to appreciate directly the effect of this action on peasant identities, although the inference is that these were suppressed people with limited power. Smith's (2009a; 2009b) study of resistant identities critiques such an impression of peasants having limited agency in relation to the formation of their own identities. In particular she considers the wearing of dress accessories by peasants, in contradiction of contemporary upper class conceptualisations of how a peasant should look; peasants were able to resist the identity which was being thrust upon them (Smith 2009a, 324–5). Further examples of resistance is identified at Wharram Percy in relation to stone robbing, poaching and household scale milling, all of which subvert in some way the primacy of lordly authority within the village (Smith 2009b, 407–9). Importantly,

Smith dismisses a contrast in the motivation of this action between social emulation and resistance, to argue that the very act of social emulation was in itself resistant within the medieval social order and therefore by acquiring and wearing these accessories peasants were able to form their own identities and subvert the forms of identity being thrust upon them (Smith 2009a, 327–8). By seeing these items not as indicators of status, but rather focussing on the social effect of wearing these items, practice rises to the foreground of processes of identity formation, allowing movement away from a simple correlation between objects and status.

It is clear that identity is an important theme within both contemporary medieval archaeology and medieval history. This chapter began by raising some concerns regarding the application of identity theory within archaeology. How successful has medieval archaeology been at overcoming these issues? Firstly it is clear that ideas of identity within medieval archaeology have become increasingly theorised. Consideration of sociological approaches to themes such as ethnicity and gender have led to a consideration of how identities were constructed, rather than seeing material culture as reflective of groups. Secondly, it has been suggested that practice has replaced objects as signifiers of identity. This does appear to be an area however in which medieval archaeology has been particularly strong, in considering the processes through which identities were formed and maintained, be that through occupying space or burying the dead in a particular way. It is clear that the relationship between identity and practice has been well explored within medieval archaeology, with an increasing emphasis being placed on variability in practice, as seen, for example through Smith's discussion of peasant resistance. I contend however there is more to be done. In particular the focus has remained on forms of constructed identities (in part due to a focus on burial archaeology), or a consideration of how through practice existing social norms were reconstructed through *habitus*. This leaves open a large area, those elements of identity which are form spontaneously, as we relate to our surroundings in particular ways, and it is these forms of identity I seek to address in the remainder of this chapter.

## Towards a Relational Approach to Identity

A relational approach to identity allows a greater appreciation of the emergence of the multi-faceted and fluid ways in which people related themselves to others (both human and non-human). This is achieved through the retention of a focus on practice, but a greater consideration of the plural effects of action on the identities of people, both those undertaking action directly and those affected by it. A key deviation from the majority of existing approaches is the move away from a focus on constructed identities, to an examination of how the agency arose for their construction, as well as an examination of the effects of objects upon people's identities. By defining identity as the ways in which people relate themselves to others (see also Jenkins 1996, 49–50) it immediately becomes a relational concept and the study of practice becomes the examination of the relationships which give rise to particular forms of identity.

A starting point in considering a relational approach to identity is Latour's (2005,

27) assertion that 'there are no groups, only processes of group formation'. Here the point is that groups, which we can take as identities, are always in a constant state of becoming (Greenhough 2010, 38); identity is not a possession of an individual or a group but rather a process of becoming something in a particular place, at a particular time. That is not to say that identities cannot be made durable, but that for this to occur there is a reliance on the material (Law and Mol 1995, 279). In order to maintain constructed identities vigilance is required, the associations which are behind an identity must be continually recognised and reproduced in order to emphasise difference, be that through particular uses of space or the repetition of particular ritualised action (Saldenha 2010, 287). These identities are not pre-configured, but are maintained through material relationships which echo what came before (Dewsbury 2010, 151–2). Furthermore, it can be considered that sub-conscious senses of identity, things which may routinely be attributed to *habitus*, are similarly formed and maintained through durable associations with the material world, whilst changes to these identities come about through material re-mapping.

This is not to say that identities cannot be constructed. A convincing argument is put forward, for example, by De Clerq *et al.* (2007) in relation to the manipulation of the material world to construct noble identities in medieval Flanders. Here the use of specific objects and the claiming of space through the planting of a town allowed an individual to build a particular sense of identity. The implication here though is that this identity arose from human agency, or intentionality, which was somehow divorced from its material setting. The action takes place within a context in which individual agents have free will to do as they like, with little consideration either of the material associations which made this individual action possible or the consequences of it. Indeed this is a general criticism of approaches to agency in which identities can be seen as constructed in isolation, with little appreciation for the effects of this action or the context in which the motivation arises (Knapp and Van Domellen 2008, 17; Voutsaki 2010, 67). From a relational perspective we consider that such an anthropocentric view of agency is unrealistic. Rather, it could be considered that the agency behind identity formation was situated within the social relationships which created a situation in which it was both possible and desirable to construct an identity in this way. Through bringing together items of material culture it was possible to *become* noble, with the maintenance of relationships with the material world making durable this constant process of becoming, which also forced others to relate to their surroundings in particular ways, both to situate themselves, but also the new lord, within a web of social connections.

We are moving towards an approach therefore where identities are not deliberately created in isolation, but are the product of the coming together of people and things, in which the agency to form identities emerges from particular processes of social assembly, in some cases manifesting as intentionality and in others a more sub-conscious conceptualisation of the self in relation to surroundings. Such an approach can find parallels in recent discussions of relational personhood. Based upon, in particular, the writing of Strathern (1988), the concept of personhood has been particularly enthusiastically adopted by archaeologists studying the neolithic and bronze age periods (*e.g.* Fowler 2001; Jones 2005; Brück 2006; Kirk 2006). The basic tenant of such an approach is that individuals are not self contained beings, but rather persons are constructed of relationships with other people and their material surroundings. Therefore rather than existing *a priori*, the individual is the product of particular relationships (Fowler 2001, 142) and the process of becoming a person is what is studied through examinations of practice (Kirk 2006, 334), with these processes simultaneously making, for example, objects and landscapes; with the artefactual record therefore both reflecting and constituting the social relations which make up the person (Fowler 2001, 148; Casella and Croucher 2011, 211; Creese 2012, 382). Rather than identities reacting to broader social changes, by considering the ways in which people, places and things constitute one another it can be considered that it is in the changing nature of these relationships in which the agency for social change is located and therefore identities are not related within or by *habitus*, but rather are created with it (Chapman and Gaydarska 2011, 37; Jones 2005, 216; Creese 2012 382; Knapp and Van Dommellen 2008, 22). A key component of such studies has been a consideration of what being a person meant within past societies, in reaction to the primacy of modern, western perspectives on the bounded individual (*e.g.* Jones 2005). Clearly within medieval society, for which a wealth of material and written evidence is available, this is a topic which is far too extensive to cover in this book. Rather than attempting this task it is my aim to use personhood as a concept to think with, to open up the multi-faceted nature of personal identities (Van Dommellen and Knapp 2008, 17), to consider the role of practice in their emergence and in particular to examine the effect of relationships with people and things through which people came to understand their place in the medieval world (*cf.* Kirk 2006, 344–5).

Approaches to personhood have great potential for understanding the dynamics of identity formation in medieval society as well as for understanding medieval conceptualisations of the person. However they have received little attention from medieval archaeologists (see for example Williams 2003). In both prehistory and historical archaeology the majority of literature relates to the mortuary sphere, in which persons were constructed through participation in mortuary rituals. Yet these concepts are equally applicable to the domestic realm, a realm which may be more complex in its variability but in which such a focus on practice and effect can prove rewarding in the interpretation of social relations in the medieval period. A particularly insightful example is Bedos-Rezak's (2000, 1531–2) examination of seals, which, through their enrolment in social relations played a role in the creation of categorical identity systems, offering a medium through which power relations could be negotiated and images of the self could be portrayed. Whilst the study does not draw directly on ideas of relational personhood, it is a good example of how in the medieval period it is possible to see components of social identity being formed through relations with the material world, rather than the material simply standing for these relations. A further example can be seen in Loveluck and Tys' (2006) examination of maritime identities in the North Sea region, in which a particular form of maritime identity and culture emerged through the performance of particular sets of social relationships, including the exchange of goods, which, through their entanglement in these relationships themselves developed particular meanings amongst these communities, although this study is not explicitly relational in its approach.

A relational approach, drawing upon ideas of personhood as well as broader considerations within relational theories in other disciplines requires realignment, rather than a revolution in the way we consider identities and their relationship to practice. What is required is to examine the ways in which the agency for identities to form, either consciously or sub-consciously, was spun through processes of social assembly and the effects of action on the ways in which people were able to perceive themselves. The shift is from seeing identity as a constant or attribute to seeing it as emergent, as a process of becoming, which is under constant negotiation as people become effected by and entangled within their surroundings in a plurality of ways.

## An Archaeology of Constructed Identities? Cooking Practices and the Norman Conquest.

We can now begin to put these ideas into practice, to explore the effect of the use of pottery in the emergence and maintenance of identities in the medieval period. The first of these considers the relationship between domestic practices and the emergence of identities following the Norman Conquest, focussing upon the port town of Southampton. It is often considered that the Norman Conquest was a major event which changed the face of English society, and which was so traumatic that its history was not immediately recorded as an act of forgetting (Van Houts 1999, 123–130). However, study of the ceramic evidence from Southampton (Jervis 2013b; Jervis 2013c) has demonstrated that the use of pottery was enrolled in multiple processes of continuity and change over the long term, in which the Conquest was a factor, but not the only driver in a process of social re-mapping. Archaeological approaches to the Conquest are, surprisingly, rare, however where undertaken have provided multiple narratives about its effect in relation to, for example, building traditions (Impey 2000), faunal remains (Sykes 2007) and burial monuments (McClain 2012). Impey (2000) for example considers the possibility that influences moved in both directions across the Channel in the post-Conquest period, arguing that seigniorial residences in Normandy are in fact influenced by Anglo-Saxon architecture. Sykes (2007) uses zooarchaeological evidence to question the visibility of the Conquest, arguing that difference is apparent in the subtleties of provisioning strategies, rather than in the nature of the animals consumed. Finally, examining the spread of burial monuments in Yorkshire, McClain (2012) argues that the adoption and adaptation of local commemorative techniques allowed incomers to build a new form of distinctly northern identity, which cut across any pre-existing ethnic differences, in what was already an area occupied by people of Anglo-Saxon and Scandinavian descent. All three cases show that the study of different forms of material culture allows the presentation of differing histories of Conquest and suggest that the paying of more attention to this period by archaeologists would prove fruitful.

The aim of this case study is not however to consider the impact of the Conquest on the ceramic record, but rather to consider how the use of pottery contributed to the emergence and formation of identities around 1066. In particular we can question whether a specific Norman or Anglo-Norman identity emerged amongst the people of Southampton in relation to their domestic practices, or whether, in fact, the agency emerged for the generation of multiple forms of identity, related to the plurality of experiences associated with this event. In order to place this discussion into context it is necessary to briefly summarise some debates about the nature of 'Norman' ethnicity. The Normans were not a homogeneous group, but rather consisted of a mixture of Scandinavian settlers and the existing Frankish population of Normandy. A Norman ethnicity was constructed in order to legitimise control and served to create an origin myth which underpinned the coherency and legitimacy of the group (Loud 1981, 104). Early medieval textual practice was to conceptualise areas as discrete polities, populated by distinct peoples, who were characterised by particular character traits or practices (Loud 1989, 114; Johnson 2004, 89). Through writing in this way a new ethnic group emerged and was reified in text. However, the motives behind the emergence of this group and its character varied through time. Initially the aim was to legitimise the groups' presence in France, building an origin myth in which the Scandinavian settlers, led by Rollo, undertook a process of Francisation, which included the conversion to Christianity (Loud 1989, 108; E. Johnson 2006, 157). However the original history, that produced by Dudo of Saint-Quentin, can be considered to have only been accessible to lay and ecclesiastical elites, familiar with both Latin and the style of writing and language (E. Johnson 2006, 157). The aim in this early stage then was perhaps to legitimise the presence of the Norman group amongst the elite and therefore of the new nobility's power. Dudo's writings formed the basis of later work however which were more accessible and perhaps intended to propagate the idea of Norman ethnicity more widely (E. Johnson 2006, 162). It must be remembered that identities were multi-layered and although Normans were distinct from, for example, Bretons, all could be referred to as French and indeed this was the term used to describe them by the English (Thomas 2003, 33). The effect of these histories, produced in Normandy, was to form a Norman identity, which emerged as a result of particular political situation and which came to be manipulated as this situation changed and as the influence of the Normans expanded. In Italian chronicles for example, an origin myth is replaced by tales of common endeavour as the string which binds the group together, shifting the emphasis from legitimising the groups' history to expressing the identity of an existing group (Johnson 2004, 100; E. Johnson 2006, 163). Furthermore, by adopting particular traits it was possible to be considered Norman and thus to become Norman, whilst the Normans were also adept at adapting to new circumstances and shifting their identity accordingly (Johnson 2004, 90). This notion is supported in histories such as the writing of Orderic Vitalis, writing in *c*.1125:

English and Normans were living peacefully together in boroughs, towns, and cities, and were intermarrying with each other. You could see many villages or town markets filled with displays of French wares and merchandise, and observe the English, who had previously been contemptible to the French, in their native dress, completely transformed by foreign fashions (The Ecclesiastical History of Orderic Vitalis book IV; *ed. and transl.* Chibnall 1969 , 257).

It should be noted however that Orderic was a product of integration and although explicitly writing about the period before 1069, is likely to be projecting conditions his own day to present a somewhat idealised version of the situation immediately following the Conquest (Golding 1994, 182). Indeed, the text may even have been taken from earlier writing, such as that of William of Poitiers, whose *Gesta Guillemi* is considered something of a panegyric to William I. Even with this caveat in mind, at face value a united, hybrid form of Normanised social identity appears to have emerged relatively quickly (within a generation) in Anglo-Norman England if this writing is taken at face value, although this quote does indicate a somewhat antagonistic relationship immediately following the Conquest.

Norman identity was also expressed more explicitly in some circumstances than others. Again in Italy, the study of naming patterns has demonstrated an increasing use of names to emphasise Norman descent in the 12th century, when the Norman identity was becoming less clearly defined as the result of cultural mixing (Drell 1999, 200). We can see then that Norman ethnicity was not fixed, rather it emerged and changed in relation to changing circumstances, indeed the histories can be seen as group formation processes rather than reflections of the presence of a discrete group, with processes of referencing, copying and reading re-forming the group, but allowing its constitution and core characteristics to shift relationally. As has been seen in Italy it was an identity which could be expressed at particular times, and furthermore, an identity which could be acquired or constructed through the adoption of practice. Clearly affiliation to the Norman elite could be expressed monumentally through architecture and through acts of political allegiance. However we can also consider that the Conquest offered opportunities for Norman identity to be constructed at the domestic scale and, furthermore, that widespread changes, for example to processes of provisioning, did not occur in isolation, but rather flowed in to the house, with household practice similarly having an outward influence, for example in relation to the emergence of new forms of pottery.

## Ceramic Use in Anglo-Norman Southampton

The discussion of artefacts necessarily requires recourse to meaningful categories which emerge through our analysis of archaeological objects. Such labels typically focus upon a ware developed through particular production processes, which, archaeological terminology implies, is relevant throughout the life of a pot. This clearly is not the case, rather the same product immediately becomes many different things throughout its life, and the pot itself is the product of processes of social assembly, in which potters themselves may have developed very different senses of what a particular kind of pottery was (Van Oyen 2013, 97). This should be borne in mind in this discussion, which focuses upon Anglo-Norman Southampton. The focus of this discussion is the most ubiquitous form of pottery to be found in Anglo-Norman Southampton, known as Scratch Marked Ware (see Brown 2002, 9), a locally produced coarseware used primarily for cooking and storage and its late Saxon predecessor, Flint-tempered Ware (see Brown 1994b, 130–1) (Figure 4.1). These categories were defined through modern analysis, and it is questionable whether they existed in the minds of medieval people. However the larger capacity of the Scratch-Marked Wares and the patterning of their distribution in Southampton does suggest that these post-conquest wares developed through a particular process of social assembly, in which pots were specifically produced to allow for particular cooking practices, bringing durability to domestic experiences and thus identities. Pots then are not clearly defined categories at any point in their biography, but develop as materialisations of messy bundles of associations, which shift in meaning as they are drawn into and out of courses of action (Van Oyen 2013, 97). Usewear analysis of these wares has indicated changes in cooking practices from the 10th–12th centuries, which may have some relation to the Norman Conquest (see also Jervis 2013b; Jervis 2013c; Jervis in prep.).

In summary, analysis of the type and location of sooty deposits on pots has demonstrated that two styles of use can be ascertained (Figure 4.2c). The first involves placing the pot in or close to the embers, leading to the accumulation of thick sooty deposits particularly around the mid portion of the pot. This is prevalent in the late Saxon period and can be seen as the dominant form of cooking practice at sites throughout Southampton. The second involves suspending the vessel over the fire, leading to thinner glossy sooty deposits, around the base and lower part of the vessel. This is particularly prevalent amongst the post-conquest Scratch Marked Wares (Figure 4.2b). Underlying these general trends however are exceptions. At two late Saxon waterfront sites instances of vessel suspension were unusually high, suggesting a form of cooking which was relatively unusual within the late Saxon town. At both sites there are high relatively quantities of imported pottery and it can be considered that these may relate to the presence of a mercantile household. Circumstantial evidence, including a noticeable trend for contemporary north French coarseware cooking vessels to have suspension holes or lugs and a depiction of a suspended cooking pot on the Bayeux tapestry (Figure 4.1), may indicate that this was a typically French cooking practice (see Flambard Héricher 2004, 285–877; Lewis 2005 for a discussion of artefacts depicted on the Bayeux tapestry); potentially French merchants within Southampton were using locally produced cooking pots in a distinctive way. The increase in incidences of this practice following the Conquest can perhaps be related to the planting of a French population into Southampton, focussed on the waterfront area around French St (Figure 4.2a). It is however, unlikely that the population of this area was entirely French and that vessel suspension was unique to French households, particularly as by the 13th century it appears to have been practiced commonly throughout Southampton. Analysis of the composition of stratigraphically post-conquest ceramic assemblages from the site at York Buildings, located in the east of Southampton and away from the

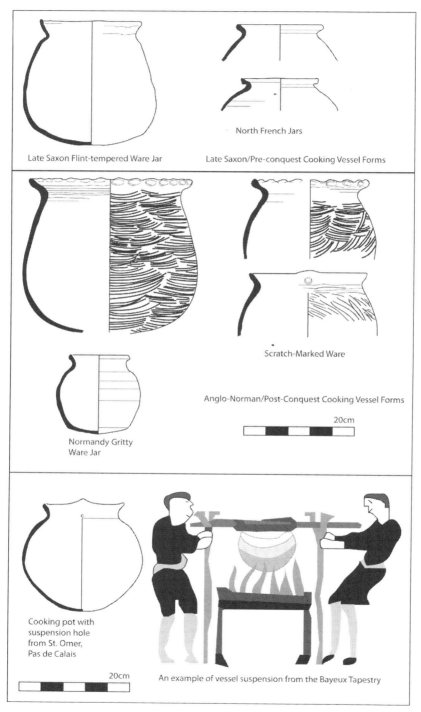

Late Saxon Flint-tempered Ware Jar

North French Jars

Late Saxon/Pre-conquest Cooking Vessel Forms

Scratch-Marked Ware

Normandy Gritty
Ware Jar

Anglo-Norman/Post-Conquest Cooking Vessel Forms

20cm

Cooking pot with
suspension hole
from St. Omer,
Pas de Calais

20cm

An example of vessel suspension from the Bayeux Tapestry

*Figure 4.1:
Examples of
late Saxon and
Anglo-Norman
cooking
vessels from
Southampton
and an image
from the
Bayeux tapestry
illustrating a
vessel being
suspended over
a fire. Pottery
redrawn from
Brown (1994
and 2002).*

*Figure 4.2.
(opposite)
A) The
occurrence of
types of sooting
at sites in
Southampton.
B) Comparison
of sooting
patterns on
late Saxon
and Anglo-
Norman vessels.
C) Examples
of 1) Black
carbonised
and 2) Glossy
black sooting.
Drawings and
photographs:
Ben Jervis.*

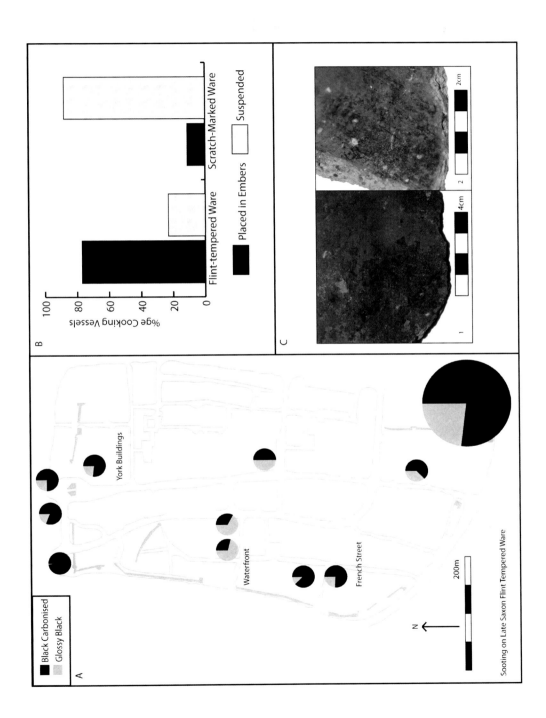

waterfront, suggests that here late Saxon vessels may have persisted for longer. A high level of fragmentation inhibited usewear analysis at this site, but it can be considered that the persistence of these types here may suggest continuity of late Saxon cooking techniques into the post-conquest period (Jervis in prep.).

These changes in cooking practice can be, circumstantially at least, related to the presence of a French community in Southampton following 1066. To see these practices as simply reflecting the presence of an immigrant group, who, through cooking practice were re-creating a form of *habitus* is overly simplistic and contributes little to our understanding of experiences of conquest and the formation of identities in Anglo-Norman Southampton. It is in moving towards this aim that a relational perspective can be utilised, to consider the plurality of identities which emerged in the early medieval town, as people related to pottery in particular ways.

## Emergent Identities in Anglo-Norman Southampton

The Norman Conquest can be considered a colonial situation, albeit one less pronounced than those which characterise later historical periods, on account of there being considerable similarities between Anglo-Saxon and Norman society and a noticeable French presence in England prior to the conquest, particularly in port towns such as Southampton (see Lewis 1994; Matthew 2005). As such our understanding of the event and its effects can be seen as being formed largely on histories which, as discussed above, are products both of the event and of particular political agendas. As Elisabeth Van Houts (1999) has ably demonstrated, histories produced particular forms of collective memory about the conquest, with a particular aim being to mitigate the historical trauma caused in 1066. Studies, particularly in relation to changes to the urban and rural landscape, including the imposition of castles (*e.g.* Lilley 2009) have ensured that the impacts of the conquest upon the existing population have been addressed to some degree, yet a relatively simple history has been presented, one in which elements of the existing population were oppressed, new power structures developed and eventually a process of assimilation occurred. It is possible though to use the study of material culture to explore alternative histories and archaeologies of the conquest which more fully address the plurality of experiences and identities which emerged in 11th and 12th century England (see broader discussions in Horning 2010, 29–30; Croucher 2010, 34). Such an approach clearly finds some parallel within the field of post-colonial archaeology, in which the concept of hybridity is key. In simple terms, hybridity is the process of cultural mixing, and is the concept which, implicitly at least, underpins our terminology, in which the period is typically defined as Saxo- or Anglo- Norman, even though such terms do not occur in contemporary sources (Thomas 2003, 71), in which people are distinctively English or French or could identify with both simultaneously, but not in a transitional sense (Thomas 2003, 73). The concept of hybridity has been utilised to demonstrate that robust cultural boundaries can be challenged, particularly in colonial situations. However if taken too simply the idea reduces down to a reliance on cultural purity, in which defined groups mix through the appropriation of particular characteristics, leading to a tangible hybrid identity (Jiménez 2011, 114), which becomes a bounded category in itself. Hybrid objects might be characterised as the effect of mixed *habitus* (Cañete and Vives-Ferrándiz, 2011, 135), with hybridization being a process of translation in which people gain control over culture to express mixing through material things (Jiménez 2011; Cañete and Vives-Ferrándiz 2011, 135).

Such a process of hybridization can arguably be seen in Southampton, with the adaptation of cooking practices through the utilisation, by an immigrant community of locally produced cooking vessels and, potentially, the adoption of French cooking practices by the existing population. If this is considered a mixing of *habitus*, and *habitus* leads to identity, they we can consider that a hybrid Anglo-Norman identity emerged, at least on the part of some members of Southampton's population. We might consider the continuity in the use of late Saxon wares by other members of the population as resistant to this identity, as this oppressed group strived to hold onto a sense of identity and maintain their own agency in a colonial setting. I do not dispute that the practices led to the emergence of new forms of identity and the maintenance of old ones. However, a simple view of a uniform hybrid identity, such as that alluded to by Orderic Vitallis, is clearly over simplistic. If, following Latour, there are no groups, but only processes of group formation, then hybridization can be considered one of these processes, which allowed people to relate to one another in certain ways, but which, rather than producing a hybrid group, spun the agency for multiple forms of identity to emerge.

Conventional post-colonial theory, although not incompatible with a relational approach, does seem to fall short for our purposes in two key areas. The first of these is a reliance on context, a continued conceptualisation that experiences happen within a colonial context, rather than courses of action forming and re-forming the context and experiences of it simultaneously (as identified by Van Dommellen 2011, 3; Villelli 2011, 89). Secondly, whilst it can be considered that groups of coloniser and colonised are not homogeneous, but formed of multiple individuals with differing ethnic, gendered or age based identities (Van Dommellen 2010, 39), the concept of cultural hybridity and of alternative histories is reliant upon the presence of some form of fixed group, the source colours which become mixed on the pallet of colonial encounters. By trying to write the history of the neglected other, post-colonialism forces us to acknowledge that the other, as a defined group, exists. However, if, as we are urged to by Audrey Horning (2010, 27) we embrace ambiguity and move away from viewing such rigid groups as existing, it is possible to create a thicker and multi-vocal archaeology of the Norman Conquest, which considers the effect of engagements on the ways in which people related to the world around them and to examine how the agency for identity formation was spun and re-spun through action. Such an approach might find parallels in archaeological applications of Bhabha's (2004, 56) concept of 'the third space', the in between in which hybridity as process occurs (*e.g.* Naum 2010). If we follow Latour in considering groups only to be discernible as processes of group formation, then the concept of hybridity becomes more useful, providing a basis from which to explore the processes of adjustment brought about by the coming together of people from different backgrounds and to consider the effects in terms of continuity and change or familiarity and unfamiliarity, rather than the emergence of a labelled hybrid identity. It also becomes crucial to acknowledge that groups of people and objects are mutually constituted, meaning that the same material thing can become completely different objects, a process masked in archaeological processes of object categorisation in which things remain within bounded groups, as different groups form (Van Oyen 2013, 88). In other words, within a relational approach the categorisation of people and things is entangled within the development of multiple social realties which form a context, rather than objects being a medium upon which meaning can be inscribed through the expression of identity, be that consciously or through betraying the influence of interaction with human others upon how people see themselves. By focussing on effect and the spinning of agency, we move away from simply observing diverse practices or analysing them in contrast to one another, to consider their effective nature and their connectivity, meaning that we can follow flows of action to examine how an entangled, diasporic, society emerged, rather than considering how different histories were established upon a pre-existing stage. By acknowledging fluidity of context we can account more convincingly for trajectories of experience and the emergence of identities. A relational approach is therefore not opposed to a post-colonial one, but offers a mechanism through which the post-colonial critique can be applied in understanding the formation of historical and archaeological contexts.

The Norman Conquest re-mapped the associations which formed 'the social' in Southampton and beyond. Whilst constantly in flux, the repetition of practices had created a familiar environment for the inhabitants of the town and allowed for identities to be continually reformed as the agency for them was perpetually re-spun. The effect of objects was restrained by *habitus*, rather than *habitus* being reflected in their use. This is a simple but key distinction, as we can consider that the agency for continuity was not deferred by humans onto the material world, but was rather re-spun through interactions with it. Therefore, the changes observed in cooking practices do not simply reflect the presence of a new group re-forming their own *habitus*, but rather of the presence of human actors who formed new associations with material culture, with effects upon both the identity of them and of others, and which reached beyond the confines of the home. Although people moved, distinct and homogeneous groups of newcomers and 'natives' did not exist *a priori*, but rather groups of individuals who experienced the world in the same way were constantly re-made through repeated action. The reconstruction of courses of action allows the identification of distinctive groups, who were joined and formed through shared experiences of food, achieved through participation in similar courses of action. Importantly, although these can be interpreted on the basis of historical evidence to be loosely related to incoming and existing populations, the groups were identified through following the evidence for courses of action through which identities emerged, rather than through seeking signatures associated with fixed cultural groups. Indeed closer interpretation suggests these courses of action led to the emergence of multiple experiences and social realities and therefore were enrolled in complex processes of identity emergence.

What then, was the effect of these associations upon these incoming people? Vessel suspension can be equated with a slower cooking technique than the placement of pots in the fire. Therefore this promoted the cooking of tenderer meat, allowing the replication of sensory sensations associated with eating amongst this group (see Sutton, 2009, 74). This can be considered particularly important when the zooarchaeological evidence, that younger and therefore more tender, animals were consumed in Normandy than late Anglo-Saxon England (Sykes 2007, 19). In reality however it is unlikely that Norman settlers undertook cooking themselves, higher class households had cooks, some of whom were sent to Normandy to learn to cook in the 'correct' fashion (Matthew 2005, 38). Therefore the identities of these people were not formed through the act of cooking, but rather through the act of eating. Through the replication of sensory experiences associated with eating particular dishes memories of past meals were cited, spinning the agency for continuity in experience and therefore in identity. Returning to the concept of relational personhood, identity did not reside within a person to be expressed through eating, but rather it was through forming relationships with the material world that the person 'became' and their *habitus* was reconstituted. For these people then, eating did not contribute to the formation of a hybrid identity in isolation, rather it was a means by which existing associations with the material world were re-formed and the agency for a particular sense of identity could be re-spun. Whilst eating in the French manner allowed a French identity to be reformed and re-made, this need not necessarily have been the result of considered intentionality, but more a product of stability in the relationships formed between people and their surroundings. It was in the effect of practice that identity emerged and was re-made with every meal. That is not to say that they did not experience hybridity in other areas of life, for example through making associations with a new physical setting, experiences and associations which de-stabilised their sense of belonging and potentially eroded any distinct Norman elements of identity (Thomas 2003, 165), either because attention was not paid to reproducing the connections underpinning this ethnicity or the materials (in the broadest sense of the term) required for the agency behind the re-forming of this identity as distinctive were not present. For example, relationships formed in office within towns have been argued to have worked the other way, with incomers adopting English identities through behaving in particular ways and building particular social networks around them (Thomas 2003, 392). To see these food practices as an expression of identity is to miss the point. Identity was re-formed through the re-making of associations and re-experiencing the world. It emerged as the effect of these interactions, along with a feeling of familiarity, which allowed for some stability in an individual's social reality, as other elements of it were re-mapped. They formed certain facets of identity, but not the whole, as the person was distributed through a wider range of associations with their human and non-human surroundings.

For those undertaking the cooking however these associations may have had a more profound effect. We can consider that households employed local cooks, as well as those brought from Normandy. For cooks who had come from Normandy it can be considered that, just as their employers experienced continuity through eating, they experienced it through the replication of the bodily actions and experiences of cooking. However the differing material properties of the vessels with which they were interacting caused a de-stabilising agency to emerge, creating unfamiliarity as they acted in unexpected ways, potentially forcing adaptation to cooking practices. For these cooks the introduction of new actors was destabilising, even if the physical processes of interaction were familiar, the result being a re-formulation of the sense of identity which emerged through cooking as experiences of the familiar and unfamiliar were mediated through practice. For local cooks, the opposite was true. Familiarity came through interaction with the materiality of the vessels, but through engaging with these vessels in new ways unfamiliarity emerged, meaning that the impact of the Conquest was perhaps profoundly felt by these individuals, even within domestic space.

In none of these cases can we consider that an Anglo-Norman identity was consciously constructed. Rather, we can see that through varying forms of interaction with the material world in the processes of cooking and dining, multiple forms of hybridized identity emerged. The agency for identity to emerge was formed through processes of assembly; cooking and eating, with the effect of material engagement being feelings of familiarity and unfamiliarity, which directly relate to senses of identity which were not formed in isolation, but for which the agency was distributed between an individual and their material surroundings. This was of course only one facet of identity, and one which was formed sporadically in the moment of cooking or eating. Only by tracing the other connections which a person undertook is it possible to consider the full effect of their human-material interactions on their sense of self and to consider the locations in which the agency for identity formation and identity emergence were spun.

As we have already seen however, Norman identity was not a fixed category, but was constructed in different ways in relation to different situations. If we consider, as is likely, that the waterfront area was not only populated by French immigrants, we can consider that in some English households French cooking practices were being adopted, potentially as a conscious means of affiliating with the incoming elite, not simply through political acts, but also through the adoption of Norman taste and practice. The social remapping associated with the Conquest, the re-making of ties between people, spaces and things, created the agency, or intentionality, for the expression of identity in this way to emerge. For those striving to affiliate themselves with the newcomers, change was perhaps mediated through the most mundane of domestic experiences, such as eating. In these households it was not only the cooks who saw their identities subtly changing, but also those consuming the food, as new tastes were experienced, destabilising experiences of the material world and causing new identities to emerge, both as people related themselves to their surroundings and others related to them in new ways. Therefore meaning in terms of identity, but also of the objects themselves, emerged through practice (Van Oyen 2013, 90). Such a conclusion finds parallels in Naum's (2010, 115) discussion of 'the third space' and pottery production. However, the implication in Naum's study is that pottery was directed by anthropogenic agency to allow people to negotiate the 'third space'. A relational perspective allows us to go one step further, removing the assumption that identity formation need be the result of human intentionality, to consider the wider reaching effects of interactions upon the identities not only of those seeking to build identity or control experience, but also the others who are drawn into this process. Crucially we move from seeking hybrid identities to tracing the emergence of the individual social realities, which emerged through differences in experiencing the world. Clearly the process was more complex, intermarrying in particular would have further stimulated these changes in identity expression at the domestic scale, and potentially have caused experiences of eating to have had multiple effects on the identities of diners even within a single home.

*Summary*

In this section I have argued that changes in cooking practice do not simply demonstrate the *habitus* of an incoming group, nor do they reflect a simple process of hybridization. Rather, it can be considered that interactions with pottery through cooking and eating had multiple effects, spinning the agency through which feelings of familiarity and unfamiliarity emerged alongside senses of identity and belonging. Such an approach finds parallels in post-colonial considerations of 'the third space', in which through material interactions unfamiliar spaces and insecure identities and transformed into familiar places and senses of belonging in a plurality of ways. At the domestic scale it can be suggested that the impact of the Conquest had the least impact on the incoming French population, for whom experiences of taste and texture cited previous meals, spinning familiarity and re-making a sense of identity in relation to the bodily experience of eating. For the cooks change was mediated through differences in the act of cooking, which were not designed as pre-mediated expressions of their own identity, yet destabilised the ways in which they experienced and related to their surroundings. Yet the social remapping of the conquest also created opportunities for new identities to be produced, spinning the agency for intentionality in the formation of a particularly Norman identity and mediating this through the manipulation of experiences of the material world through eating. We can see therefore that a simple, hybrid Anglo-Norman identity did not emerge, nor were hybrid identities a reflection of social context. Rather, action spun the agency for multiple experiences of domestic life to occur, leading to the emergence, formation and re-formation of identities and processes of continuity and change, weaving 'the social' as a fluid bundle of individual social realities, which were directly effected by objects (see also Van Oyen 2013, 98–9). Importantly this is reliant on an appreciation of historical processes. Following Austin (1990, 30–1) the methodology applied here has been explicitly archaeological, however turning to historical knowledge we can gain some understanding of the biographies of the individuals enrolled in these processes, and therefore gain a stronger understanding of the processes at work. There is clearly a place for cross disciplinary research in identity studies, but one in which history does not provide *a priori* groups, but rather offers some explanation for the patterning identified in the archaeological record. Of course these domestic entanglements were only a tiny part of the wider web, which created individuals and 'the social' and further research must focus on tracing other connections to further understand the ways that multi-faceted senses of identity emerged as individuals were continually re-formed through entanglement with their material surroundings.

## Identities of Dominance: Pottery, Space and the English Castle

A second case study can allow us to focus more on the constructed elements of identity, through a consideration of the use of material culture and dining spaces within two medieval castles. Castle studies have been characterised by an unconstructive polarisation between those who advocate their defensive function and those who prefer to adopt a more balanced, interpretive perspective, in which castles are vibrant spaces which materialise multiple purposes and influences (Platt 2007; Creighton and Liddiard 2008). Platt's (2007) contention that castle studies have been 'hijacked' by followers of Charles Coulson and Matthew Johnson, obsessed with considering castles as fashionable accessories rather than defensive fortresses is however untrue. Whilst Coulson's historical research and Johnson's archaeological interpretations of castle spaces have stressed the non-defensive elements of castles, their effect has not been to negate defensive issues entirely, but rather to force scholars to consider castles in new ways (Creighton and Liddiard 2008). Largely this has been through the consideration of castle spaces. Gilchrist (1999) for example has explored feminine spaces, exploring the relationship between women and private spaces and the ways in which contemporary *habitus* is reflected and enacted through the design and use of castles. Hicks (2009), drawing on textual as well as archaeological information, creates a more elaborate picture, considering how castles were perceived in different ways by individuals from varying social backgrounds, and considering how public and private, masculine and feminine spaces were not fixed, but were fluid, coming into being as such at particular times and in particular circumstances.

Creighton and Liddiard (2008) rightly argue that castle studies have suffered from a lack of focus on the material culture of castle life. This is partly due to the fact that few castles have been the subject of extended programmes of excavation, particularly using modern techniques. Analysis does hint at castles having distinctive signatures in some respects, for example both Thomas (2006) and Albarella (2005) have shown that faunal assemblages from castle sites are distinctive from those of urban and rural settlements, particularly in relation to the quantity of wild animals consumed (and particularly birds in later periods), a pattern which is interpreted as relating to high status feasting and hunting by castle communities.

Varying depositional practices within castles however mean that in some cases it is possible to identify material culture related to particular spaces within the castle and, if these groups are interpreted in relation to these spaces, the people who populated them and each other. Therefore through the study of these groups it becomes possible to explore how identities were formed within the castle through the undertaking of practices associated with the use of varying types of material culture.

## Pottery and Identity in Two English Castles

Castles were undoubtedly a symbol of power and wealth and the activities which went on within them contributed to the emergence of identities of power and status. It was in the public spaces in which the agency to construct and display an image or identity of power and wealth was spun, and this was achieved through the display of rare and valuable objects, the consumption of particular foodstuffs and the gathering of people. The presentation of power and wealth did not occur in isolation however, and had an effect on others who inhabited this space. By controlling the space, the lord could determine rules of etiquette, which, through being constantly or intermittently enacted, forced people to relate to them in particular ways. This could be displayed, for example, through reflecting and re-enforcing social hierarchy in the order in which food and drink were taken (*e.g.* Phillips 2005, 147). Therefore, by controlling the dining space individuals were able to express their own identity, whilst at the same time forcing others to relate to the world around them in particular ways, leading to the emergence of particular forms of identity, for example of dominance and submission (see Jenkins 1996, 22). These spaces then were not just static locations in which identities could be displayed, but were spaces in which multiple identities emerged through engagements with material culture. Studies of pottery and space in historical archaeology have shown the potential that exploring the relationship between spaces, identities and portable material culture. Dellino-Musgrave (2005), for example, has demonstrated how the restricted use of English tewares amongst the crew of British Navy ships allowed a plurality of meanings and identities to occur, in relation to concepts of British-ness, but also in relation to the creation and maintenance of social memory and hierarchical identities onboard the vessel. By considering pottery not as a reflection of such identities, but as enrolled in the emergence of difference, the social dynamics of the castle can be further investigated.

The two castles under discussion have been extensively excavated, leading to the recovery of large ceramic assemblages. The first is Barnard Castle (County Durham), excavated between 1974 and 1981. During the 13th–14th centuries the castle was under the tenure of the de Balloil family, functioning as the centre of their estate, and passing to the Earl of Warwick around 1330 (see Austin 2007a; 2007b). The second is Launceston Castle (Cornwall), the centre of the Earldom of Cornwall and held by Richard, Earl of Cornwall and his successors from the 13th century (Saunders 2006). Contrasting approaches have been taken to the analysis of the pottery from these sites. The Launceston assemblage has been catalogued by ware, being placed into a broader regional context, particularly in terms of exchange patterns, with a core aim of the analysis being the understanding of the chronological patterning of the pottery present (Brown *et al.* 2006). A different approach was taken at Barnard Castle, which was deliberately set up in opposition to traditional practice. An exhaustive catalogue of the pottery was created, with a particular emphasis on understanding the distribution of the different types throughout the castle. This has allowed the identification of several functional groups, which relate to activities being undertaken in different areas of the castle, as well as providing details about waste disposal (Austin 2007b).

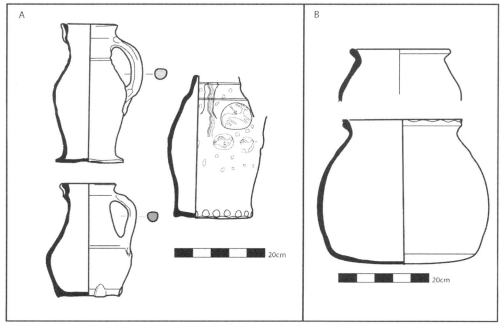

*Figure 4.3. Examples of jugs and cooking vessels from Barnard Castle. Redrawn from Austin 2007b.*

    A first group of pottery from Barnard Castle is interpreted as being associated with
the Lords' table. It was found in association with glass and consists primarily of highly
decorated ceramics (Figure 4.3). The assemblage is taken as a direct reflection of lordly
status and as a symbol of elite dining and display (Austin 2007b, 498–9). Whilst it
can be considered that the pottery does indicate the relative status of this area of the
castle, by considering the interactions which people had with this material, and the
effect of these engagements, it is possible to create a thicker understanding of the ways
in which identities formed through dining in the castle. Analysis of the assemblage
from Launceston also hints at spatial patterning in the consumption of ceramics. The
majority of pottery from 13th century phases was recovered from the yard area and the
Lesser Hall. The Lesser Hall is argued by the excavator to have functioned primarily as
an administrative space, whilst the Great Hall would have been the location of feasts.
The pottery from the Lesser Hall consists primarily of local coarseware vessels, which
dominate the assemblage as a whole, with quantities of jugs produced regionally and
a small quantity of imported wares. This is indicative of some ceramic use within the
Lesser Hall and it is possible that the Great Hall was only used for dining on specific
occasions, perhaps when Richard was in residence. Very small quantities of mid-13th
century pottery were recovered from the kitchen and Great Hall, with the majority
being excavated from features and surfaces in the yard area. It is noticeable that the
distribution of imported wares, consisting of Saintonge- and North French- Whiteware

jugs, cluster around the Great Hall (Figure 4.4a). This pattern can also be observed into the 14th century, with, in relative terms, imported wares being most common in deposits associated with the Great Hall and, to a lesser extent, the Lesser Hall; for example only 4% of the assemblage consists of imported wares, yet 23% of the small assemblage from the Great Hall consists of this pottery. At both castles then spatial analysis of the pottery suggests that the consumption of highly decorated tableware was limited to specific contexts within the castle, whilst its low quantity may indicate that it was consumed only on specific occasions. At Launceston this can tentatively be suggested to be on occasions when dining took place within the Great Hall, perhaps when the Earl was in residence.

How then, can we think about the consumption of tableware, principally ceramic jugs, but alongside glass and metal vessels, in terms of identities? First of all we need to consider the objects themselves. As we have already discussed (chapter 3) pottery was not inherently valuable, either in economic or social terms, yet through being enrolled in the expression of lordly identity through the act of dining it can be considered that these vessels became enacted as socially valuable objects. They presented an opportunity for the Lord to display his wealth and connections, not simply through the vessels, but through their contents and their association with Italian glass and other exotic or visually impressive items. Furthermore the use of these vessels was regulated, through unwritten or written rules of etiquette. Rules, it can be considered, are not inherently meaningful, but must be continually enacted, or re-made, to retain their power (see the discussion of Latour (2010) in chapter 3). Through being enrolled in courses of action these rules limit action, allowing social structures and identities to be re-made and retained, creating a relentless snowball of agency until they cease to be enacted. Rules therefore reduced the ways in which people could relate to one another and were therefore enrolled in processes of identity creation, however this agency could only be spun through the presence of a range of material relationships, including those with the dining space (or spaces), vessels and foodstuffs. By being enacted therefore it can be considered that they effected the emergence of multiple forms of identity of dominance and submission. By participating in dining a feeling of exclusivity could be created, whilst for those who could not participate identities of exclusion may have emerged. Yet within the dining hall the ways in which peoples engagements with food, pottery and each other were limited also served to mediate relationships of dominance and submission, for example through the enacting of rules relating to the order in which food or drink could be taken, or in the gestures surrounding service. At Launceston, the spatial context may also have played a role, with a distinction perhaps occurring between those who ate in the Great Hall and those who dined in the Lesser Hall. Within the context of the castle dining hall pottery does not simply reflect identities. By building a relationship with it and associated objects, within specific spaces, a lord could express dominance, directly impacting upon the ways in which people could relate to their surroundings and therefore the senses of identity they might experience. Whilst the lord enrolled material culture and space to build and present an identity, for others their sense of self, of personhood, emerged relationally, as the agency for them

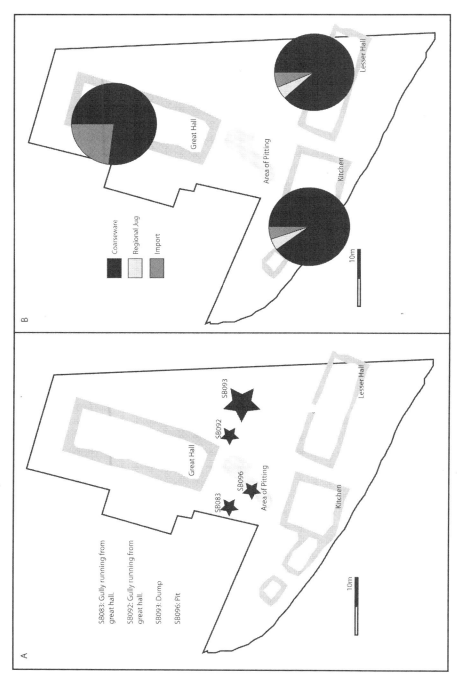

*Figure 4.4. Pottery distributions at Launceston Castle. A) Distribution of imported pottery (size of star relates to quantity of imported pottery). B) Composition of pottery assemblages from different areas of the bailey by weight. After Saunders 2006.*

to perceive themselves in particular ways came to be distributed through themselves and their surroundings.

The presence of plainer, local pottery within the Middle Ward at Barnard Castle is taken as a reflection of the lower social status of this area of the castle and of those who inhabited it (Austin 2007b, 499). The same can be seen at Launceston, with locally produced coarseware pottery dominating the assemblage from the kitchen area, for example (Figure 4.4b). Certainly there seems to have been little financial expenditure in the acquisition of functional kitchen wares, with the local types represented at both castles most likely being the most economical option available. Yet just as the use of jugs in the dining areas fostered senses of identity, so did the use of these vessels in particular spaces. The 'backroom' staff were excluded both from fine dining and particular spaces, creating divisions within the castle. The space of the kitchen or ancillary buildings and interactions with these plain, utilitarian formed the fabric of the lives of members of the castle staff however, with these experiences leading to the emergence of very different experiences of castle life and of identities related to it. Yet, for the upper echelons of castle society, these interactions were removed from view, these were invisible, non-objects, and, potentially, by extension, those who used them may even be seen as non-people. Clearly the distribution of pottery reflects functional spaces within the castle, yet it does more than reflect social identities. Rather, pottery was intimately related to the identities of its users, with these courses of action not only differentiating people, but also differentiating the relative social value of particular forms of pottery in relation to them. Whilst cooking pots were most likely of low social or economic value to the lord and his immediate entourage, for the servants who used them these experiences were central to how they understood the world around them, distributing the agency through which they were constructed as persons through specific relationships with the material world.

This has been a necessarily brief analysis, hindered, to a degree, by the quantity of published information available. It has though demonstrated that by taking pottery from castles as more than dating tools and indicators of the relationship between the castle, its estate and its hinterland, we can begin to shed new light on the dynamics of castle life. Rather than seeing pottery as reflecting identities, we can consider its effect, how the formation of promiscuous relationships between pots, people and other things in dining spaces and in kitchens formed the agency for multiple identities to emerge, being enrolled in relationships of dominance, the negotiation of hierarchy and the breeding of familiarity in castle life, with pottery both being used conspicuously to build identities, yet also effecting the ways in which people related to their surroundings. The key point however is that pottery did not act alone; for example, it did different things in different spaces, it acquired meaning through various associations with other objects and developed the capacity to cause particular effects through being associated with rules of etiquette. It is clearly possible to answer Creighton and Liddiard's (2008) call for greater vibrancy in castle studies through the integration of studies of material culture, however to achieve this we need to be prepared to look at the material more deeply and attempt to unlock the connections which secured its place in castle life.

## Summary

Identity is a key theme in medieval archaeology, and one which pottery has often been used to address. In this chapter I have emphasised the need to have a clear definition of the term and to conceptualise identities as the effects of practices and not their equivalent. In general terms I have argued that medieval archaeologists have, on the whole, been reasonably successful at making this distinction, yet they have been limited by an anthropocentric perspective, in which objects are tools for conscious processes of identity formation. Through drawing upon ideas of distributed personhood I have created a model through which the agency for the emergence of identities is distributed through connections with the material world; in which the agency to create a particular identity can emerge, but in which we are also able to allow for the effect of objects upon the ways in which people perceive their place in the world. We have seen, for example, at the medieval dining table, that the creation of a particular identity had implications for how other diners could relate to the world around them, whilst experiences of dining in Anglo-Norman Southampton created different experiences of continuity and change, which did not lead to the development of a simple hybrid identity, but plural experiences of what it was to become 'Anglo-Norman'. The identities of people and of things then are entangled with one another, being effective upon each other and leading to the world being a web of personal experiences, through which single practices or actions, could effect identities in a multitude of ways.

# 5

# EMERGENT LANDSCAPES: POTTERY, PEOPLE AND PLACES

Ceramic and landscape archaeology are considered to be discrete sub-disciplines within medieval archaeology and within archaeology as a whole. This chapter aims to conflate the key difference between artefacts and landscapes, scale, to consider how they were mutually constituted through being entwined within courses of action. Neither artefacts nor places exist in isolation, rather they can be considered as constructed through the same processes of social assembly, and thus enrolled in the formation of 'the social'. The chapter begins with a short critique of approaches to landscape archaeology, drawing heavily on the work of Matthew Johnson. A framework for a relational archaeology of landscape is then proposed, which is inspired by non-representational approaches in contemporary human geography. Such an approach provides the method to conflate scale and consider the entanglement of places, pots and people. Finally, two case studies are presented which examine how processes surrounding pottery relate to the emergence of landscapes, through discussions of resource procurement in the Anglo-Saxon period and depositional practices in medieval towns.

## Landscape Archaeology: A Summary of Contemporary Critiques

It is not my intention to summarise the entire history of medieval landscape archaeology, indeed Matthew Johnson (2006) has ably done so. I do however wish to summarise what Johnson identifies as the major issues within the field, as well as briefly discuss the implications of some contemporary approaches which have primarily been utilised in relation to the prehistoric landscape. The intention of this is not to demean the work of landscape archaeologists, but to explain how I have reached the conceptualisation of landscape which is painted in the second part of this chapter.

Johnson identifies three core problems with historical landscape archaeology in Britain. Firstly, as we have seen with the field of medieval archaeology as a whole, when 'interdisciplinary' approaches have been taken, history has largely had primacy over archaeology (M. Johnson 2006, 134). Archaeology has therefore been used to answer historically determined questions and to corroborate historical evidence, rather than to consider the archaeology of a landscape on its own terms. Secondly, approaches to the landscape have largely been functionalist, focussed on agricultural regimes or settlement patterns as systems, which sometimes has the effect of dehumanising the landscape (M. Johnson 2006, 129). Perhaps the largest problem though has been the insular nature of historical landscape archaeology, both in terms of its geographical and temporal outlook. The result has been a failure to engage in theoretical debates about the constitution and perception of landscape (M. Johnson 2006, 120). Landscape characterisation has been a core focus and whilst an important endeavour in relation to managing the historic landscape, such approaches, focussed on mapping, can lead to a static understanding of the landscape (Rose and Wiley 2006, 476). Two reasons are commonly put forward to explain historical landscape archaeologists failure to immerse themselves in the theoretical elements of study. The first is the familiar nature of these landscapes, in contrast to prehistoric landscapes, meaning that theoretical frameworks are simply deemed unnecessary (M. Johnson 2006, 137). Such a standpoint is untenable as all interpretation is reliant upon some theoretical, or interpretive, framework (McClain 2012, 138) and, as we shall see, geographers have created such frameworks in which to understand contemporary landscapes. A second reason is that, compared to prehistorians, historical archaeologists simply have too much data to work with and therefore direct their effort towards its synthesis and presentation, rather than going beyond it to build interpretations (Finch 2008, 513).

A major emphasis within prehistoric landscape archaeology in the last two decades has been the adoption of a phenomological approach (*e.g.* Tilley 1994). Such approaches are intended to emphasise the human experience of landscape and are therefore highly anthropocentric and based upon the experiences of the modern researcher, rather than of past populations. An example is Tilley's (2004) discussion of barrows in the landscape of bronze age Wiltshire, which argues that the placement of these features acts as a metaphor for the cosmology of death and commemoration, relating to the harnessing of the variability of the natural landscape, to form a significant man made landscape. Whilst such an approach has utility, particularly in that it allows landscapes to be viewed at a particularistic rather than general scale and to explore the processes behind its formation, the approach has been critiqued, particularly in responses to the paper by Brück (2004) and Barrett (2004). Both argue that this modern reading of archaeological features in the modern landscape is ignorant to processes of temporality, by reading a finished rather than transient version of the land, as well as failing to account for changes in the natural landscape (such as vegetation) and also that this account privileges a cosmological or ritual reading of the landscape over a more pragmatic, functionalist one. Critiques of the phenomological approach as a whole go further still, questioning the methodological and interpretive perspectives upon which such approaches are built (Fleming 2006, 275), and certainly the impenetrable style of writing and lack of supporting data support such a critcism (*ibid*, 276). In order for such approaches to be convincingly utilised detailed landscape characterisation is required, to understand what was being experienced in the past. It is surprising therefore that phenomological studies have failed to integrate scientific data, particularly in relation to environmental studies into their narratives, effectively denying a world beyond the human experience of the manmade landscape (Walsh 2008, 547). Where studies of material culture and the environment are included it is largely to create a backdrop against which humans acted and experienced, denying the material realm in all its forms an active role in the creation of landscapes in the past (Walsh 2008, 548; Edmonds 1999, 485). This human centred approach is not just common within deeply theoretical studies however. The role of finds and environmental data is typically marginalised in archaeological reports, which focus upon 'built' elements of the landscape (in the form of archaeological features), largely using this data in relation to the economy or to illustrate social trends (Walsh 2008, 548; see chapter 1). Such an approach has marginalised both material culture and environmental remains in the study and understanding of the landscape, emphasising it as a consistent backdrop against which action unfolds, rather than as a dynamic and unfolding phenomena.

It is wrong to place the problems with landscape archaeology at the doors of phenomenologists and specialists in landscape characterisation. They each take valid approaches to specific problems. Scholars have simply identified more problems to tackle, a process which requires new methodologies and outlooks. Perhaps what is lacking most of all is a definition of landscape. In order to devise one it is necessary to consider that the landscape is not a constant, it is always in motion, being constituted and re-constituted through human action, action which leaves the material and documentary sources which underpin our studies (M. Johnson 2006, 120; 139). Reading the landscape does little more than allow us to link the past and the present however, it does little to inform us about how the landscape was encountered or experienced in the past, leading to an arrogant landscape archaeology, which is centred on our own experiences (Finch 2008, 528; Allen 2011, 247). Instead we need to concentrate on understanding the processes of action and assembly which bring a landscape into being and the effect of these processes on a range of social actors, which go beyond the human. Landscapes are assemblages and as such can develop agency. Therefore they make people as much as people make them, meaning that rather than the landscape being a static backdrop, it is a dynamic assemblage with which we exist in a reciprocal relationship (Finch 2008, 512; M. Johnson 2006, 145). Because landscapes are formed relationally they are multiple, the same physical space can be experienced in a multitude of ways, creating partially connected landscapes, defined through a variety of streams of action (Finch 2008, 528; Hinchliffe 2010). People are therefore not anonymous and disembodied within their surroundings, they are enrolled in a process of landscape creation, through building associations with physical features and material culture (Walsh 2008, 550; Edmonds 1999, 485). Defining landscape is a difficult task. The term invites ideas of large scale spaces, which are formed through human and non-human action but that have long term durability, masking dynamism and fluidity with stasis and sedentism. By seeing a landscape as emerging, being maintained and changing relationally though we can see a landscape as another social assemblage, one which is assembled through action and has the potential to act by being drawn into future associations. Landscape archaeology then needs to move from mapping static worlds to paying attention to dynamic and changing worlds, worlds which are lived and formed by lively beings, but which act upon these beings (Greenhough 2010, 41). The second part of this chapter is concerned with defining relational landscapes more closely.

## Relational Landscapes

In order to put forward a relational conceptualisation of landscape there are several key areas to consider. The first is the nature of the landscape, the second is temporality and flow and the third is the effect of the landscape. Firstly we can continue to work towards a definition of landscape. Traditional landscape archaeology can be characterised as an archaeology of the land, but the first crucial distinction to make is that the landscape is not land, although land is enrolled in the process of landscape creation. Whereas land is quantitative and homogeneous, something which can be mapped, landscape is the opposite, qualitative and heterogeneous, it is subjective and formed simultaneously in many different ways (Ingold 1993, 154). Because landscape is not land, landscape cannot be viewed as a stage or backdrop for action, instead landscapes, or places emerge, they come into being through action (Gregson and Rose 2001, 441). Rather than be interested in characterising landscapes then, we can focus on the process of world (or place) forming (Dewsbury 2010, 150). In doing so the landscape comes to exist of connections, of ongoing localised interactions which shape the landscape and are shaped by it, which bring durability but can also mediate change (Conradson 2005, 339); the only thing which landscape ever is is the practices which animate it and make it matter (Rose 2002, 462–3). Just as a distinction can be perceived between things and enacted objects, so too it may be useful to distinguish between spaces and enacted places, formed of space, but also of further networks of association. To use ANT language, landscapes are actor-networks, formed through action rather than existing *a priori* awaiting action (Allen 2011, 278). Crucially, landscapes are not static, they are not the result of action, but emerge through it and then must be sustained through further action. Spaces are constantly in the making, they are never finished (Whatmore 1999, 33; Rose 2002, 465).

We have then acknowledged that landscapes are fluid, dynamic bundles of relationships. It should have become clear already that culture and 'the social', like landscapes, emerge relationally and do not pre-exist action. Therefore, just like artefacts, landscapes cannot be read as static representations of culture, although they could be viewed as a process of the re-presentation of culture, through the repetition of the practices which make 'the social' durable (Rose 2002, 457). As the landscape is not sustained we can question what there is to read (Rose 2002, 463). In language, words can be seen to acquire their meaning through their contexts of use, they are not inherently meaningful (see chapter 3). Similarly, meanings are not attached to landscapes and therefore they cannot be read. Instead meanings are gathered from the landscape through its formation, its form and meaning are taken on through incorporation not inscription (Ingold 1993, 155). Places are the nexus of social relationships and as such spaces in the physical world come to being in multiple ways, creating partially connected multiple worlds enacted through different relationships (Ingold 1993, 155; Hinchliffe 2010, 205). Similarly the affordances of a space emerge relationally, as the same space becomes enrolled in multiple, but connected, processes of landscape formation (McCormack 2010, 208). As spaces are enrolled in multiple processes of place formation, places can threaten or contaminate each other, as they become joined through action (Gregson and Rose 2001, 442). Therefore, whilst multiple landscapes emerge through action, they are also joined by action, with the landscape forming as partially connected bundles of relationships. As such, these places are not bounded, having the effect of diminishing scale. Landscapes are an assemblage like any other and therefore can be acted upon by other landscapes (as Actor-networks) or any of the relationships which comprise them (Conradson 2005, 339). Rather than reading the landscape then, our role as archaeologists is to use our evidence to reconnect and resuscitate these landscapes to understand the processes through which they were formed and the ways in which they became joined. Our usage of the term changes from it being a noun, standing for a static phenomenon, to a verb, acknowledging the fluid and mobile nature of landscapes (Dewsbury *et al.* 2002, 439).

Once the landscape is acknowledged as processual, it becomes inherently temporal (Jones 2009, 105). Archaeologists do, of course, acknowledge the temporality of landscape through the presentation of phased plans or computer models. But these represent the landscape at a very coarse resolution, they do not acknowledge the constantly changing nature of the landscape or the variety of temporal rhythms which form through action (see Ingold 1993); places are constantly in motion as they are sustained or develop through action, the world never comes to rest (Rose 2002, 457; Dewsbury *et al.* 2002, 437). Therefore landscapes are always temporary entwinements of threads of action, they are unfinished stories which continue to emerge through further action (Massey 2006, 46). We can view these threads as unravelling, but as being intertwined as they move forward at different rates across scale, remaining connected to past engagements but depending upon future activation to either re-activate these connections or form new ones; the process of connection is constant but not consistent, meaning landscapes emerge rather than being sustained; whilst places can be durable, they cannot last (Thrift 1999, 317; Thrift 2008, 201; Rose 2002, 462). In any landscape there lies the potential for new events to form, opening up a variety of possible trajectories of action which can be taken and therefore a variety of landscapes which can emerge, action then opens up the possibility of new relationships, but also leaves a wake which limits the range of relationships which can be formed, introducing some element of continuity into the landscape (Halfacree and Rivera 2012, 95). The emerging and progressing threads which make up the landscape form a compendium of lived moments and it is in the wake of this motion that the potential for a landscape to evoke memory lies latent, ready to be re-activated through action, cuing memory of past experience of a landscape and distributing the agency to create memory and knowledge through it (Jones 2011, 6; see also Edensor 2005). Landscapes then are constantly evolving, but in a connected and distributed fashion, forming and progressing through entangled actions (Conradson 2005, 340). The world can be seen as existing in relation to itself, to what came before and what comes after, as action re-presents the landscape and 'the social' through the re-forming of connections and the effect of this process of assembly on the future (Dewsbury 2010, 152).

It is to the effect of landscapes that we can finally turn. I have already briefly discussed how memory is effected through the interactions which make a landscape and more generally in going beyond landscape characterisation it is necessary to ask what landscape did and what it asks for (Rose 2002, 465). In other words, as well as emerging through performance, space has active qualities (Thrift 2008, 16). This is an important consideration because the effect a landscape has on our lives is directly related to how it comes to be significant as a network of meanings and relations and is inherently related to the formation of multiple landscapes and experiences of space (Rose 2002, 456; Gregson and Rose 2001, 441). The processes of self-making and world-making are mutually constitutive (Jones 2009, 105); both emerge through relationships and therefore the effect of landscape is keenly felt in ourselves. I do not offer a methodology for understanding the effect of landscape beyond the tracing of connections and considering how these act back upon people. Indeed an acknowledgement of the effect of landscape is not greatly removed from contemporary phenomological approaches, however it is built on more solid foundations, allowing the data to lead us and acknowledging the active role of the landscape in a symmetrical ways, which directs us away from an anthropocentric discussion of landscape and towards an understanding of landscape as a dynamic process and the human role within it.

It is in the understanding of the landscape as a social assemblage that we can relate pottery and the landscape. Following Law (1992) we can see that the processes through which pottery and landscape as assemblage form is the same, as things are brought into affective relationships. Thinking in such a way removes scale as a factor, localising all action as contributing to the formation of the web of relationships which make up 'the social'. In the remainder of this chapter I want to explore how interactions with clay and with pottery contributed to the process of landscape formation and to explore the relationship between these two social assemblages as processes.

## Potting Landscapes

The most obvious way to explore the emergence of landscapes through the study of pottery is through the analysis of resource procurement. Understanding clay sources is a major focus of ceramic studies and a wealth of techniques, such as thin-section petrology and chemical analysis have been utilised to map sources of clay onto the landscape (see Vince 2005 for a review of their application to medieval ceramics). Typically this understanding has then been used to understand the supply of pottery to settlements and thus the scale of manufacture. What has not been studied in such detail

*Figure 5.1. Examples of Anglo-Saxon organic-tempered pottery. Photographs: Ben Jervis.*

is the effect of resource procurement in terms of the emergence of landscapes and this is the route I wish to explore here (although see Jones 2002, 122–39 for a prehistoric example). Within the later medieval mindset (and probably earlier) humans and the environment appear together (Allen 2011, 275) and therefore to create an arbitrary distinction between people and the space they inhabit can be argued to mask the mutually constitutive effects of interactions with the land in this period. The two case studies I will present relate to the early medieval period, the first develops a previous study of Organic-tempered pottery in the 6th–7th centuries (see Jervis 2012) and the latter concerns the late Saxon burh of Chichester (West Sussex).

## Organic Tempered Pottery: A Choice not a Compromise?

Organic-tempered pottery is something of the ugly duckling of medieval material culture. These dull, soft and friable vessels are typically seen as being of limited functional or interpretive value and placed within a narrative in which pottery was relatively unimportant in Anglo-Saxon domestic life (Figure 5.1). Whilst this statement does seem to be true, with documentary, pictorial and archaeological sources providing evidence for vessels in a range of materials, pottery is a consistent find on sites of the period and therefore must have played some part in the creation of the early medieval 'social'. The origins of this pottery remain a matter of some debate. It is clear that they emerged after the migrations of the early-Saxon period, probably in the later 6th–7th centuries, based, for example, on chronologies from sites such as Mucking (Essex) and Puddlehill (Bedfordshire) (Hamerow 1993; Matthews and Chadwick Hawkes 1985). These wares are likely therefore to be an Anglo-Saxon development, although small quantities are known from coastal regions of the Low Countries (Hamerow *et al.* 1993) and northern France (Soulat *et al.* 2012), probably attesting to some form of continuing connections between south-east England and this area in the period. The exact origins of the ware however remain unclear (see Jervis 2012).

It is worth briefly considering the technical elements of these wares. The Organic-temper of their name is likely to be derived from a variety of sources, including dung (Brisbane 1981, 235), chaff (Hurst 1976, 292–4) or grass (Farley 1978, 193). In contrast to mineral inclusions, the nature of these inclusions is not the subject of rigorous scientific study, with terms seemingly coming in and out of fashion depending upon the results of the latest experiments or scientific approach (Jervis 2012). This has the effect of homogenising a heterogeneous group of pottery. What we can say however is that vessels were tempered with organic materials which were easily available in an agricultural community, something of key importance when considering the effect of the production of these wares in the emergence of landscapes. The addition of organic material to clay has a number of functional advantages. It can increase the workability of a 'short' clay, whilst the presence of voids increases the thermal shock properties of low fired ceramics to a certain degree (Rye 1977, 33–4; Skibo *et al.* 1989, 131). Vessels are also very light (Skibo *et al.* 1989, 126). This technology is highly suited to particular situations, particularly to mobile, perhaps agricultural, communities who do not have access to a reliable clay source. Indeed ethnographically the occurrence of this type of pottery can be related to mobile communities (Skibo *et al.* 1989).

In a previous review, (Jervis 2012) I demonstrated that the occurrence of these wares can be closely related to rural sites, situated on poorer quality agricultural soils in southern England (Figure 5.2). Settlement shift is a well attested early-Saxon phenomenon and it is primarily from sites with short structural sequences or evidence of settlement shift (such as Mucking) which this ware is recovered. In areas where settlement patterns were more stable these wares did not emerge, or are present for a shorter period of time. It can be argued then that Organic-tempered pottery emerged with a transitory lifestyle and declined as settlement patterns stabilised in the 8th–9th centuries. We can propose then that this type of pottery emerged from a particular set of relationships and was maintained by them, dissolving once these relationships were re-negotiated. Yet, this pottery did not emerge out of nothing. The earliest Anglo-Saxon pottery types are Sandy Wares, similar to those used in the Elbe and Wesser valleys, the traditional Saxon 'homeland'. Several factors can be proposed to explain the decline of these wares and the emergence of a new pottery type. The first is plague, which may have led to a decline in potting skill and knowledge, forcing people to build new

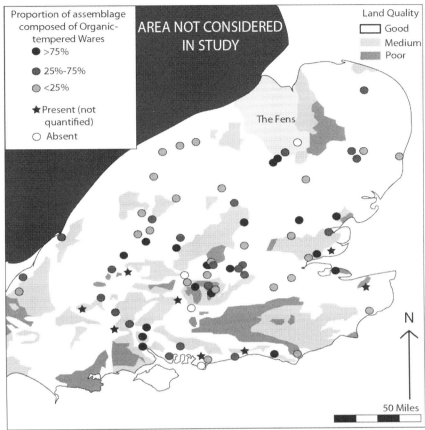

*Figure 5.2. Distribution of organic-tempered pottery in south-east England. Image: Jervis 2012.*

relationships with clay. The second is the increased mobility of communities, which meant that they no longer had access to reliable clay sources, which, when coupled with the presence of agricultural by-products had the potential to cause this new type to emerge. Clearly these wares are a product of a particular context, whilst their manufacture underpinned the making durable of this context.

Studies of resource procurement are largely based on a notion of space as static and unchanging. I propose however, that within the context of a mobile community, that the process of resource procurement contributed to the re-making of landscapes and places in new spaces. We have acknowledged that landscapes emerge and worlds are formed through action and that landscape is animated by practice. Resource procurement is one such practice. Let's take a hypothetical moment of resource procurement. A relationship is formed with a particular clay source, potentially one which has not been used before, whilst agricultural waste, be it dung or chaff, is gathered to be added as temper. In this moment meaningful relationships are formed with two spaces, the clay source and the 'farmyard' (for want of a better term), probably located within or close to the settlement. This landscape is temporary however, formed and maintained through action, meaning that without the pot standing for this connection it is a landscape which would be easily missed. How then does this landscape develop? The mobile nature of settlements means that this same place likely develops in a new space, as the actions of resource procurement are re-enacted in a new physical space. It can be argued that landscape, that a sense of place, is maintained through this repeated action. Landscapes are temporary entwinements of a range of actors, of which space is one; the process of resource procurement entangled a different range of actors, which worked to make a place, and more importantly a social, durable. Memory emerged through this process for example, the agency for this not residing in a particular clay source or particular space, but being activated through action, or more specifically interaction, with clay and tempering materials. The effect of this action was to re-make a world, bringing about stability to what we might perceive as an inherently mobile and unstable settlement pattern. Drawing settlements on phased maps of a landscape then tell a different story to that which emerges through action. Rather than seeing discrete, bounded, settlement phases we can see the re-making of places in multiple spaces.

Landscape emerged through the actions of resource procurement and was sustained through continued action. This landscape though was not permanent, a conclusion which can be drawn from the decline of Organic-tempered pottery and the increased permanence of settlements through the mid- and late- Saxon periods. The formation of estates and the related changing provisioning strategies (see Sykes 2007, 38–9) fundamentally altered what was required of pottery (in terms of cooking practice) and the relationships formed in its manufacture, as people made durable links with reliable clay sources, revisiting spaces. These changing relationships caused one landscape to dissolve and new landscapes to emerge, a process which will be discussed in more detail in the second case study of this chapter.

Landscapes are inherently local, they are formed through localised action and take place in localised spaces, those with which we are able to form relationships or associations. Localising the landscape, seeing it as made up of connections, allows us to collapse the scalar differentiation between the pot and the landscape, to see the pot as the only surviving trace of an emergent landscape. This brief study of Organic-tempered pottery has done two things. Firstly, it has guided us along the route taken in the emergence or formation of a landscape, allowing us to consider the connections which created the conditions in which this pottery and by extension the landscape of its production could emerge. Secondly, it has allowed us to consider the effect of this action, in making a temporary place, made durable through repeated action in multiple spaces but never lasting as this durability was enmeshed within action.

## *Multiple Landscapes: Clay Procurement in Late Saxon Chichester*

The second case study concerns resource procurement in the later Anglo-Saxon period. Three broad ceramic phases can be identified in late Saxon Chichester, West Sussex (see Jervis 2009a). The first relates to the pre-burghal settlement (7th–9th centuries), in which the small quantity of pottery present is relatively homogeneous in regard to fabric. These are reduced Shelly Wares, probably produced from the eocene clays found to the south of Chichester and tempered with beach sand (including shell). The second phase relates to the foundation of the burghal settlement (9th–10th centuries). It is characterised by a high level of variability in the fabrics present, which include mixed-grit, flint-tempered, sandy and chalk-tempered wares, produced from a range of clays found around Chichester. Tentative links can be drawn between this pottery and that used at nearby rural settlements, although at least in some cases, there is evidence for production within the town, rather than vessels being brought in from these settlements. It seems then that this phase is characterised by small scale, household production (Jervis 2009a, 71). The final phase (10th–11th century) sees the establishment of the pottery industry at Chapel Street, the products of which dominate the latest Saxon assemblages from the town (Figure 5.3). In this discussion I wish to focus on the last two phases, to explore how resource procurement led to the emergence of multiple landscapes in the same space, through similar patterns of action and how the landscape was re-formed through a range of actions in the later phase.

It is well established that a range of factors influence a potters' choice of clay, including the accessibility of the resource and changing technological imperatives (for example wheel-throwing requires finer clay than coil building) (see Arnold 2000). Assuming that these factors are constant, the core choice can come down to the potters experience and perception of clay, selecting materials based upon characteristics and texture, which may have little impact upon the actual quality of the clay (Arnold 1971, 21). The variability in the clay sources utilised across Chichester, which can be seen between households rather than areas of the settlement (Jervis 2009a, 75), suggests that people who settled in Chichester brought with them knowledge and perceptions regarding suitable potting clays and their place in the surrounding (spatial) landscape. People's varying experiences of clay is also reflected in the variety of tempering materials used which include sand, shell and gravel, all of which have different material properties and effect the clay in different ways (for example in relation to plasticity and thermal shock; see Rye 1977). Migration into Chichester clearly had a destabilising effect on the landscape. People moved from familiar spaces in which their action created familiar places, to a new setting where new social relationships and identities emerged and at least some elements of life changed. Resource procurement appears to be one set of engagements however where people were able to introduce stability into this landscape, by re-forming relationships with spaces and resources the landscape re-emerged through this action, as people acted on their knowledge of available clays and tempering materials. New and old landscapes came to be connected through this action.

The process of resource procurement re-activated landscapes. Plotting the sources of clay on a geological map represents a single landscape in which people acted within multiple spaces (Figure 5.4). We can consider though that these different trajectories of action led to the emergence or maintenance of different, multiple landscapes. Experiences of clay procurement differed between households then, with each potter

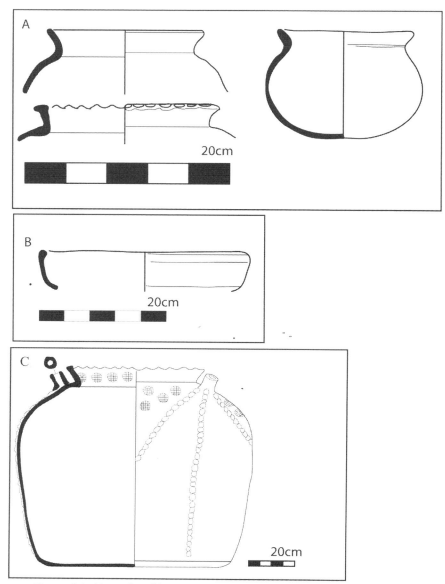

*Figure 5.3. Examples of late Saxon pottery from Chichester. After Jervis 2009.*

building their own 'cognitive map' (Arnold 1971), linking them to individual spaces and resources. Interactions with these spaces and resources cited previous engagements, enacting memory and knowledge, both in relation to the qualities of the clay and linking their past lives in rural settlements and their present in an emerging urban centre. These multiple landscapes were joined through a common set of actions in their formation and through an anchoring point, Chichester, but these were not closely meshed threads, they did not contaminate or threaten each other, forming as relatively discreet and individualised worlds. Household potting is a part-time activity and this action unfolded within a temporal cycle, probably taking place in the driest months of the year (May–July). This action not only re-formed places then but was active in the maintenance of a temporal rhythm, which was likely mediated through participation in a range of other seasonal and everyday activities (what could be termed 'settlement time'). Clay procurement can perhaps even be seen as disruptive to the daily cycle of events, creating a course of action where people connected to their past, re-made past landscapes by stepping out of the regulated realm of 'settlement time'.

The process of migration into Chichester was not a discrete and bounded process (see Halfacree and Rivera 2012 for a discussion of migration in relational perspective). It was a fundamentally disruptive process, which forced people to abandon spatial relationships and led to the emergence of new landscapes through action in new spaces. Furthermore the imposition of burhs into spaces served to unsettle identities within the rural hinterlands as well as within these new centres themselves, as people struggled to re-align their identities within a changing social landscape (Astill 2006, 250–51). The exact circumstances of this process are unclear, but may even amount to a forced re-settlement, emphasising this disruptive effect (Abels 1988, 75). The foundation of a new settlement clearly built multiple potential avenues for action and led to the emergence of new relationships and thus worlds, identities and landscapes. Clay procurement can be framed in opposition to this re-forming of the world, acting as a medium through which people could return to spaces, re-make places and thus elements of themselves, through evoking memory and maintaining the ties which activate a place and make it significant. Clay procurement though was not the only action going on in these spaces and it is to the making of multiple landscapes in the same spaces which we must turn to now.

In relation to clay procurement the space around Chichester was not a single landscape, but a loose tangle of related trajectories of action through which multiple landscapes emerged. But in any one space in this landscape clay procurement was not the only set of actions taking place (see Hinchliffe 2010). These were managed spaces and agricultural spaces. Historical evidence provides clues to one set of relationships which made alternative places from these spaces. Charter evidence demonstrates that the land around the Chichester Channel was under the possession of the manor of Bosham (Salzmann 1953, 138) for example and much of the remaining land to the south of the town was controlled by the church, under the control of the Bishop of Selsey (Barker 1947, 52–4). In the tenth century land ownership to the north of Chichester as well as within Chichester itself changed, for example land in the southern part of Chichester was granted to the Bishop of Selsey (Barker 1947, 142–8; Livitt 1990, 1). We can hypothesise that people's access to clay resources was limited by tenurial and ownership relationships (see Neuport 2000 for an ethnographic example), directing action and entangling resource procurement strategies in other processes of landscape formation. It is through this entanglement that different places emerge in the same spaces, places which have the potential to contaminate or threaten each other (Gregson and Rose 2001, 442). Around the tenth century the re-organisation of land tenure created new places, which replaced some old places and threatened others. Changing land ownership and use may have made certain clay sources inaccessible, limiting the potential for the continued re-making of places through resource procurement. At the same time Chichester was emerging as an urban place, in which people were increasingly able to develop specialisms in certain crafts, of which pottery was one, with clear implications for elements of identity formation, as people became urban persons and specialist persons through changes to the ways in which they related to their changing surroundings. These developments cannot be considered in isolation, nor can a simple relationship of cause and effect be put forward. The development of Chichester as a town stimulated the re-organisation of the landscape, but this re-organisation fundamentally altered processes of place-making and resource procurement around Chichester, playing a role in sustaining and furthering the development of craft specialists, who would appear to have had exclusive access (or perhaps exclusively accessed) clay sources. New places emerged through action, the urban place of Chichester and the new places enshrined in and remade through the enforcement of charters. Just as documents do not determine values (chapter 3), nor do they determine landscapes or reflect places. Rather, through being enacted and enforced, they were enrolled in the processes through which landscapes emerged and were made durable. They can be considered to have had effect in two senses, on the one hand physically demarcating ownership of land and thus potentially limiting access and secondly by being drawn into economic relationships they played a direct role in establishing the economic base of Chichester, through which craft specialism could emerge. These places threatened the existing landscape, by cutting the connections which re-formed them, forcing clay sources, as places, to be re-negotiated through action, an action which simultaneously led to the emergence, or sustained the presence of, groups including craft specialists and the landed elite. Place making, self-making and pot making cannot be separated. They emerge through the same trajectories of action, causing material and human actors to become entangled in new ways, causing old places and old selves to dissolve and new ones to emerge.

Clay procurement created multiple but relatively discrete landscapes through the enactment of multiple courses of action, allowing people to re-make places, possibly in opposition to the new relationships forming within Chichester and outside of the passage of 'settlement' time. Although discrete, these landscapes were entangled within other processes of place making, such as those surrounding the ownership of land and resources. This entanglement endangered places, creating or limiting the potential for the actions which re-made places through clay procurement. We can see then that clay procurement created multiple places, but action within spaces also created multiple, entangled places. The re-organisation of land division, coupled with a range of other factors limited action, being enmeshed in the process of specialist identity formation and re-mapping the relationships behind the formation of places through clay procurement.

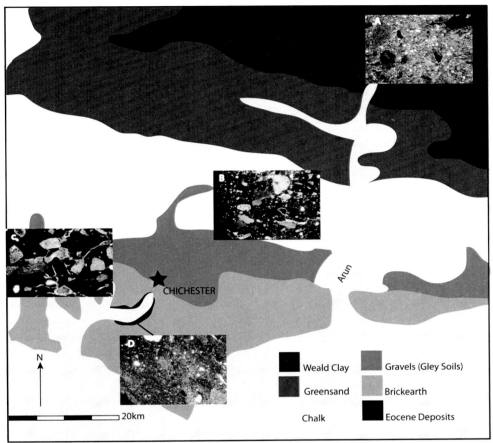

*Figure 5.4. Geological map of the Chichester area, indicating the areas from which resources may have been sourced. Drawing and photographs: Ben Jervis.*

## Making Urban Landscapes: Pottery as Waste

Clay procurement is a relationship which characterises the conception of a pot. The end of a vessels biography (until, at least, its recovery as an archaeological object), the act of deposition, provides an equally fruitful area in which to consider the relationship between objects and spaces. Depositional practices are the processes through which the majority of the archaeological record is formed (Schiffer 1987), but, like any other set of human-object interactions were processes through which meaning emerged, identities formed and places created. In chapter 6 ideas of waste are considered in more detail. The present discussion is focussed on the role of disposal in the creation of urban landscapes, drawing on evidence from a number of medieval towns, to explore the entanglements between people, rubbish, spaces and documents.

*Reconstructing Action: Methodologies*

The methods for reconstructing waste disposal practices are perhaps less well known than those for provenancing ceramics, and certainly have had less impact on the wider discipline. On the whole the main purpose of understanding how deposits form has been to inform the interpretation of stratigraphy, identify patterns of residuality and therefore to create firm foundations for the construction of dated sequences (Brown 1994a; Vince 1994). Yet these methods also allow us to reconstruct effective courses of action and therefore to consider in some detail the effects of waste upon people's perceptions of space (the emergence of landscapes) and themselves (the emergence of identities). The bulk of the case study discussed below is drawn from the authors work on the ceramic assemblage from the medieval port of Southampton (see also Jervis 2013d), which is supplemented by research undertaken in other towns, particularly Worcester and Norwich. The key to any methodology is the integration of pottery and contextual information, to allow a reflexive understanding to develop in relation to the methods of deposition and the resulting formation of archaeological deposits. Two techniques form the basis of the study presented. The first is an analysis of fragmentation and the second is the analysis of cross-fits.

Schiffer's (1987) seminal work on depositional practices identified three types of waste; primary (waste recovered from in situ contexts, such as items trodden into a floor surface), secondary (waste dumped directly into a feature, such as a pit) and tertiary (waste re-deposited into a feature, for example from a midden) waste. A fourth type can also be identified, provisional waste, that is material categorised as waste, but with a lingering presence, meaning that it can be drawn back into a course of action (see Hayden and Cannon 1983). An example might be material built up as a midden. There is very little concrete evidence for primary waste, and therefore it will not be considered further. Where it does occur it is in exceptional circumstances, for example in relation to a house fire, and therefore does not reflect a 'typical' depositional trajectory. Secondary and tertiary waste can be considered to be associated with different levels of fragmentation. Secondary deposits of pottery can be considered to have a low level of fragmentation, as sherds were dumped into the ground soon after breakage, and therefore have not had the opportunity to abrade or fragment further through processes such as trampling. Tertiary waste is likely to be considerably more fragmented and abraded, having been exposed on the surface to further attritional processes. Therefore by calculating an index of fragmentation, the mean average sherd weight (which can be productively combined with the use of other statistical measures, such as range or standard deviation), it is possible to consider the relative levels of fragmentations of different types of pottery and the pottery from specific features, to identify differences in the types of deposit present (see Orton, Tyers and Vince 1993, 178–9).

Cross-fitting relies upon the identification of joining sherds between contexts, either in the same feature or between features (see Brown 1985). Identification of cross-fits within features may provide evidence of residuality or, alternatively, of a quick process of dumping, where the layers of a pit represent a rapid succession of dumping events. Identification of cross fits between features is likely to indicate the presence of tertiary waste, as material is likely to have accumulated on a surface deposit, before being spread across a number of features. By setting this evidence against the level of fragmentation it is possible to further reconstruct the depositional processes at play.

Further, less statistical, methods are also available. Principally a simple analysis of the composition of a deposit may allow the identification of material derived from a discrete ceramic phase, or the presence of mixed, residual or intrusive sherds (see Vince 1994, 9). Correlation with the stratigraphic record is also vital, in order to understand the relationship between dumping and the original function of the feature (for example a cess pit may be filled very differently to a disused quarry pit or a boundary pit) and the formation of deposits within them, for example capping layers, from which no material culture was recovered, may be present. Reconstructing these practices not only allows for the trajectory of pottery as waste to be considered as a phase in a vessels biography, but provides a mean to consider the relationship between object biography and the biography of archaeological deposits, which, like objects break down into a multitude of phases, in which their meaning, nature and the influences behind their formation vary (Morris 2011). For the later middle ages, documents such as town ordinances also provide valuable information on attitudes to waste within towns and the correct treatment of it. By being enacted (see chapter 3), they can also be considered as enrolled in the process of deposition. By drawing all of this data together it is possible to reconstruct depositional practices in some detail, and I identify patterning in the treatment of waste.

*Waste Disposal in Medieval Towns*
Typically waste disposal in towns is associated with pits, often termed 'rubbish pits' by archaeologists. Research following extensive excavations in Worcester brought this concept into focus, by questioning whether such a category of feature actually existed (Buteux and Jackson 2000). It was considered that pit dug specifically for rubbish would comprise secondary deposits, the material for the deposition of which the feature was excavated, a phenomenon observed in only 1 of the numerous pits excavated at the Deansway site, an unusual deposit, seemingly associated with a house fire (Dalwood and Bryant 2004, 87). Rather, the material excavated from pits at the Deansway site was highly fragmented and often abraded, with few cross-context joins, attributes which were also observed amongst the faunal remains (*ibid*). It was inferred therefore that much of the waste deposited within these features was derived from surface deposits, the presence of which is confirmed by the results of analysis of soil formation, with it being likely that the majority of waste was removed from the town and dumped elsewhere, on extra-mural waste tips or into the river. Analysis of later medieval and early post-medieval regulations relating to the treatment of waste in Worcester support this archaeological viewpoint, with the simple model seeming to be that waste accumulated on middens in backyards or on vacant plots, before being transferred to larger communal dumps at the edge of the city (Bryant 2012, 4–5). Similar processes can be seen in the build up of waterfront revetments in towns such as London (Vince 1985, 26–7) and Reading (Underwood 1997, 157). Furthermore it

is likely that a great deal of recycling took place, as elements of waste were re-used for particular craft processes (Bryant 2012, 5).

The comparative value of the results from Worcester is limited however, due to the fact that excavations have not considered such wide areas of the urban landscape as in towns such as Norwich or Southampton (Dalwood and Bryant 2004, 89). Summarising the evidence from Southampton, Brown (1999, 162) has identified differences in the types of materials recovered from sites of varying social status, whilst in a later study he identifies changes in the way that waste was treated through time (Brown 2002, 150–1), principally a shift from deposition in pits in the 13th–14th century to deposition in surface deposits as the population and density of occupation in Southampton declined following the Black Death and the onset of recession, with deposition into negative features once again increasing into the 15th century. General trends in depositional practices can then be related to contextual changes and the social map of a town. However, in order to understand the impact of depositional practices on the individual social realities of town dwellers, and thus their role in the formation of urban landscapes and 'the social' more generally, it is necessary to consider whether differences in depositional practices are observable within a single snapshot of time, therefore determining whether the model from Worcester can be applied across a whole town, or even between towns.

Excavations in both Southampton and Norwich have provided evidence for depositional practices in a number of households, and provide a means through which to identify differences in the ways that rubbish was treated and therefore to consider the effects of these depositional practices. The site at Botolph Street, Norwich, was a centre of iron working and can be considered to be of relatively low status when compared to the wealthy mercantile households occupying other areas of the town. It occupied a peripheral location in Norwich, being characterised by the excavator as a 'semi-rural backwater' (Evans and Davison 1985, 142). The majority of the 13th–15th century material recovered at Botolph Street was residual, dumped in disused quarry pits or spread over surfaces, sometimes as make-up layers (Evans and Davison 1985, 107–8; 143). A similarly marginal site at Alms Lane was also used for rubbish dumping until the 13th century, with assemblages from throughout the medieval period being characterised by the presence of significant proportions of residual material. Parallels can be drawn with peripheral sites, often associated with dangerous, or polluting, crafts such as iron working, in Oxford (Underwood-Keevil 1997, 249–50) and Hereford (Shoesmith 1985). Detailed analysis of a similar site in Southampton, that at York Buildings, provides evidence for similar treatment of waste (see also Jervis 2013d). This site, which occupies a series of plots on a road known in the medieval period as 'the street of the smiths', and from which evidence for iron working and low density pottery manufacture are known (Kavanagh unpub.). The gravelled yard area of one tenement was defined, associated with a number of pits and a ditch, which may have formed a tenement boundary. Behind this, garden soils had accumulated, indicating that cultivation took place within Southampton, possibly at a neighbourhood scale, as no evidence of property boundaries was observed as extending into this area. Some

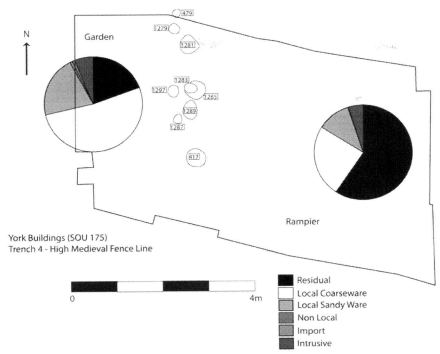

*Figure 5.5. Comparison of the composition of pottery assemblages from either side of a fence line at York Buildings, Southampton. Drawing: Ben Jervis.*

spatial patterning was observed in the distribution of particular types of pottery (see chapter 6), however in general terms it appears that kitchen waste, including sherds of pottery, were spread onto these garden areas as fertiliser. Analysis (see below) suggests this deposition respected boundaries, particularly the boundary ditch and the interface between the tenement and the rampier, a communal space belonging to the town, between the rear of the tenement and the town wall (Figure 5.5). This contrasts with the distribution of waste associated with metal working, which is focussed within the yard area. The material recovered from pits was highly fragmented, and it is possible that material was dumped into these, to allow decay of the organic material (with pottery sherds potentially facilitating aeration), prior to the pits being emptied, with their contents being spread onto the gardens, a suggestion supported by evidence for the lining of these pits with wood. The evidence from these peripheral sites supports the Deansway model, that waste was not dumped in specifically excavated rubbish pits, but rather that it was used to fill redundant features or was spread on surfaces, perhaps finding utility as fertiliser.

The picture at these sites is contrasted however by the evidence from mercantile households in both Southampton and Norwich. The site at Westwick in Norwich is noteworthy because it is 'the only site in Norwich where the undoubted wealth of

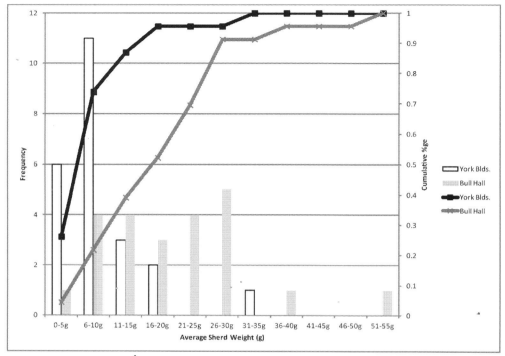

*Figure 5.6. Comparison of the level of ceramic fragmentation in pit assemblages from York Buildings and Bull Hall, Southampton. Drawing: Ben Jervis.*

the occupants can be demonstrated by the remains of their pottery vessels' (Jennings 2002, 134), chiefly this comment relates to the presence of imported wares in higher quantities than elsewhere in the town. The depositional practices undertaken at this site differ greatly to those at the peripheral sites outlined above. Areas appear to have been kept clear of waste, with this management being related both directly to the wealthier status of the sites inhabitants, but also to the pressure on space created by the high rents which could be charged in this area of the town (Jennings 2002, 143). Similarly, the evidence from York Buildings in Southampton can be contrasted with that from the site of Bull Hall, a tenement owned by the English merchant Thomas le Halveknight, but possibly rented out to a merchant of Gascon origin (Brown 2002, 165). The primary contrast with York Buildings is the fact that the majority of pottery was recovered from pits. These were not dug as rubbish pits, but rather for specific functions (for example as lime kilns or quarry pits), with the relatively lower level of fragmentation and the presence of cross-fitting sherds between features and contexts within individual features, suggesting that these were filled rapidly, having the effect of closing these features (Figures 5.6 and 5.7). It is likely, given the evidence from

*Figure 5.7. Plans indicating the location of cross-fitting sherds at Bull Hall, Southampton. Data from Duncan Brown. Drawing: Ben Jervis.*

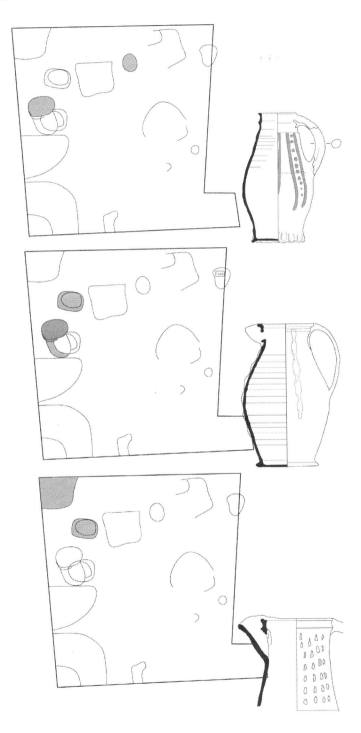

other sites of similar status in Southampton, such as West Hall, the capitol tenement of Thomas le Halveknight, that, as in Norwich, sites within the merchant's quarter of Southampton were largely kept clear of waste, with deposition occurring only in specific circumstances; when there were features present which required closing.

As in Worcester, depositional practices in Southampton and Norwich were regulated through town ordinances. The Oak Book of Southampton is one such document, dating to around 1300 (see Studer 1910). In relation to waste it states that:

> '42. That no butcher or cook throw into the street any filth or other matter under pain. And that no butcher or cook throw into the street any filth or other matter whereby the town or the street become more dirty, filthy or corrupt; and if any one do this and be attained, he shall pay a fine of twelve pence, as often as he shall offend in the manner aforesaid'

> '43. That no man have before his house muck or dung, or pigs about. No man shall have any pigs going about in the street or have before his door, or in the street, muck or dung beyond two nights; and if any one has, let whoever will take it away; and he who shall have acted contrary to this statute shall be grievously fined'

It is clear from the documentary sources that there was a concern with the treatment of waste on the behalf of the civic authorities, with these materialising as rules designed to control the ways and spaces in which waste was deposited. Clearly the role of such rules within the practices of deposition and the processes of place-making which emerged through them must be considered, in order to fully understand the effect of depositional practices.

### Waste and the Urban Landscape

Having reconstructed the processes through which waste was disposed of in medieval towns, we can now consider the effect of these processes as regards the emergence of places. The gardens and backyards in which these processes occurred were not pre-existing stages upon which action occurred, but rather unfolded as places as these spaces became entangled, through action, with people, waste and regulatory documents (see above). Furthermore, the differences observed in depositional practices at different sites in Norwich and Southampton do not simply reflect social difference, but rather were enrolled in processes of identity formation, as action simultaneously led to the emergence of people, places and also categories of waste, which will be considered in more depth in chapter 6.

Drawing upon the relational approach outlined at the beginning of this chapter we can consider that depositional activity did not lead to a single urban landscape, nor did it develop a specific meaning (Pollard 2001, 317) but rather was enrolled in the emergence of multiple urban *landscapes*, in which waste and space formed nodes through which heterogeneous, qualitative places developed. Deposition was one process which animated spaces, a process of assembly through which a variety of actors were drawn together with multiple effects. The replication of these processes brought durability, whilst in some cases the agency for deposition developed intermittently, as spaces afforded it. The urban landscape, and the individual tenements of which it is formed can be considered as connected, transient, bundles of action, of connected processes of place-making, within which the deposition of waste was enrolled.

The garden and yard area at York Buildings for example did not emerge as a single place, but rather, different places (related, for example, to craft, domesticity and civic politics) formed, made from different, but connected things. The spaces take shape through action and makes shape as it is enacted in future courses of action (Hinchliffe 2010). Clearly domestic waste was only enacted in some of these processes, however these different forms of place can be considered as effective upon one another. It is possible to isolate three forms of place which emerged at York Buildings, in order to consider how different but separate places emerged and therefore how urban landscapes became.

The first of these is the emergence of the yard as an industrial place, through this being a space in which metalworking was undertaken. Although occurring within the domestic tenement, it seems that this action was limited to specific spaces, based upon the distribution of ironworking waste (Kavanagh unpub.). The undertaking of this activity forced people to relate to the space in particular ways, experiencing the obnoxious fumes and loud noises associated with the craft, constituting a distinctive place, but also a distinctive category of person occupying this space, the smith, which was formed and maintained along with this space. The use of space for metalworking may have constrained the areas which could be used for deposition; however otherwise there appears to be little direct relationship between depositional practices and the enacting of this industrial place.

However, when we consider the broader processes at play it becomes apparent that the industrial place serves to localise a web of action which stretches throughout the town, as these crafts came to be marginalised in peripheral locations, so too did the identities of the people who operated in these places. By becoming marginalised industrial places were undesirable, their position at the edge standing for the position of this craft (Lilley 2009, 155), as well as the very real dangers which it brought to the urban environment. Yet this marginalisation was closely woven into the emergence of the yard and garden as domestic and horticultural spaces. The lower status which emerged in association to this area of the town ensured there was less pressure on space, creating areas in which horticulture could develop, whilst the comparatively low income received from craft activities also directly contributed to the emergence of this second form of place. Crucially, this organisation of space ensured that contamination of landscapes did not occur. Whilst civic rules and policies played a role in marginalising these communities (see Lilley 2009, 144–5), it was only through being enrolled in the performance of craft that the desires of the urban elite were enacted in the simultaneous emergence of liminal places and marginal identities within the broader urban landscape.

Depositional activity did not occur in isolation, being closely associated, in this instance, with provisioning strategies, which in turn relate to the level of wealth which could be achieved by the inhabitants of these sites. Therefore, depositional practices can be related to the trajectories of action through which these craft activities were pushed to the margins and as tied to the necessity of the occupants of these sites to cultivate gardens (see Dyer 1994). The practices observed therefore both arose from and contributed to specific processes of social assembly, through which these households were formed and their inhabitants came to experience urban space. These comings-together formed the intentionality, the agency, required to cultivate these spaces and treat waste in a particular way, the effect being to form a domestic place which was very different to those experienced in the merchant's quarter, where it is apparent that different process of place-making emerged, as is demonstrated, for example, through depositional practice. The processes which made this place industrial were closely tied to those which made it domestic, whilst the effect of domestic/horticultural place-making simultaneously led to particular experiences of urban life and, thus of urban identity, materialising as the semi-rural urban fringe which has been observed at similar sites in Norwich (see also Jervis 2013d). This domestic landscape was not inherently durable, but was re-formed with the associations which constituted it; with the emergence of this landscape localising the far reaching connections which resulted in, and maintained, the lower income and marginal nature of the inhabitants of the site, associations through which the agency to re-make this place continually re-formed. Furthermore, this activity can be considered to have had a mnemonic role, standing for the general rhythm and flow of life (Pollard 2001, 323), as this repeated activity served to reform the domestic place through the maintenance of the associations, shifting from a landscape which became, to one which was constantly becoming.

The final form of place to be considered is the emergence of the tenement as a contested or civic place. It is here we can consider the effect of the Oak Book ordinances, as well as those of the physical boundaries which have been identified on the site. Documents, such as the Southampton Oak Book, serve to 'black-box' decisions made by the civic authorities regarding the best way to mitigate against the disruptive impact of waste upon urban space more widely. The Oak Book expresses clear concern with waste causing blockages, whilst it may also be possible to identify the document arising from the enacting of contemporary attitudes regarding hygiene and cleanliness (R. Jones 2011, 145). As we have already seen (chapter 3), these rules were meaningless unless enacted however. In turn the agency for the townsfolk to enact the rules must have emerged through courses of action within the town, whilst it might be that the development of social relationships built civic pride, and thus instilled the motivation to follow and enact these rules, it can be considered that the looming threat of punishment for failure to follow the rules also loomed large. Therefore, experiences of household spaces were not limited to the direct material associations formed within the tenement plot between people and their waste, but spilled over as action was constrained or enabled by the lingering presence of civic authorities. A further element to consider is the respect of boundaries, principally the fence line, which separates the tenement from the rampier (Figure 5.5). Although the rampier is not explicitly mentioned within the Oak Book, it is likely that similar rules prevented the build up of waste within this space, as is demonstrated by differences in the composition of deposits on either side of the fence line marking this boundary. Whilst the boundary was metaphysically enacted through the enacting of such regulation, it was also physically enacted as it was respected through practice. This was not a material property of the space, but an emergent one, which was maintained only for as long it was enacted. The tenement was re-produced as a contested, civic, space through the continued enacting of rules, as they were drawn into regulatory courses of action. By the mid 14th century the stratigraphic evidence suggests that this process changed, as this boundary was no longer enforced, demonstrating that the associations which maintained it were no longer being re-formed, likely being the result of a general relaxation of concern in civic defence which in turn was the result of relative peace, action which was spatially distant (being enacted through activity in court for example) but localised through this most mundane of household activities. Waste is often seen as disruptive and polluting (Douglas 1966). Interactions with waste can be considered to have had disruptive effects, with the enforcement of regulations serving to prevent these effects. As such, by being enrolled in processes of place-making, they prevented the contamination of the public place of the rampier by the domestic and industrial places within the tenement, however once these ceased to be enacted, the processes behind the re-formation of the domestic place physically over-spilled, contaminating the defensive place and reducing its capacity, as can be best illustrated by the results of the French raid in Southampton in 1338, where the defences were clearly demonstrated to be woefully inadequate.

The backyard area at York Buildings was a simple space, but one which was enacted as multiple places, through being caught up in plural courses of action. This was not a space represented in multiple ways, but a space which became different things, through connected processes, which were effective upon each other. Furthermore people and places were mutually constituted, the effect of deposition being to re-form marginal identities and to allow identities of power to be enacted through regulation. The example of the rampier shows that these places had the potential to endure for as long as the courses of action which brought them into being were sustained, but that once these ceased, so did the agency which brought these places into being. A relational approach forces us to turn our view of landscape around. Rather than reflecting change, it, like material culture, was enrolled in it. The places which emerged permitted and constrained action, iron working contributed to the emergence of particular domestic spaces for example, whilst the enacting of regulations constrained the forms that action, and thus this place, could take, whilst also forcing the inhabitants of York Buildings to relate to their surroundings in particular ways, sustaining a particular form of (marginalised?) urban identity.

This brief analysis of depositional practice at a single site has shown that depositional practice was not simply related to the lower status of its occupants, but considered it to be enrolled in the emergence of various places or landscapes within a single space. Landscapes are not expressions or reflections of identity, but are formed with them. Both of these processes localised far reaching associations and were effective upon each other, bundling them together into a dynamic urban landscape, which was constantly in flux, with the agency for its reproduction being spun through the enrolment of waste in deposition, as an act of social assembly, and of regulatory documents, for example. The benefit of such an approach is to move from a static representation of urban space, to be able to trace the myriad of concerns, associations or connections which contributed to the emergence and maintenance of towns as distinctive places, which were in turn formed of distinctive places, the occupants of which developed particular forms of identity grounded in the myriad of ways in which urban populations experienced their surroundings (see also Hall 2006, 189).

Finally, it might be worth returning to the concept of the rubbish pit and questioning the utility of this term. Clearly at Bull Hall in Southampton and at Westwick in Norwich, pits did function as receptacles for waste. They were not dug for this purpose however, and as such the act of deposition can be considered a specific point in their biography, when they no longer fulfilled their intended use. Whilst in use these pits, as with the boundary feature at York Buildings, did not afford deposition, they were being enacted as something else, through different courses of action. However, once these courses of action ceased, or they ceased to be enrolled within them, new affordances developed; they became suitable for deposition and became rubbish pits, or rather became waste in themselves, as they lost their utility. The process through which things and features became rubbish and the effects of these processes will be considered in further detail in chapter 6.

## Summary: The Place of Pottery in Landscape Archaeology

The aim in this chapter has been to explore the implications of a relational approach for our understanding of landscapes. Such an approach provides a means to overcome many criticisms of contemporary approaches, on the one hand being empirical in nature, demanding us to reconstruct the processes at play in space. On the other, it provides a means to understand the plurality of experiences and the effect of place-making on the identities and experiences of past populations. Considering resource procurement demonstrated how landscapes, as the product of action, can be re-made in different spaces, removing the concept of landscape from its spatial anchor by identifying the processes behind their formation through the study of things than of the land, and allowing them to be considered as the effect of doing, rather the stage upon which action occurs. A temporal element was also considered, allowing an exploration of how the processes of place-making occur at varying temporal rhythms. In both the case of resource procurement and depositional practices the role of documents, as 'black-boxing' land division or attempts to regulate the use of space, played a particular role in preventing the contamination of places. An examination of waste disposal in medieval towns identified that various processes were at play. Specific consideration of those processes in relation to one site showed how these practices were enrolled in multiple, but connected forms of place-making, which bundle together to form a dynamic urban landscape. It is unlocking the effect of courses of action on the making and connecting of places that the utility of a relational approach to landscape archaeology lie, allowing us to consider how places unfold at multiple scales, rather than seeing spaces as stages which are fashioned by purely anthropogenic means.

# 6

# POTS IN MOTION:
# POTTERY, MEANING AND CHANGE

The preceding chapters have explored how pottery becomes meaningful through the relationships formed with people, documents and things (chapter 3) and how pots as meaningful objects, identities and landscapes came to be mutually constituted through the entanglement of pottery, people and spaces (chapters 4 and 5). The focus of this chapter is fluidity, considering how the meaning of things changes through time and how not only the properties of things, but the things themselves as materialisations of these properties, emerge as the products of the social contexts which they then go on to alter or maintain. The first case study explores the concept of biography in relation to pottery, focussing upon the end of its life by exploring how pottery came to be understood as waste and the effect of this process of categorisation. This expands upon the case study presented in the previous chapter, in which the role of waste deposition in the emergence of meaningful places was considered. The second case study explores the relationship between the emergence of new architectural forms and new ceramic forms, arguing that the two emerged together as the result of specific social relationships, which could be made durable through the presence of these forms. In both cases the fluidity of the social and of the way things became meaningful with it is emphasised. In order to develop these case studies it is first necessary to expand upon the concepts of biography and emergent properties which have been introduced in chapter 2 and have been implicit within a number of the case studies presented in chapters 3, 4 and 5.

## Biography and Categorisation

The concept that the properties of things are emergent has already been considered throughout this book. The idea was introduced in chapter 2, through the assertion that meaning develops through action and therefore that the affordances, or performance characteristics, of materials and things emerge through practice, allowing the same item to become meaningful in multiple ways. This was illustrated in chapter 3, through considering how pottery vessels became meaningful through their associations with text and enrolment in magical practice, whilst the concept of the skeuomorph was utilised to show how, following Conneller (2011), materials are understood through technology and the relationships which emerge between different substances. In chapter 4 the properties of people, defined in terms of identity, were seen as emerging through food practices, with vessels playing multiple roles in identity formation whilst in chapter 5 vessels were entangled in processes in which spaces became meaningful places through practice. Because properties are emergent they are inherently unstable, changing throughout the life of a thing, as it is caught up in bundles of action which are constantly in flux, with the same thing changing meaning through time, but also as it is enacted in multiple ways at the same time. Throughout their lives therefore, objects come to be understood, or categorised, in different ways, with their identities as objects, as well as their affordances being defined relationally. The concept of biography allows us to explore the trajectories through which things gain and lose meaning and develop performance characteristics and affordances which vary throughout their lives.

## Object Biography

Biographical approaches are now commonplace in archaeological interpretation, having first been brought to the archaeologists' attention through the work of Appadurai (1986) and Kopytoff (1986). The approach, based upon tracing the 'life history' of an object, and exploring the ways in which it was enacted at various points along this trajectory, provides a framework in which the fluidity of meaning can be appreciated. In considering the process of commodisation Kopytoff (1986) illustrated that meanings emerge and dissolve as an object negotiates its biographical trajectory, but at the same time what came before influences what can come after (as was shown, for example, in the varying effects that forms of pottery could have on elements of identity in chapter 4). Importantly, the life histories of objects do not take place in isolation, but rather the biographies of people, places and things are entwined within each other (Gosden and Marshall 1999, 169; Mytum 2010, 244). These trajectories are not simple linear progressions however, through the use of objects time is manipulated (Gosden 1994, 17) and things are caught in cycles of use, acting as nodal points in webs of associations, meaning that their life history, like that of humans, is a patchwork of associations and meanings, which manipulate time in a number of ways, be it through cycles of daily use or longer processes of decay (Joy 2010, 12; Mytum 2010, 245).

Pottery is a relatively ephemeral artefact type. Vessels typically have a short lifespan (see DeBoer and Lathrap 1979, 127) and as such their material durability is potentially limited (Jones 2007, 83). We can consider though that a range of temporal flows are present in the life history of an object (Gosden 1994, 17). In the first instance we have the history of the vessel itself, as it moves from production, through distribution to use and finally deposition, with potential for further re-use after breakage. Gosden (1994,

16) has termed chains of action 'structures of reference', through which time flows at different rates. For example some activities may be timed in relation to the duration of a process (waiting for a pot to boil), others may relate to a time of day (such as set meal times), or some element of biological time (eating foodstuffs before they go off). At a given time vessels may be present in a household, which are at varying points in their linear lives, meaning that engagements with some objects generate different temporal flows than those with others. Therefore, whilst an individual object may be ephemeral, a degree of durability is introduced by people interacting with different versions of the same object at different points in their lives (Jones 2007, 83). Whilst this can act to introduce durability, we also need to account for developments both in production and use.

One limitation of the approach is a tendency to study generalised life histories (Jones 2002, 85; Tilley 1999, 248), rather than studying the history of an individual artefact. This is necessary when dealing with an object such as pottery, as the evidence may not be present in a single sherd to reconstruct the biography of an individual pot. However, throughout their lives, objects can come to be enacted through entirely different sets of relationships. An example of this are silver beakers, which change from being simple commodities when in the hands of one Romanian ethnic group, to increasingly becoming fetishised objects and symbols of identity for another group, as the object develops what has been termed a 'social career' (Berta 2009, 194). Generalisation is especially true of objects such as pottery, which occurs in bulk, however by adopting methods which allow the associations into which these vessels were drawn to be reconstructed in detail (for example through use wear analysis as in chapter 4 or through the study of depositional practices as in chapter 5 and below), it becomes possible to create a more nuanced understanding of this fluidity within what, on the surface, appear to be fairly homogeneous groups of material. The aim of the two case studies presented in this chapter is to explore further how the biography of pottery is entangled with that of the actors with which it comes to be associated, considering how categories and the affordances of things emerge through varying processes of social assembly at different points in an objects life.

## Becoming Waste: The Many Meanings of Rubbish

The final case study in the previous chapter examined the role of waste disposal in the making of landscapes, considering how this action drew together multiple actors and enacted a single place in multiple ways, demonstrating that not a single urban *landscape*, but multiple urban *landscapes* emerged through action. In this section I wish to focus on how pottery became meaningful through its categorisation as waste and how, through this process, it developed varying performance characteristics, as well as constituting people and places through enrolling them in this process, which formed at a specific point in a vessels biography.

*Thinking About Waste*

In the previous chapter the varying categories of waste categorised by Schiffer (1987) (primary, secondary and tertiary, with the addition of provisional waste) was used primarily as a means of distinguishing different trajectories of deposition, to understand the processes through which archaeological deposits formed. However, these categories of waste also have implications for considering how waste was perceived by those disposing of it. The dumping of secondary waste into negative features suggests that it was intended to be forgotten, as it is removed from consciousness through concealment. Not all secondary deposits need represent disposal of waste however, as into this category fall deliberately placed deposits, such as the foundation deposits mentioned briefly in chapter 3. Provisional waste (and by implication tertiary waste), as well, arguably, as primary waste had a lingering presence (Edensor 2005, 316), allowing it to be caught up in new courses of action, perhaps through recycling, or as manure as we saw at York Buildings in Southampton (chapter 5). Variation in depositional practice suggests that not all 'waste' was perceived as 'rubbish' (see Beck and Hill 2004, 305 for an ethnographic example), but rather these were categories which emerged through engagement with the material, through which it was determined as having or lacking utility in a given place (as a bundle of social associations) at a given time. The type of utility is highly variable however. Whilst in some societies a midden may be considered a pile of materials to be re-used in craft activities, in others they may have functioned as spatial barriers or as indicators of wealth (Needham and Spence 1997, 84–5). Indeed, just as spaces could be enacted in multiple ways (chapter 5), so to could the same deposit, as it was drawn into varied social realities. Therefore, whilst secondary deposition can perhaps be seen as an objectification of negative value, the value of waste is not fixed nor is it a single homogeneous category, rather, unless removed entirely from consciousness through concealment, it has the potential to be resuscitated and made meaningful once again (Reno 2009, 30; Edensor 2005, 316).

Waste can therefore be considered an ambiguous category of material. On the one hand it is the residue of society, a group of undesirable things, but on the other it is a collection of discrete things, waiting re-enactment as meaningful objects. As such it can be described as:

> "a mulch of matter, which profanes the order of things and their separate individuality, or their membership of a category of objects" (Edensor 2005, 318).

In other words, waste is a category in which things lose their identity, but one from which they can exit, being re-born as new objects. The ambiguity of waste is further tempered by the process of decay, in which things can revert to substances, or develop new physical properties, through which new performance characteristics can emerge through their being put to use. The process of categorisation as waste therefore is about more than human perception, it is a coming together of anthropogenic and natural forces which act together (Edensor 2005, 320), forming the agency through which waste as a category of meaningless, valueless material emerges, but which must be considered to extend back, through the previous courses of action which constitute an objects biography.

Deposition therefore is a process through which objects lose their identity and power, a process of neutralisation in which their properties can be re-negotiated. The ambiguous and varying nature of the affordances of waste is well demonstrated by scavenging, in which one interpretation of an item as waste is replaced by another's interpretation of the item as having some utility, with it becoming re-enacted as something of value (Reno 2009, 32; Edensor 2005, 317; Douny 2007, 313). Interactions with waste not only have implications for how waste is comprehended however. As we have seen, waste played a role in enacting spaces differently. Constraints on waste management varied even within single settlements (Beck and Hill 2004 316), meaning that the processes through which waste could be categorised as valuable or valueless consisted of more than the relationship between people and materials, but also through the extended relationships which were enrolled in this process (particularly pressure on space which, as we have seen in the case of Southampton) played a role in determining how people could manage their waste (see also Brück 1999a, 256 for a prehistoric example). Identities too are entangled within people's interactions with waste. Whilst from the outside scavengers may be seen as poor or dirty, for the individuals undertaking such activity these engagements can lead to the emergence of identities based upon skill and creativity (Reno 2009, 35; Crane 2000, 24). Waste therefore has the potential to affect people in different ways, for some it is a destabilising presence to be dealt with, for others it opens up a realm of potential courses of action and experiences (Edensor 2005, 324). Therefore categories of place, waste and people can be considered as mutually constituted, because deposits are formed of a myriad of ontological connections, associated not only with how waste material comes to be understood, but also how the spaces of action and the people performing it 'become' (Pollard 2001, 322). The concepts of value and disposability can therefore be considered as relationally constituted (Brück 1999b, 330), forming through processes which also enacted people (in the form of particular identities) and places, making deposition a process of mediation, transformation and classification, not only of objects, but of all of the actors drawn into this activity (see Hill 1995, 126).

## *The Medieval View of Waste*

The town ordnances discussed in chapter 5 suggest waste to have been considered undesirable within medieval towns. It was thought of as a disordering and disruptive presence, which reflected negatively upon the image of the town and was associated with dirt and disease. The archaeological evidence suggests however that, in some households at least, waste was re-categorised as a resource, being spread onto gardens to assist in horticulture. Evidence for the re-use of waste is considerably more abundant in the medieval countryside, where manuring patterns can be reconstructed through the patterning of pottery recovered through fieldwalking (see R. Jones 2005; Gerrard 1997). Typically the date of pottery has been utilised to identify differences in land use through time. However, Richard Jones (2011) has sought to understand the patterning in a more nuanced manner, by considering medieval perceptions of waste. Jones (2011, 147) draws upon historical sources to question whether waste was uniformly used in this way, in particular, he highlights that a thirteenth century source, Walter of Henley's 'Husbandry', describes the process of manuring in some depth, but makes no reference to household waste. Archaeological evidence demonstrates clear variation in disposal practice within villages (Jones 2011, 149–50). One distinction which can be made is between the waste from peasant households and that from elite households. Whereas peasants are unlikely to have differentiated their waste, based on archaeological patterning of pottery and animal bone remains, there is some evidence that elite households separated waste, in particular food waste appears to have been treated differently to non-organic materials such as pottery (Jones 2011, 150–1). This separation, it is suggested, relates to the ways in which these varying categories of material were considered to have utility within a medieval worldview in which humoral theory was a key component. The physical properties of varying forms of waste therefore can be considered to relate to particular elements and have led to them being utilised in different ways to neutralise different kinds of soil. Warm, damp soil, for example, may be cooled with cool, dry materials such as animal bones, whereas cool and dry soils may have been treated with warm and wet manure (Jones 2011, 152). We can see then that within these households waste become seen as having utility based upon the enacting of knowledge (black-boxed in text) and through its enrolment in action (agricultural activity). From Jones' study three things emerge. Firstly, waste pathways are complex and must be reconstructed in detail, as was demonstrated in chapter 5. Secondly, there is a great deal of variation in the ways in which waste was enacted as manure based upon the associations into which the material was drawn through action and thirdly this relates to a wide array of associations, which are not limited to people and space, but also to documents and other objects and substances, returning us to the points discussed above regarding waste loosing its identity. This was clearly not a universal phenomenon, but rather categories of waste formed in multiple ways, which in some cases could be a homogeneous, anonymous mulch of matter, but in others could be meaningful assemblages of material, the agency behind which extended beyond the physical relationships of waste disposal. With this in mind we can now return to medieval Southampton, to consider the variety of ways in which waste was categorised, the agency behind these processes and their effect on the identities of the town dwellers and urban space.

*Becoming Waste: Categorising Rubbish in Medieval Southampton*
The depositional practices discussed in the previous chapter in relation to Southampton can be traced back to the origins of the settlement following the decline of the earlier site at Hamwic in the mid 9th century. In its initial phases at least, this settlement of Hamwic appears to have been fairly dispersed and, although the majority of waste has been recovered from pits, the levels of fragmentation suggest re-deposition from surface deposits in the closing of features, although there is considerable variability in the pace of filling, with some features being filled episodically and others in discrete

dumping events. The the majority of deposition appears to have been onto middens in the first instance, with waste finding utility as filling material as features went out of use (Jervis 2011, 254). By the post-conquest period the pattern observed in the high medieval town appears to have developed, with secondary deposition into pits and other abandoned features being most common in the densely occupied waterfront area, with tertiary deposition and the spreading of waste on gardens being more common in the east (Jervis in 2013c). From this evidence it can be considered that features came to afford deposition in different ways and that waste came to be categorised as such in a manner which varied with the social associations into which it was drawn, having effects upon identities and, as we have seen, the emergence and maintenance of places.

Provisional deposition, be it onto surface deposits such as middens, into lined pits or other areas in which material could re-enter the social fray, is a key moment in the re-categorisation of material. Through breakage objects lose their utility; they can no longer be re-enacted as what they once were, losing their affordances. As we have seen, in such a deposit they occupy a transient, ambiguous state, being part of a malaise of thingness, an anonymous component of a mulch of waste matter. It is through engagement in new processes that they become new objects, affording new things, as these performance characteristics emerge through situated action. The settlement of Hamwic appears to have been provisioned through a tributary system (see discussion in Bourdillon 1980) and there is no evidence of agriculture within the settlement, even in those areas which were not densely occupied, which recent research suggests were allowed to grow wild (Stoodley 2012). The agency to undertake horticulture within the new settlement of Southampton (evidenced by the build up of garden soils which continue into the high medieval period, for example at York Buildings (see chapter 5)) can be seen to have arisen through the remapping of the connections through which these settlements were maintained. The shift of the settlement materialises this process of remapping in which one settlement dissolved (or rather ceased to become) and another emerged through the retention of some associations (such as trading connections) and the formation of others (for example those associated with the emergence of a defensive burh). The remapping of provisioning strategies, including, perhaps, the need for a defended settlement to be self sufficient, gave rise to the practicing of horticulture within the settlement, whilst a further stimulus may have been the ambiguity felt by urban dwellers in relation to rural settlements given the changing role and character of urban centres (Astill 2006, 250). It was through this re-mapping that waste came to afford a role in this process, as the settlement and this re-categorisation of material as manure became together and were therefore mutually constitutive, with the dispersed layout of the settlement affording horticulture and the agency behind this emerging through the wider remapping of the associations of which it was constituted, including those through which waste became something else.

Waste was not only deposited as fertiliser however, it is, of course, chiefly recovered from archaeological features. As has already been discussed (chapter 5) 'rubbish pits' in the sense of features dug specifically for the deposition of waste are exceptionally rare in high medieval towns, and this conclusion can also be drawn both for late Saxon

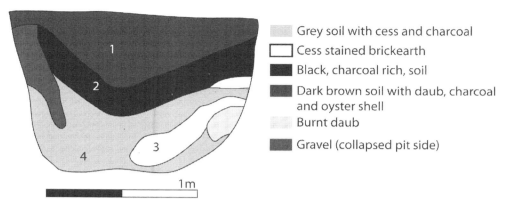

*Figure 6.1. Comparison of the levels of fragmentation in pits at Melbourne Street, Southampton (Hamwic SOU4). Redrawn from Holdsworth 1980.*

Southampton and the earlier settlement of Hamwic. Throughout the medieval period features can be considered to come to afford deposition at various points in their biographies. Boundaries, such as the ditch or gully separating plots at York Buildings, did not afford deposition as in order to function they had to actively be kept clear of waste. This is well demonstrated through the fact that little material was recovered from the feature at York Buildings and similarly, in Hamwic, boundary pits contained little material in their lower fills, with small sherds (which occasionally cross-fit between pits) dominating these small assemblages, suggesting they occasionally acted as useful receptacles into which the residue of sweeping could be concealed, but did not afford deposition, as their boundary role was re-enacted through practice (Figure 6.1). In Hamwic there are numerous instances of these features being dumped into the latest phase of the settlement, demonstrating that as the boundaries ceased to be enacted these features moved to a new phase in their biography, affording deposition of waste in their closure (Jervis 2011, 257). Similarly cess pits needed to be kept clear of waste material in order to function. The filling of these often demonstrates the presence of discrete bands of waste, sometimes sealed with layers of oyster shell, demonstrating that these features only afforded deposition intermittently. If waste was allowed to build up as provisional deposits (as is suggested by the level of deposition), it was always to hand and therefore this intermittent filling would appear to relate to more than waste simply becoming available, for example as the result of a large scale consumption event. Rather these pits came to afford waste at specific moments in their life, perhaps when the smell became too much to bear and the agency to fill developed from the effect of the pit on its users – the pit literally demanded filling. We can consider therefore that pits do not always afford deposition, but rather these affordances emerged at specific points in their biographies, as they demanded filling for some reason, including as they ceased to be enacted as what they once were.

Just as these features did not permanently afford filling, neither did waste continuously afford deposition as filling material. Rather the biographies of features, pottery and the settlement as a whole were entangled within each other. Pits afforded deposition as waste came to afford a role as filling material, just as waste afforded use as fertiliser as the settlement came to afford horticulture. The utility of waste was therefore relational, as it was re-enacted through being enrolled in new forms of action, where it exited the ambiguous thingness of rubbish to fleetingly become a new object with new affordances. People too were made through this activity. Deposition can be considered to have had a mnemonic role, as there were similarities between depositional practices in Hamwic and late Saxon Southampton and interaction with surface deposits and deposition into cess pits may have been action through which continuity was mediated in the face of dislocation. Yet, through the undertaking of horticulture, this activity may have mediated change as well, re-configuring what it was to become urban in Southampton by breaking down the contrast between urban consumers and rural producers. Indeed, if Southampton was peopled not only from Hamwic, but also its surrounding countryside, this activity could have had multiple effects depending upon an individuals biography, for some being de-stabilising, but for others bringing continuity of rural life into an alien urban setting. We can then, begin to see how engagements with waste mediated continuity and change in people's lives, as these provided a means through which they could engage with their surroundings and thus through which senses of identity developed and were maintained.

Certainly by the Anglo-Norman period and probably before, the affordance of waste as having utility for horticulture was not recognised by the entire population, or at least not everyone enacted waste in this way. Increasingly there is evidence for secondary deposition around the waterfront area and it can be argued that here a concept of disposability emerged. Such a concept again links the biographies of pottery, spaces, features and people and can be considered to have mediated difference. Anglo-Norman deposits from the waterfront area, like those from the high medieval period, are characterised by the presence of large and unabraded sherds. There does not appear to have been a clear provisional stage in the biography of this waste, rather it was rapidly re-categorised as useless waste. In certain instances this waste was used to close features, developing this affordance with the features into which they were dumped, however on the whole rubbish appears to have quickly been removed from sites. At Southampton Castle there is evidence for the presence of middens. Tertiary waste was used to close some features, particularly a garderobe (Brown 1985), but on the whole, as in the domestic tenements, this waste does not appear to have developed any other utility. In the fifteenth century a workman was paid to dump waste into the sea (Platt 1973, 171) and it is likely that this practice may extend into earlier periods. The removal of waste may also be indicated by the presence of unusually high quantities of imported pottery from deposits found in agricultural layers at Cook Street and Orchard Place, outside of the walls, suggesting that this material was derived from the merchant's quarter, rather than from the poorer households who may have lived in this suburban area (Russel 2010). Through the Anglo-Norman and high medieval periods in the wealthier areas of Southampton waste appears to have been perceived as disposable. Unlike in the east of the town it did not develop new affordances through being directly enacted in agricultural activity (although the spreading of waste on fields outside of the town suggests it was re-enacted once away from domestic tenements), and it only occasionally developed utility as filling material. In simple terms this can be seen to reflect the wealthier nature of the inhabitants of this area, however, we can consider that the entwinement of the biographies of pottery, people, spaces and features extends into this area of the town too, but with very different effects.

The waterfront area was chiefly utilised as a mercantile area. This activity generated wealth and, just as the periphery become undesirable (see chapter 5), this area attracted growth and development as it developed into the economic and political heart of the town. Further pressure on space developed from far reaching chains of action, such as the settlement of a new population in this area following the Norman Conquest, which was the result of associations stretching back as far as the royal courts in England and Normandy. Building activity placed pressure on space, meaning that this area did not afford horticulture and the presence of large dumps of waste would be disruptive, providing a physical obstacle but also creating undesirable associations with the poorer areas of the town. The generation of wealth meant that households did not need to undertake horticulture and therefore the agency for spaces which could afford this activity was not spun in this area. Waste here became the residue of household life and a disordering presence, an undesirable mess for which the agency did not emerge for re-enactment. Rather this material became disposable, as no agency emerged for it to develop new affordances, except in the occasional instances where it was required to fill pits dug for quarrying or other purposes. None of these developments can be considered in isolation. The development of mercantile identities, the building up of the town and the concept of disposability emerged with each other, through the same sets of action into which people, spaces and waste were drawn. Therefore, a concept of disposability and this treatment of waste does not reflect the identities of those living in this area, but rather emerged with them, as the effect of action through which wealth was generated and distinction emerged, both between urban people, but also between urban places.

So far I have argued that the biographies of people, spaces, features and pottery are entangled within each other, all are caught in processes of becoming through which affordances emerge with identities and places. Finally, I wish to return to the work of Richard Jones to consider the trajectories of waste, returning again to the site of York Buildings (see chapter 5). Jones argues that different elements of waste could develop different trajectories, effectively affording different things, a process which was reliant upon the enacting of knowledge which can be considered to have been made durable (or 'black-boxed') in text. Analysis of the distribution of different types of pottery at York Buildings suggests that different forms of waste were enacted in varying ways, demonstrating that waste is more complex than a simple amalgamation of all material, but rather emerges as categories of material through complex courses of action. The material dumped over the gardens as fertiliser consists primarily of jars used as cooking pots and plain jugs, indicating that this material comprises waste from cooking and food processing. Pottery does not appear to have been separated from the organic material and the evidence for this waste having a provisional phase in a lined pit suggests it maybe fulfilled a specific role, aerating the organic matter and allowing it to decompose more quickly. The distribution of some jugs, particularly whitewares most likely used for drinking, is skewed more towards the frontage and yard areas, suggesting that, in some cases, this waste was treated separately, rather than being amalgamated with the 'kitchen' deposits. For example one pit contained a near complete profile of a Laverstock-type jug. Some jugs are still found their way into the garden area, but in certain instances it appears that these drinking vessels developed particular affordances as filling material for redundant features, presumably because they lacked the organic qualities of the kitchen material. Whilst there is no evidence that the residents of York Buildings were separating their waste in the elaborate and intellectual style identified by Jones at manorial sites, it does appear that depositional activity indexes the emergence of different affordances in relation to broken pottery, depending upon the trajectory of its biography. Therefore although one stage in a vessels biography, deposition must be related back to earlier stages in an objects life, to consider the processes through which it was considered to afford deposition in a particular way, which may relate more to the relationships which it formed in its life (for example with kitchen waste) than its specific material properties.

### Summary
This section has focussed on a particular stage in the biography of pottery, deposition. It has been argued that the biography of a vessel is entangled with that of people, places and features and that through this entanglement particular affordances emerge, which determine not only how a vessel may be disposed of, but also the effects of this activity in relation to identities and senses of place, including the emergence of particular physical forms. In the final case study these ideas will be developed further, to consider how the emergence of particular ceramic and architectural forms is entangled with each other.

## Mutual Emergence: Pottery and Buildings
The concept that forms and categories emerge and become meaningful together can be further explored through an analysis of the relationship between pottery and buildings in the medieval period.

### Approaching Medieval Buildings
The study of medieval buildings has been a particularly rich area of theoretical research over the past two decades. The roots of study were laid by scholars such as Faulkner (1958) and Pantin (1963), who focussed on refining the typology of house forms, considering how they developed through time and varied in accordance with setting. Pantin (1963) examined medieval town house forms, arguing that they developed from existing rural forms, a conclusion which has been critiqued, for example by Schofield (1994) and Rees Jones (2008), who argue that distinctively urban forms of housing

developed, in response to the demands of urban living. Contemporary approaches to buildings draw upon a range of theoretical approaches, particularly considerations of *habitus* and the concept of translation, to explore how houses became meaningful spaces and to consider the ways in which they are related to other elements of medieval society. In particular, techniques such as access analysis have moved from a consideration of the physical characteristics of a house to thinking about houses as socially structured spaces, in which contrasts emerge, for example in relation to gendered or public and private spaces (*e.g.* Schofield 1994; Gilchrist 1999, 144).

Access analysis is a means through which the steps required to access areas of a building can be reconstructed, allowing the complexity of structures to be presented visually and providing a means through which contrasts can be drawn between open, accessible spaces and deeper, private ones. Schofield (1994) uses such analysis to argue that town houses in later medieval London were designed with specific binary oppositions, between public and private and clean and dirty in mind. Crucially such an approach allows similarities to be drawn between houses of varying physical form, with it being the use of space which is important, rather than the exact morphology through which it is divided. This has been demonstrated, for example, in relation to Viking houses, where structures of seemingly differing form have been shown to be structured by similar patterns of access and use of space (Price 1995, 123–4; Boyd 2009). Although a methodological technique, rather than a theoretical framework, access analysis has allowed a re-conceptualisation of spaces, including public (Giles 2000) and religious (Gilchrist 1994) buildings as well as houses, as places in motion, which are experienced in different ways through action, rather than static, unchanging structures.

Such approaches have begun to see houses as somehow beyond representational. As with portable material culture, there has been a realisation that buildings are not inherently meaningful structures that can be 'read' – indeed it can be questioned whose text we are reading in attempting to do so; those commissioning it? The architects? The builder? The inhabitant? Instead, buildings must be considered in a biographical manner. Rather than having meaning inscribed within them, it emerges as a series of translations, as a concept becomes materialised and the building then goes into use, re-use and decay (Whyte 2006). Therefore, although typological study may identify similarities in buildings, we need to understand how these similarities translated into meaning, either through similar buildings being enacted in similar ways, or through buildings drawing upon elements of other types of structure but enacting them differently. Evidence of the latter phenomena can be seen within later medieval and early post-medieval merchant houses, in which architectural motifs and elements of the use of space (such as the division of open halls into 'high' and 'low' ends) can be seen to transcend boundaries between domestic and ecclesiastical architecture (a process which occurs both conceptually but also materially, through the re-use of elements of church architecture) (King 2007). The division of space within such dwellings also imitates that within aristocratic dwellings. However this can be considered as more than simple copying, but rather a process of translation as particular spatial configurations are enrolled in different courses of domestic action, through which they come to have very different effects as mediators of social relationships which constitute urban, rather than rural settings.

The beginnings of an adoption of this concept of translation can be seen in post-processual approaches to medieval architecture. Johnson's (1993) work on later medieval housing in Suffolk argues that variability in domestic architecture is the result of more than economic practicalities. Whilst building an argument that house forms develop social meaning and therefore that social values are reflected in the form of domestic structures (Johnson 1993, 30) and attempting to read these meanings through contextual analysis, Johnson also considers that house forms can 'act back'. For example, the open hall form was not only being structured by, but also structured behaviour, producing, symbolising and maintaining social distinction within the home (Johnson 1993, 59), generating *habitus* through the process of dwelling. Changes towards more closed forms of architecture are considered to be an expression of ambiguities and tensions within the domestic sphere, relating to wider processes of social differentiation along lines of, for example, gender and class, and the associated developments of concepts of privacy, meaning that, unlike in the earlier part of the study period when wealth and status could be closely linked to the size of a house, in the later period it was the number of distinctive spaces within the house which symbolised the social complexity of a household (Johnson 1993, 150). Transcending scales, Johnson argues that variation in housing stock relates to processes of social distinction which can also be seen in the layout of the landscape, particularly through processes of enclosure, arguing that this process was as much social as it was economic. This contrasts with prevailing arguments which privileged an economic explanation for this phenomenon. A process of translation is more explicitly addressed in Gilchrist's (1994) discussion of female religious houses, in which parallels are drawn between the use of space in these institutions and in the noble houses from which the inhabitants would have been drawn (contrasting the distinctions between the use of space in male religious houses and domestic architecture). Similarly, Giles (2000) identifies elements of translation between domestic houses and guildhalls in York, which in turn also find parallels in church architecture. In both cases, the concept of *habitus* is introduced to explain these processes of translation as more than simple copying. Both Giles and Gilchrist argue that the layout of these buildings is underpinned by a subconscious knowledge of how space should be used, which in turn is embedded in the reproduction of contemporary divisions in society, for example along the lines of gender or status. Referring back to the ideas discussed in chapter 4, these similarities allow the social relationships through which identities are established and maintained to be translated between locations.

Discussing the similarities in the use of space between houses of varying status in medieval York, Rees Jones (2008, 83) argues that a nested process of translation can be identified, in that despite differences in the size of houses, the use of space translates as households were structured by similar sets of social relationships (for example between the householder and the dependents). Such an engrained understanding of space and its relation to the structure of society is considered by Grenville (2008, 108–9) to explain the flexibility of the tri-partite house plan (the division of space into a hall with service rooms at one end and chambers at the other, found in both rural and urban households). Indeed Grenville (2008, 111) identifies a similar set of translations in rural households to those identified by Rees Jones in relation to urban ones. This process of translation, Grenville (2008 118) argues, offers an element of 'ontological security' to those experiencing a space for the first time, coming to understand it in relation to other similar spaces, which have similar patterns of access even if they are in some ways different in their physical form. In other words, buildings can be 'viewed as the realisation of ideas about domestic space' (Gardiner 2008, 39). *Habitus* can, therefore, be closely related to the concept of durability, with action in buildings coming to form the agency for continuity through providing a means through which social relationships can be re-formed in varying physical spaces. Yet the *habitus* can also lead to a somewhat unsatisfactory 'social' explanation. Grenville (2008, 119) questions whether we might see *habitus*, rather than functional need, as structuring space, however this perhaps reduces down to a contrast between a 'social' or a 'functional' explanation. *Habitus* though is not an explanation, but rather a concept which provides a vehicle for the process of translation, from which the building forms emerge and are maintained. This is perhaps well evidenced by the development of the buildings occupied by the urban poor, consisting of single celled rooms which are not paralleled in the countryside. Rather than reflecting the development of the urban poor, outside of the realms of existing *habitus* (Grenville 2008, 121), such structures can be considered to have emerged with the urban poor and been enrolled in the maintenance of them as a specifically differentiated group within urban society.

The relationship between urban and rural housing is discussed further below, but the process of translation provides a means by which the use of space and its relation to the social order can be used to frame this relationship, rather than relying upon the presence of material similarities and differences between the structures themselves. Just like landscapes, houses are made meaningful through action coming to be different things in different places. But this is a process which, just like identity formation, is not reducible to *habitus* (Chapman and Gaydarska 2011, 23), rather *habitus*, drawing upon memory and learning, provides a means through which we come to terms with the world, with the agency for new forms of *habitus* emerging through enrolment in changing patterns of social relationships, leading to the emergence of distinctively urban people, places and, potentially, pottery, through the entanglement of the biographies of these diverse actors.

## Developments in Domestic Architecture

Before discussing the emergent relationship between pottery and house forms it is necessary to briefly discuss the emergence of the tri-partite house form and the relationship between urban and rural housing. Halls were the pre-dominant pre-Conquest form of housing in England, although debates have examined the exact ways in which spaces were configured. Initially it was considered that two storey buildings consisted of a multi-purpose hall over a cellar, perhaps with ancillary buildings. Blair (1993) questioned this interpretation, considering instead that the upper room was

*Figure 6.2. Schematic plan of the tri-partite hall. Image: Ben Jervis.*

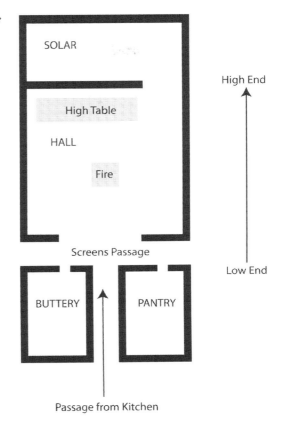

in fact a chamber, with the hall occupying ancillary buildings. By 1200 a new form of domestic form was firmly established, in which two separate service rooms were present (the buttery and pantry) off a main hall, with a chamber at the other end (the so called 'tripartite' plan) (Gardiner 2008, 40) (Figure 6.2). My aim in this section is to explore how the agency for this new plan emerged in conjunction with the agency for new forms of pottery, principally the glazed jug. Drawing on documentary sources, Gardiner (2008, 46) considers the tripartite form, and particularly the distinction between the pantry and the buttery, to relate to a deep-rooted distinction between items associated with drink (pantry) and those associated with the setting of the table (the buttery), with enrolment in these processes leading to the establishment of professional identities (of butler and pantler). The agency can be considered to have emerged then in part through this distinction, in which these identities were made durable through interactions with particular spaces (*cf.* Gardiner 2008, 48). Prior to the establishment of the tripartite form it is considered that undercrofts were used for the storage of wine and ale, consumed privately in the chamber above (Gardiner 2008, 56–7). The development of the pantry and buttery as distinctive spaces, accessed from the hall rather than the chamber, may be related to changes in dining practice, in

particular an increase in the ceremony of dining, as this activity cited the ceremony of
the church (Gardiner 2008, 59). Therefore, the adoption of the use of space within the
hall as a translation of ecclesiastical spaces can be considered to have emerged from the
translation of courses of action, associated with the establishment of particular forms
of identity and the control of social relationships in dining (see chapter 4), including
the gestures associated with serving and eating. Text played a role in this increasing
formality, through the publication of etiquette books, which were enacted in the act
of dining (Gardiner 2008, 61). It can be considered that the agency for these spaces
emerged with that for these books, as well as the material culture required for the
undertaking of this action, and the identities which formed with them, with this being
black boxed within and re-formed through the performance of regulations, although
the component parts of this agency are unclear. The entwinement of people, spaces,
things and texts through action served to formalise the distinctions between elements
of house form and materialised as a tripartite form which translated between houses of
varying status and setting. Gardiner (2008, 64) considers development in the church
to be key, with the ritual of dining not only citing that of the church, but with the
distinction between the buttery and the pantry relating to the contrast between bread
and wine in the Eucharist. The agency can then, perhaps be traced back to an increased
awareness of Christian belief and practice, perhaps as a means to come to terms with
rapid socio-economic change (Jolly 2002, 20–1), which in part developed through the
foundation of increasing numbers of religious houses as a means to disseminate ideas
of 'proper' behaviour through text.

The development of house forms cannot therefore be separated from other
developments which contributed to the changing 'social' of the 12th–13th centuries.
The Norman Conquest can perhaps also be considered a stimulus, not in the sense that
new forms were imported directly, but rather that a dialogue existed between English
and Norman forms (Impey 2000). More importantly, the Conquest was a stimulus for
the broader socio-economic changes through which the connections which formed the
agency behind the emergence or persistence of domestic forms were re-mapped. It is of
particular relevance to consider the distinctions between urban and rural housing. In
considering this relationship Rees Jones (2008) suggests a more subtle understanding
of this relationship than those posited by previous scholars; chiefly that urban builders
copied existing rural forms (Pantin 1963) or that new forms developed in towns and
were transferred, due to social emulation, to the countryside (Pearson 2005). Rather,
Rees Jones (2008, 90) argues that particularly urban patterns of urban house and
tenement developed, translating some elements of rural plots into urban settings, but
also being influenced by social competition and freedom afforded by urban living and
the ability to express and maintain this freedom through the emergence of documents
such as charters. Houses do more than reflect *habitus* and represent 'society'. They were
drawn into the processes through which *habitus* developed and morphed, not simply
re-making social distinction, but contributing to the courses of action through which
distinction emerged. Crucially the agency for particularly urban forms of housing or
for the development of new forms of house did not develop in isolation, but rather

was the result of far reaching sets of associations, which brought new houses, places, identities and forms of material culture into being. Houses therefore were enrolled in and enacted through the processes of social assembly through which society 'became', and therefore in order to understand their emergence we must consider more closely how their biographies are entangled within those of the people who built and occupied the and the objects which were used within them.

## The Emergent 'Social': Pottery and Buildings

The relationship between buildings and objects is rarely discussed. In his discussion of the buttery and the pantry, Gardiner (2008) does highlight that particular objects would be associated with these rooms, but on the whole such distinctions are largely limited to historical archaeological approaches which rely upon documentary evidence (principally probate inventories) to examine where objects were used in the home (see also chapter 3). An exception is Mellor's (2004) examination of pottery and interiors, which considers how decorated pottery emerged alongside other forms of decorated material culture, particularly textiles; however, whilst considered to be linked to the development of particular concepts of taste and refinement, the focus is on aesthetic effect rather than the emergence of new forms. Both Brown (2005, 91) and Mellor (2004, 157) consider that the introduction of tripod pitchers and jugs from the 10th century onwards reflects a change in lifestyle or dining practices. Such a conclusion seems unsatisfactory, as it does not explain these social processes. Rather we need to consider the relationships through which these new ceramic forms developed. From a chronological perspective a relationship can be considered to exist between the development of the tripartite house form and these jugs, as is illustrated by case studies from the port town of Southampton and the palace site at Cheddar in Somerset.

In both of these settings the tri-partite form was established by 1200. Excavations at the medieval palace of Cheddar identified several phases of building and uncovered a large ceramic assemblage (Rahtz 1979). The early phases of the palace are characterised by a complex of hall-type building, but around the 10th–11th centuries elements of the tri-partite form begin to develop, with these being firmly established by around 1200 (Figure 6.3). The ceramic assemblage largely consists of local types, however from the 11th century new spouted forms are present. These are initially scarce, but by the 13th century jugs are an established and significant component of the ceramic assemblage. Throughout the Anglo Saxon period and immediate post-conquest period Cheddar was a royal palace, visited in a regular, but infrequent, manner, by the King. In 1204 the palace was granted to Hugh, Archdeacon of Wells (Rahtz 1979, 18) and it stayed as a bishop's manor throughout the 13th century. Given Gardiner's (2008) identification of a relationship between ecclesiastical influences and the development of the tri-partite form it may be telling that it is in period 5 (dated to the early 13th century) that the earliest version of a tri-partite hall develops at Cheddar. Elements of the identities of the bishops who owned the palace can be considered to have been developed through particular social relationships; the occupation of particular spaces (the church) in which relationships between people and things were closely

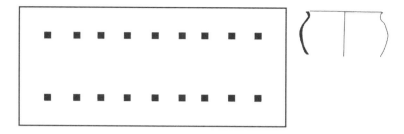

Phase 4 (Late 11th-early 12th century)

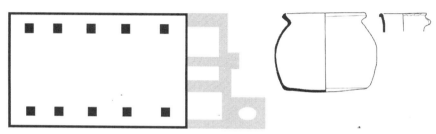

Phase 5 (Early 13th century)

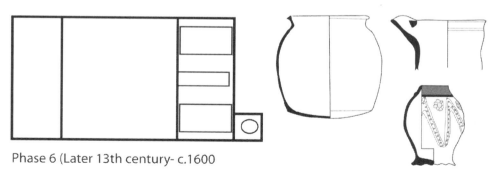

Phase 6 (Later 13th century- c.1600

*Figure 6.3: The development of the hall building at Cheddar, with examples of typical pottery from each phase. Redrawn from Rahtz 1979.*

regulated through ceremony and written and unwritten rules (for example in the form of processions or the performance of the liturgy). The emergence of the tri-partite form at Cheddar can be considered a translation of ecclesiastical into domestic space, affording similar social relationships to be formed and underpinning social hierarchy and identities, in a similar way to that observed at Barnard Castle and Launceston Castle in chapter 4. It was in the entanglement of particular people, constituted of certain sets of social associations, that the agency for the tri-partite form to emerge at Cheddar was developed. The development of the form does not therefore reflect the changing ownership of the site, but rather emerged with it. By extension, I would argue that the agency for the development of the jug form at Cheddar also emerged through this process of entanglement. The tri-partite form asked different things of pottery. In purely functional terms, vessels were required to move liquids around the hall and also to mediate social relationships through serving activity (see chapter 4). Action within these structures spun the agency for the emergence of a new vessel type, the jug. Whereas in some cases the agency for a new industry developed through patronage (for example in the case of the Pound Lane pottery in Canterbury; see Cotter 1997) – the need for a particular type of pottery within particular households leading to the emergence of new forms, the jugs used at Cheddar are largely of Ham Green type (see Barton 1963), with Cheddar benefiting from the development of an industry to supply the port of Bristol. Here, as we shall see in the case of Southampton, the emergence of jugs may have been related to changes in architectural form, but the act of serving translated differently between the bishop's manor at Cheddar (where they were enrolled in the translation of ecclesiastical practice into domestic settings to maintain an identity through the making durable social relationships which transcended the divide between the ecclesiastical and domestic spheres) and merchant houses in ports such as Southampton or Bristol; through particular processes of entanglement therefore the jugs came to afford identity formation and the underpinning of hierarchy in different ways.

Evidence of later Anglo-Saxon domestic buildings in Southampton is scarce due to the ephemeral nature of these timber structures. However, the evidence which survives implies the presence of fairly simple, hall-type structures. As at Cheddar, by 1200 more complex architectural arrangements, built around the tri-partite model emerged and are apparent in surviving stone structures (see Faulkner 1975). Similarly, this period of architectural development is accompanied by the development of new ceramic forms. In Southampton tripod pitchers are a distinctive component of post-conquest ceramic assemblages (Brown 2002, 136), with locally produced jugs being common from around 1250. Here the development of the tri-partite form can be considered to have emerged from a distinctly urban form of agency. The Norman Conquest stimulated a number of changes in Southampton, not least the development of the Guild Merchant and the eventual transition of the town from royal to guild administration, but also expanded trade, leading to the development of wealth in the town. The Conquest appears also to have stimulated the re-building of the town in stone, partly the result of increasing wealth, but also of the opening up of the market for the import of large quantities of building stone from northern France (Jope 1964, 112). Commercial activity was a key set of social associations between people, spaces and things which underpinned the emergence of a distinctively urban form of 'the social' in Southampton, and these associations both spun the agency for and underpinned the maintenance of particular architectural forms, in which shops were included in house frontages. These buildings became a nexus of agency, a coming together of the human and non-human in a way which means they cannot be separated. They emerged with the urban 'social', and with the landscapes, identities and things which came to constitute it. As Rees Jones (2008) argues for York, houses in Southampton developed from a specific set of comings-together, the translation of the tri-partite form from the rural manors, held by many of the wealthy burgesses of Southampton, and particular urban sets of associations between people, spaces and things. Although similar in form, the interiors of urban tri-partite houses likely differed greatly from those at Cheddar (although the material culture of the palace does not permit further discussion). In Southampton, for example, zoomorphic and heraldic imagery permeated various forms of material culture, including pottery and architectural ceramics, images which were not inherently meaningful, but were enrolled in networks of citation associated with knighthood and high status activities such as hunting (see for example Pluskowski 2007, 36) (Figure 6.4). The distribution of jugs in medieval Southampton shows that these are most prevalent in the area around the waterfront (Jervis 2009b; Jervis 2013a) and therefore it can be considered that this form (along with associated forms of material culture, such as glass drinking vessels; see Tyson 2000), within the context of Southampton, emerged with these households. In this light, the translation of the tripartite form into the urban setting, a form commonly associated with high status rural manor houses in the first instance (Gardiner 2008) worked along with these portable elements of interior design to build an atmosphere which had varying, but particular effects upon those who experienced it. Whilst citation can be traced between the manor house and the peasant home, the sparseness of these spaces (see chapter 3), meant that the form was enrolled in the development of a very different atmosphere, and by extension the emergence and maintenance of different forms of social identity, even if elements of household organisation translated between these homes, as suggested by Grenville (2008, 118). In mercantile houses the ceremony of dining was a translation of influences from the worlds of the church and the rural manor, which did not directly re-create the social associations underpinning mercantile identity, but provided a medium through which not only could identity work be managed (see chapter 4), but also in which, through citing ecclesiastical practice, afforded merchants the opportunity to build a particular image of themselves, transmitting an image not only of wealth and power, but also the connected characteristic of virtue (see Thrupp 1948, 15; Tyson 2000, 25). This is particularly apparent in the presence of vessels, such as Saintonge Redware pegaus, vessels which contained large quantities of liquid, which may have assisted in the construction of an image of wealth and generosity when consumed in mercantile houses, particularly in the case of a vessel in Southampton which carries an inscription to Saint Geron, the patron saint of headaches – perhaps alluding to the effects of wine consumption at social gatherings, and maybe, like those inscribed vessels discussed in chapter 3, being enacted as a magical or animistic object which was considered to be able to protect drinkers from these effects (Figure 6.5) (Brown 2002, 28).

It is therefore my contention that the tri-partite form and the jug form developed together. Whilst jugs can be considered in simple terms a product of supply and

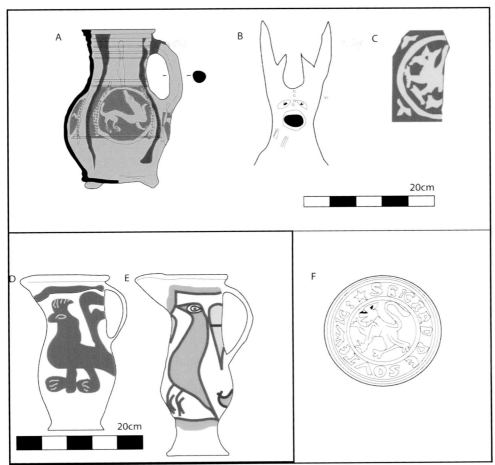

*Figure 6.4. Examples of zoomorphic and heraldic motifs on material culture from the merchants quarter of Southampton. A) Seine Valley Zoomorphic Ware jug. B) Zoomorphic roof furniture. C) Zoomorphic floor tile. D) Saintonge Sgrafitto Ware jug. E) Saintonge Polychrome Ware jug. F) Seal of Richard of Southwick found in a pit at Cuckoo Lane (not to scale). Redrawn from Platt and Coleman-Smith 1975.*

demand, we have seen in the case of Cheddar that the agency for the development of industries was the result of associations in the market or directly between wealthy householders and tenant potters (as can be seen, for example, in the development of the pottery industries of the Saintonge; Musgrave 1998). Far from reflecting a social change, these emerged *with* change, with agency being spun through both the entanglement of local assemblages of people, things and places, which meant that the agency behind these developments was, for example, very different at the bishop's palace at Cheddar to in mercantile houses in Southampton, but also of further reaching sets of social associations, for example between the household at Cheddar and the urban

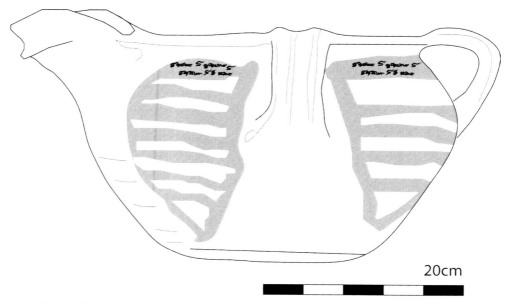

*Figure 6.5. Saintonge Redware pegau from Southampton. Redrawn from Brown 2002.*

market in Bristol. Both pottery and buildings are therefore enrolled in the emergence of a changing social, being part of connected courses of action with multiple and unpredictable effects. Buildings are a materialisation of a set of connections formed between humans and non-humans, which are the effect not only of the formation of direct linkages (*e.g.* through the building of a wall) but also more partial connections, the results of processes of translation, such as those which effect the character of spaces. It is not only people and the fabric of buildings which define their form therefore, but a whole bundle of associations formed inside and outside of the structure, both within a tenement and further away. The rooms without objects are meaningless empty shells, just as objects divorced from any other connections are isolated, meaningless things. It was the interactions between people, spaces and these objects which enacted them, not only leading to their performance characteristics or emergent properties being defined relationally, but also enacting spaces, making them into places through action and having far reaching effects, for example in the negotiation of identities and practicing of devotion, as we have seen in other examples in this book. The relationship between pottery and the tri-partite form was complex. Neither reflects social change but were produced by shifting connections and contributed to this process. Whilst a relationship can be drawn between the emergence of jugs and a functional need to move liquids around the home, this was not a simple case of human agency and the agency of the building coming together, but the spinning of agency through the coming together of these as distributed actor-networks, jugs therefore being the product of far reaching connections, being defined not as functional objects but as social ones. The agency behind their emergence developed through far reaching, entangled, associations. Whilst buildings and artefact assemblages between sites may appear at a superficial level to be similar, we can consider that the processes of social assembly which brought them into being differed greatly, the effect of these processes of entanglement being the emergence of connected but different built spaces and social realities.

## Summary

The aim of this chapter has been to show that the meanings of pottery vary situationally throughout their lives and as they are enacted as objects in different settings. In the case of rubbish it has been argued that categories of rubbish emerged as the result of different courses of action, which extend far beyond the direct associations between people and pottery. The categorisation of pottery however relates directly to the categorisation of the people interacting with it and the features into which waste is dumped, with material coming to afford treatment in particular ways through these interactions. In the case of buildings it has been argued that although superficially similar, varying translations of the tri-partite form emerged in medieval England, with these spaces, as well as the ceramic jugs which emerged with them coming to afford the development of different, but related atmospheres and processes of identity formation and maintenance. In this final set of case studies therefore it has been demonstrated that in order to understand the full meanings, affordances and effects of pottery they must be studied in context, to understand how the meanings of people, spaces and things were mutually constituted in the past and that different effects can emerge from what, might on the surface, appear to be similar courses of action or archaeological signatures.

# 7

# AN EMERGENT
# DISCIPLINE

The aim of this book has been to explore how pottery studies can re-establish itself as a central component in medieval archaeology, through the application of new theoretical concepts allied to existing methodologies, and a consideration of the connected nature of human-material-textual worlds. That is not to say that I sought to give pottery an elevated status which it clearly did not hold in the medieval period, but rather to view it as a conduit through which interpretive thought can flow, as a nexus of the connections which can be conceptualised to have underpinned medieval society. In this final section I wish to briefly discuss the implications of the work presented here for the role of pottery studies, history and theory within medieval archaeology.

## Pottery in Medieval Archaeology

The need for pottery studies, and artefact studies more generally, to be a central component of medieval archaeology has been acknowledged since the 19th century (Pitt-Rivers 1890). However, today much negativity surrounds medieval pottery studies as specialists, particularly those working outside of academic institutions, often feel marginalised from wider research agendas (Blinkhorn and Cumberpatch 2012), whilst non-specialists are often considered to have been ignorant to the interpretive potential that pottery holds. In longer term perspective however, ceramic studies have grown in parallel with the maturing discipline of medieval archaeology, as shown in chapter 1 and also through the discussions which have prefaced each chapter of this book, in which there is a blossoming and growing body of work which seeks to interpret medieval material culture in a variety of ways. Within what we might term the modern field of medieval archaeology the interpretive potential of medieval pottery has long been recognised (Blake 1980; Orton 1985; Moorhouse 1986; Brown 1988a; Davey 1988), but for various reasons this has not been fully realised. A key reason for this has been the need to characterise, date and understand large quantities of material, to put the building blocks in place from which interpretation can develop; indeed the wealth of data available which makes pottery such a valuable resource to archaeologists studying the medieval period has also proved a hindrance as it has necessarily taken generations to build an understanding of typology, chronological sequences and production centres. However, whilst our knowledge of some areas remains limited (see Irving 2011 for regional overviews), those building blocks are largely now in place, thanks in particular to the publication of large corpuses of material from major towns such as Exeter (Allan 1984), Southampton (Brown 2002), Lincoln (Young and Vince 2005), London (Vince 1985) and Norwich (Jennings 1981).

There is still a need to ask questions which specifically relate to the pottery itself, to better understand how it was made, where and for how long, where it was traded to and how it was used. However, by exploring the further potential of the material, by asking questions relating to medieval society which can be answered through the study of pottery, rather than asking questions about the pottery itself, and underpinning the approaches to addressing these questions with an explicit theoretical or interpretive framework, it is now possible for pottery studies to become re-established as a central component of modern medieval archaeology. It has been a failure to adequately explore this potential which has, in part, led to the marginalisation of ceramic studies within the discipline today. In chapter 1 the development of specialist publications was posited as a further reason which pottery studies has become marginalised. However, it is important that such publications remain and that specialists continue to develop the skills and knowledge required to work with pottery. The methods utilised in this book, including petrological analysis and use wear analysis, require specialist expertise, however by interpreting the results, and using scientific data as a means to an interpretive end, rather than the end in itself, it becomes possible to explore broader themes in medieval archaeology using pottery as primary source material. Central to achieving this aim is to move beyond specialist reports as the main form of dissemination and to move towards integrating ceramic studies more closely into discursive or synthetic works, making the data central to interpretation, rather than providing illustrative supporting information to the grand narrative provided by the integration of history and stratigraphic or landscape scale data.

These proposals are not revolutionary in themselves however. The study of identity has been particularly well served by the study of medieval pottery (Blinkhorn 1997; Naum 2011; Kyle 2012; Vroom 2011; see chapter 4). These studies have examined how people engage with pottery through production and use, critiquing prevailing concepts in which material culture reflects identity, to explore the various ways in which practice may have contributed to the emergence and maintenance of identities in the past. In the preceding chapters I have sought to explore new areas in which the study of pottery can contribute to the wider fields of medieval archaeology and medieval studies. The adoption of elements of a biographical approach within a relational framework has been key to exploring broader themes of landscape, architecture and identity through pottery studies. By asking new questions of pottery it has been possible to conceptualise and categorise it in different ways, being more than formal typology and fabric series, to being objects which were enacted and enrolled through processes of becoming. By seeing pottery as a multi-facetted research resource in the present, we are also able to explore the fluidity of pottery and other items of material culture in the past, by tracking the various ways in which it was drawn into relationships with people, things, spaces and documents throughout its use-life we can explore its multiple effects and how pottery as a meaningful object was mutually constituted with meaningful places and identities.

We have the methodologies required to explore these inter-relations. Petrological analysis for example can be used to relate pottery to the land, use wear analysis, combined with the study of food remains links us to issues of diet and cuisine and depositional analysis allows us to consider the afterlife of pottery. The study of skeuomorphs in chapter 3 highlighted that in studying pottery and objects in other materials we need to be open to blurring divisions and overcoming modern concepts of materials being complementary to one another, to consider issues of sameness, formed as material properties are experienced and items develop situational performance characteristics which may cut across modern divisions. The only way to achieve such an outcome however is to work in an integrated manner, exploring the relationships and interconnections between objects through true interdisciplinary study, rather than addressing the same question through the cross-disciplinary analysis of varying sources of information. The same is true of the relationship between pottery studies and history; as demonstrated in chapter 3 and also through the discussion of rules of etiquette in chapter 4 and charters in chapter 5, there is much to be gained through an analysis of the relationships between people, things and texts, rather than taking text as a passive reflection of the role of material culture in medieval society. By focussing on these connections, and turning pottery studies into an outward looking, rather than insular, endeavour, ceramics automatically become woven into the discipline of medieval archaeology. In doing so, it also becomes possible to move beyond seeing pottery as simply reflecting medieval life, but to explore the effects it had upon the everyday experiences of people and the development of the patchwork of associations which constitute the medieval social.

## Medieval Archaeology and Medieval History

The presence of text poses a challenge for the medieval archaeologist, not faced by our prehistorian colleagues. As we have seen in chapters 1 and 3 the relationship between medieval archaeology and medieval history has been a difficult one, as archaeology has sought to emerge from the shadow of history. Interdisciplinary research, in various guises, is becoming increasingly common, however, more accurately the majority of this work is cross disciplinary (see Wicker 1999), in that it utilises archaeological and historical material in support of each other, rather than exploring the fundamental links and relationships which developed between these sources in the medieval period. Such an approach is designed to play to the strengths of each discipline, to generate more rounded understanding of the past. However, in chapter 3 I outlined a different approach, one which allows archaeologists to engage with history on equal terms through exploring the connectedness of texts and things, which allows us to explore the effects of these comings-together on the emergence and maintenance of the medieval 'social'. It may seem odd at first that a book which uses pottery as its core source material should pass comment on the utility of text for archaeologists. However, by focussing on the relationships through which pottery developed meaning and had effects within and upon medieval society, text has been an ever present actor which demands inclusion in discourse. This has been seen, for example, through the role of courtesy texts in the negotiation of identities at the medieval table (chapter 4) and in the charters and rules which play a role in the emergence of landscapes (chapter 5). Documents are an ever present in medieval archaeology, although the may be present in different guises and quantities. If we are to fully understand the medieval past we must take them seriously in archaeological discourse, by understanding how the production and use of these documents influenced action and therefore the form which 'the social' could take, and the formation of the archaeological record.

The most tangible and direct discussion of this relationship however was presented in the discussion of peasant inventories (chapter 3). By exploring the interplay between pottery, text and people, it became clear that the meaning of the text was reliant on the objects, whilst the meaning of objects was negotiated and made durable through the formation and use of text. This is not simply text-aided archaeology. Rather I have outlined the beginnings of an approach in which action and the formation of relationships becomes central, allowing us to not simply reconstruct how things were, but to understand the process through which they became and stayed that way. This is where the core potential of this approach lies. By forcing archaeologists to consider the presence of text in social relationships, as more than representational parts of the material record of medieval life, we can acknowledge that documents do not simply say how things were, but, just like objects, were fundamental in making them that way.

The role of text as material culture deserves to be the subject of a book in its own right (see for example Andrén 1998), however what is vital to building a relational understanding of the past is acknowledging its presence. Certainly documents have very different material properties to other forms of material culture, but, just like any other object, their meaning is reliant upon constant re-enrollment in social action. Like any other forms of material culture, they emerge through particular courses of action, which other actors are enrolled into, and have biographies where they are variously enacted as different objects at different times. Sometimes this is done consciously whilst at others, documents act as a 'black-box', moderating durability in the background, as they retreat to the malaise of thingness, being present but enrolled, but not consciously enacted in courses of action. Empiricist, cross disciplinary, historical archaeology certainly has a role to play in building our understanding of the past. However, if we wish to be truly interdisciplinary we must develop mechanisms through which we can explore the inter-relationships and interplays between texts, objects and spaces in the past, by engaging with text as part of the courses of social action through which medieval society was assembled and maintained, rather than being somehow separate to it. A relational approach, in which our methods force us to explore the connectedness of various forms of evidence provides an opportunity to break down this disciplinary barrier, to situate pottery studies not just within medieval archaeology, but within a wider discipline of medieval studies.

## Theory and Medieval Archaeology

Medieval archaeology can no longer be considered to be a-theoretical (leaving aside the fact that all interpretation has some kind of implicit theoretical assumptions behind it). Over the last 20 years or so medieval archaeologists have become increasingly aware of theoretical developments in other branches of archaeology and have sought to develop these ideas further, for example through the adoption of ideas of structured deposition (Hamerrow 2006; Morris and Jervis 2011), gender archaeology (Gilchrist 1999) or animism and distributed personhood (Williams and Nugent 2012). Whilst many of the ideas presented in this book are influenced by the application of Actor-Network Theory and associated interpretive frameworks in prehistoric and historical archaeology, the main source of inspiration has been the social theory, particularly that of Bruno Latour, and application of this in other disciplines (particularly human geography). This has been a quite deliberate return to the source material, to allow the development of a relational medieval archaeology, rather than a simple transfer and adaptation of archaeological theory, developed through work in relation to other periods or places. This is best demonstrated through the discussion of how text may be woven into a relational medieval archaeology, by developing an interpretive approach which is tailored to the specific character of medieval archaeology. Furthermore, medieval archaeologists are in a considerably stronger position than (certainly British) prehistoric archaeologists to take the lead in developing theory of relevance to all branches of medieval archaeology – we have considerably more data available to us and a great deal of information available to contextualise this data, principally in the form of text. The challenge for medieval archaeologists is therefore not to *become* theoretical, but rather to *develop* relevant and specific forms of archaeological theory, through embracing insights from other disciplines, and to make developments from which archaeologists of other periods may seek inspiration, taking the lead as a mature contributor to the wider discipline of archaeology, rather than being a timid follower of interpretive trends.

The approaches taken in this book have allowed the exploration of this approach and has identified a number of benefits to such an approach. In particular, they allow us to move from a static and anthropocentric view of medieval society, to explore issues of fluidity and material agency. The adoption of the metaphor of material culture as text has ultimately led to the adoption of the concept of *habitus* in the analysis of medieval material culture (*e.g.* Blinkhorn 1997) and built spaces (*e.g.* Gilchrist 1994; Giles 2000) and has meant that material culture has come to be viewed as a symbol, with contextual meaning to be unravelled, for example in the case of pottery decoration (Richards 1986; Cumberpatch 2006) or town plans (Lilley 2004). Such approaches are anthropocentric, privileging human experience, action and understanding over the material properties of the 'stuff' under discussion (Ingold 2007). The approach adopted here seeks to re-instate the importance of material properties, alongside the emergent properties of things, to explore the fluidity of the meaning of things (in terms of their affordances or performance characteristics), whilst balancing this against the restrictions placed on action by these material properties. This has been seen for example in the discussion of the affordances of waste in chapters 5 and 6 and the exploration of the relationship between ceramic and metal vessels in chapter 3. The approach therefore shifts meaning from being entirely arbitrary and contextual, to emerging through action, as context emerges with meaning, through the engagements between people and material things (see Boivin 2004; Malafouris 2004). Following such an approach, the concept of *habitus*, as a structuring influence must be viewed in critical perspective, by acknowledging that it does not pre-exist action, but rather the agency for it forms through action (Chapman and Gaydarska 2011, 23), meaning that it too is not the force which methodically maintains 'the social', but rather a form of translation in which past experiences are drawn together with material properties to determine the emergence of affordances and the development of heterogeneous, but connected social realities.

In moving away from an anthropocentric view of the world, to one in which the material world is enrolled, the concept of agency has been reconfigured, shifting from being the property of humans, to a force which develops through the comings-together of action (see chapter 2). This has allowed the effects of things upon people to be explored, but also, through a discussion of magic and animism in chapter 3, provided a means through which it might be possible to archaeologically explore medieval ontology, in which, in certain circumstances, the modernist division between person and non-person may have not been present. A re-configuration of the concept of agency allows us to examine the multiple effects that action might have; both the intended and unintended consequences, which allow us to form both a thicker and more pluralistic understanding of past societies. By opening up this possibility, a relational approach offers a way of looking at data in which we can begin to address issues raised by broader theoretical critiques, such as the post-colonial critique, which demand us to address plurality, but do not necessarily provide a toolkit with which to achieve this aim archaeologically. This has been seen in particular through the discussion of identity in chapter 4, where the multiple effects of cooking practices in relation to experiences of continuity and change surrounding the Norman Conquest were considered, to demonstrate that the same or related courses of action could cause people to see themselves very differently in relation to their surroundings. Furthermore, by exploring how the agency to build identities develops at the medieval dining table, the effects of calculated interactions with material culture on people drawn into action have also been explored, to demonstrate how the agency for identity formation may not reside within an individual, but rather forms through their relationship with their surroundings. Such an approach draws upon ideas of relational personhood, and allow us to re-conceptualise ideas of identity, from a focus on pre-defined groups relating to gender, ethnicity or social status, to explore the ways through which groups form through people interacting with their surroundings, meaning identities can be traced archaeologically through the re-construction of action, rather than being sought out in the analysis of archaeological material.

A focus on tracing courses of action integrates theory and method, as we seek to reconstruct the entangled biographies of people, places and things. We have methods available to achieve these aims, as discussed above, but in order to draw broader conclusions it is necessary to explore the effects of these courses of action. By following action we come to appreciate the fluid nature of meaning, as things are enacted as objects, with specific affordances and effects, which become something else, perhaps simultaneously as they are pulled in another direction. A focus on action and connectivity forces us not only to embrace an interpretive framework compatible with concepts of fluidity, but also forces us to work in a symmetrical manner, identifying connections and treating data with equal weight. The advantages of such an approach in relation to historical and archaeological data have been discussed above, but it is equally relevant in archaeological practice. An acknowledgement that people, places and things are mutually constituted through the formation of associations through action collapses scales, as landscapes and things are formed in the same way. Such a perspective automatically draws the study of material culture into the study of landscape (chapter 5), or the study of people (identity) into the analysis of pottery (chapter 4). Therefore a relational medieval archaeology is one in which method and theory are reliant upon each other, and one in which specialists are not marginalised, but work together in a symmetrical manner to identify the connections between their materials, rather than discussing them in terms of others (for example the common practice of discussing material culture in terms of stratigraphic data). Tracing connections and considering the effects of the actions through which these associations forms allows us to create not a single understanding of medieval society, but a dynamic patchwork of mutating associations, in which varying but connected social realties emerged, with multiple understandings of objects, places and identities.

It is not my intention to convert all medieval archaeologists to a relational approach. Rather, I have sought to demonstrate that by closely integrating method and theory it becomes possible to develop a framework in which the fluid and multiple realities of life can be explored, and in which data is interrogated to develop new ideas, rather than being used as an illustrative representation of existing concepts of what the past was like. Medieval archaeologists should not be afraid of change, rather by embracing new ideas it becomes possible to ask new questions, to use old data in new ways and, crucially, to allow specialists to move from the margins to becoming enrolled in the emergence of a discipline in which all material residues of human life are considered together, and the actions which led to the formation of these residues are understood not as happening within a social context, but as the components of that context.

## Summary

This book has utilised a relational approach to explore how pottery can be used as source material for medieval archaeology, rather than supporting interpretations developed through the study of landscapes, buildings or documents. By focussing on reconstructing action it has been possible to explore the relationships formed between pottery, other objects, people, spaces and documents, which do not reflect medieval society, but were constitutive of it. The advantage of such an approach is that it allows us to explore variability and fluidity and therefore build a thicker, multi-layered understanding of a 'social' which was constantly in a transient state. Such an approach has allowed us to traverse scales, from people, to landscapes and back to domestic spaces, to consider how interactions with pottery played a role in the emergence of people, places and documents and how the meaning of pottery emerged from this interaction, meaning that it was far from being a simple meaningless tool. The aim has not to be to give pottery importance, but rather to use the study of pottery as a way into developing an approach in which the relationships between things are understood as the threads which hold society together. In doing so, pottery becomes a central component of medieval archaeology, which has much to offer as metalwork, buildings or landscapes, and which must be studied not in isolation, but as enmeshed within these other components of the medieval 'social', which include text. A relational approach therefore not only offers an interpretive framework, but also a methodological impetus to undertake integrated study, in which we are all medievalists first, archaeologists second and pottery specialists third – in which we set out to write about medieval society and pottery's role within it, rather than marginalising ourselves by writing about pottery from a medieval context.

# BIBLIOGRAPHY

*Primary Sources*
Chibnall, M. (trans; ed). 1969, *The Ecclesiastical History of Orderic Vitalis*. (6 vols), Clarendon Press.
Studer, P. (ed). 1910, *The Oak Book of Southampton of c. AD1300, Volume 1*, Southampton Records Society.

*References Cited*
Abels, R. 1988, *Lordship and Military Obligation in Anglo-Saxon England*, University of California Press.
Abrams, L. 2012, 'Diaspora and Identity in the Viking Age', *Early Medieval Europe* 20(1), 17–38.
Albarella, U. 2005, 'Meat production and consumption in town and country', in K. Giles and C. Dyer (eds), *Town and Country in The Middle Ages. Contrasts, Contacts and Interconnections, 1100–1500*, Society for Medieval Archaeology Monograph 22, 129–48
Alberti, B. 2012, 'Cut, Pinch and Pierce. Images as Practice Among the Early Formative La Candelaria, First Millenium AD, Northwest Argentina', in I.M. Back Daniellson, F. Fahlander and Y. Sjostrand (eds), *Encountering Imagery. Materialities, Perceptions, Relations*, Stockholm Studies in Archaeology 57, 13–28.
Alberti, B. and Bray, T. 2009, 'Introduction', *Cambridge Archaeological Journal* 19(3), 337–43.
Alberti, B. and Marshall, Y. 2009, 'Animating Archaeology: Local Theories and Conceptually Open-Ended Methodologies', *Cambridge Archaeological Journal* 19(3), 344–56.
Allan, J. 1984, *Medieval and Post Medieval Finds from Exeter*, Exeter University Press.
Allan, J. 1994, 'Imported Pottery in South-West England, c.1350–1550', *Medieval Ceramics* 18, 45–50.
Allen, D. 2011, 'On Actor-Network Theory and Landscape', *Area* 43(3), 274–80.
Anderson, B. and Harrison, P. (eds) 2010, *Taking Place: Non-Representational Theories and Geography*, Ashgate
Andrén, A. 1998, *Between Artifacts and Texts. Historical Archaeology in Global Perspective*, Plenum Press.
Appadurai, A. 1986, 'Introduction: Commodities and the Politics of Value' in A. Appadurai (ed), *The Social Life of Things: Commodities in Cultural Perspective*, Cambridge University Press, 3–63.
Arnold, C. 1986, 'Archaeology and History: The Shades of Confrontation and Cooperation', in J. Bintliff and C. Gaffney (eds), *Archaeology at the Interface: Studies in Archaeology's Relationships with History, Geography, Biology and Physical Science*, BAR Int. Ser. 300, 32–9.
Arnold, D. 1971, 'Ethnominerology of Ticul, Yucatan Potters: Etics and Emics', *American Antiquity* 36(1), 20–40.
Arnold, D. 2000, 'Does the Standardization of Ceramic Pastes Really Mean Specialization?', *Journal of Archaeological Method and Theory* 7(4), 333–75.

Astill, G. 2006, 'Community Identity and the Later Anglo-Saxon Town: The Case of Southern England', in W. Davies, H. Halsall and A. Reynolds (eds), *People and Space in the Middle Ages 300–1300*, Brepols, 233–54.

Attreed, L. 2002, 'Urban Identity in Medieval English Towns', *Journal of Interdisciplinary History* 32(4), 571–92.

Austin, D. 1990, 'The 'Proper Study' of Medieval Archaeology', in D. Austin and L. Alcock (eds) *From the Baltic to the Black Sea. Studies in Medieval Archaeology*, Routledge, 9–42.

Austin, D. 2007a, *Acts of Perception: A Study of Barnard Castle in Teesdale Volume I,* The Architectural and Archaeological Society of Durham and Northumberland Research Report 6.

Austin, D. 2007b. *Acts of Perception: A Study of Barnard Castle in Teesdale Volume II*, The Architectural and Archaeological Society of Durham and Northumberland Research Report 6.

Austin, D. and Thomas, J. 1990, 'The 'Proper Study' of Medieval Archaeology: A Case Study', In D. Austin and L. Alcock (eds) *From the Baltic to the Black Sea. Studies in Medieval Archaeology*, Routledge, 43–78.

Baart, J. 1994, 'Dutch Redwares', *Medieval Ceramics* 18, 19–27.

Back Daniellson, I.M., Fahlander, F. and Sjostrand, Y. 2012, 'Image Beyond Representation' in I.M., Back Daniellson, F. Fahlander and Y. Sjostrand (eds), *Encountering Imagery. Materialities, Perceptions, Relations*, Stockholm Studies in Archaeology 57 1–12.

Bailey, M. 2001, 'From Sorcery to Witchcraft: Clerical Conceptions of Magic in the Later Middle Ages', *Speculum* 76(4), 960–90.

Bailey, M. 2006, 'The Meanings of Magic', *Magic, Ritual and Witchcraft* 1(1), 1–23.

Bailey, M. 2008, 'Concerns over Superstition in Late Medieval Europe', *Past and Present (sup. 3)*, 115–33.

Barker, E. 1947, 'Sussex Anglo-Saxon Charters', *Sussex Archaeological Collections* 86, 42–101.

Bartlett, R. 2001, 'Medieval and Modern Concepts of Race and Ethnicity', *Journal of Medieval and Early Modern Studies* 31(1), 39–56

Barton, K. 1963, 'A Medieval Pottery Kiln at Ham Green, Bristol', *Transactions of the Bristol and Gloucestershire Archaeological Society* 82, 95–126.

Barton, K. 1966a, 'The Medieval Pottery of Paris', *Medieval Archaeology* 10, 59–73.

Barton, K. 1966b, 'Medieval Pottery ay Rouen', *The Archaeological Journal* 122, 73–85.

Barton, K. 1974, 'The Medieval Blackwares of Northern France', in V. Evison, J. Hurst and H. Hodges, (eds), *Medieval Pottery from Excavations: Studies Presented to Gerald Clough Dunning*, John Baker, 167–82.

Barton, K. 1977, 'Some Examples of Medieval Oxidized and Decorated Earthenwares Occurring in North-Eastern France', *Medieval Archaeology* 21, 47–67.

Barrett, J. 2004,' Response to Round Barrows and Dykes as Landscape Methaphors by C. Tilley', *Cambridge Archaeological Journal* 14(2), 199.

Baumgarten, E. 2008, 'A Separate People? Some Directions for Comparative Research on Medieval Women', *Journal of Medieval History* 34, 212–228

Beaudry, M. 1988, 'Words for Things: Linguistic Analysis of Probate Inventories', in M. Beaudry (ed), *Documentary Archaeology in the New World*, Cambridge University Press, 43–50.

Beck, M. and Hill, M. 2004, 'Rubbish, Relatives and Residence: The Family Use of Middens', *Journal of Archaeological Method and Theory* 11(3), 297–333.

Beddel, J. 2000, 'Archaeology and Probate Inventories in the Study of Eighteenth-Century Life', *Journal of Interdisciplinary History* 31(2), 223–45.

Bedos-Rezak, B. 2000, 'Medieval Identity: A Sign and a Concept', *The American Historical Review* 105(5), 1489–1533.

Beresford, G. 1979, 'Three Deserted Medieval Settlements on Dartmoor: A Report on the Late E. Marie Minter's Excavations', *Medieval Archaeology* 23, 98–158.

Berta, P. 2009, 'Materialising Ethnicity: Commodity Fetishism and Symbolic Re-Creation of Objects Among the Gabor Roma (Romania)', *Social Anthropology* 17(2), 184–97.

Bhabha, H. 2004, *The Location of Culture*, Routledge.

Binford, L. 1968, *New Perspectives in Archaeology*, Aldine.

Bintliff, J. 1986, 'Archaeology at the Interface: An Historical Perspective', in J. Bintliff and C. Gaffney (eds), *Archaeology at the Interface: Studies in Archaeology's Relationships with History, Geography, Biology and Physical Science*, BAR Int. Ser. 300, 4–31.

Blackmore, L. and Pearce, J. 2010, *A Dated Type Series of London Medieval Pottery: Shelly-Sandy Ware and the Greyware Industries*, MoLAS Monograph 49.

Blair, J. 1993, 'Hall and Chamber; English Domestic Planning 1000–1250', in G. Meirion-Jones and M. Jones (eds), *Manorial Domestic Buildings in England and Northern France*, Society of Antiquaries Occasional Paper 15, 1–21.

Blake, H. 1980, 'Technology, Supply or Demand?', *Medieval Ceramics* 4, 3–12.

Blake, H., Egan, G., Hurst, J. and New, E. 2003, 'From Popular Devotion to Resistance and Revival in England: The Cult of the Holy Name of Jesus and the Reformation', in D. Gaimster and R. Gilchrist (eds), *The Archaeology of Reformation 1480–1580*, Maney, 175–203.

Blinkhorn, P. 1997, 'Habitus, Social Identity and Anglo-Saxon Pottery', in P. Blinkhorn and C. Cumberpatch (eds), *Not So Much a Pot, More a Way of Life*, Oxbow, 113–124.

Blinkhorn, P. 1999, 'The Trials of Being a Utensil: Pottery Function at the Medieval Hamlet of West Cotton, Northamptonshire', *Medieval Ceramics* 22–23, 37–46.

Blinkhorn, P. 2012. *The Ipswich Ware Project. Ceramics, Trade and Society in Middle Saxon England*, Medieval Pottery Research Group Occasional Paper 7.

Blinkhorn, P. and Cumberpatch, C. 1998, 'The Interpretation of Artefacts and the Tyranny of the Field Archaeologist', *Assemblage* 4. http://www.assemblage.group.shef.ac.uk/4/4bln_cmb.html

Blinkhorn, P. and Cumberpatch, C. 2012. 'Not so Much a Pot, More an Expensive Luxury: Analysis and Archaeology in the 21st Century', Paper given at the Theoretical Archaeology Group Conference, University of Liverpool, December 2012. http://www.academia.edu/2310508/_Not_so_Much_a_Pot_More_an_Expensive_Luxury_Pottery_analysis_and_archaeology_in_the_21st_century_

Boivin, N. 2000, 'Life Rhythms and Floor Sequences: Excavating Time in Rural Rajasthan and Neolithic Chatalhoyuk', *World Archaeology* 31(3), 367–88.

Boivin, N. 2004, 'Mind Over Matter? Collapsing the Mind-Matter Dichotomy in Material Culture Studies', in E. DeMarrais, C. Gosden and C. Renfrew, (eds), *Rethinking Materiality: The Engagement of Mind with the Material World*, Cambridge: McDonald Institute Monograph, 63–71.

Boone, M. 2002, 'Urban Space and Political Conflict in Late Medieval Flanders', *Journal of Interdisciplinary History*, 621–40.

Bourdieu, P. 1977, *Outline of a Theory of Practice*, Cambridge University Press.

Bourdillon, J. 1980, 'Town Life and Animal Husbandry in the Southampton Area, as Suggested by the Excavated Bones', *Proceedings of the Hampshire Field Club Archaeological Society* 36, 181–191.

Boyd, R. 2009, 'The Irish Viking Age: A Discussion of Architecture, Settlement Patterns and Identity', *Viking and Medieval Scandinavia* 5, 271–94.

Braithwaite, M. 1982, 'Decoration as Ritual Symbol: A Theoretical Proposal and an Ethnographic Study in Southern Sudan', in I. Hodder, (ed), *Symbolic and Structural Archaeology*, Cambridge University Press, 80–8.

Briggs, C. Forthcoming, 'Manorial Court Roll Inventories as Evidence of English Peasant Consumption and Living Standards, c.1270–c.1420' in A. Furió and F. Garcia-Oliver (eds) *Pautas de Consumo y Niveles de Vida en el Mundo Rural Medieval*, University of Valencia Press.

Brisbane, M. 1981, 'Incipient Markets for Early Anglo-Saxon Ceramics: Variations in Levels and Modes of Production' in H. Howard and E. Morris, (eds), *Production and Distribution: A Ceramic Viewpoint*, Oxford, BAR Int. Ser. 120, 229–42.

Brown, B. 2001, 'Thing Theory', *Critical Inquiry* 28(1), 1–22.

Brown, D. 1985, 'Looking at Cross Fits', *Medieval Ceramics* 9, 35–42.

Brown, D. 1988a, 'Pottery and Archaeology', *Medieval Ceramics* 8, 15–22.

Brown, D. 1988b, 'Some Medieval Archaeology', *Scottish Archaeological Review* 5, 95–7.

Brown, D. 1994a, 'Contexts, Their Contents and Residuality' in L. Shepherd (ed), *Interpreting Stratigraphy* 5, http://www.york.ac.uk/archaeology/strat/pastpub/95nor.htm

Brown, D. 1994b, 'Pottery and Late Saxon Southampton', *Proceedings of the Hampshire Field Club Archaeological Society* 50, 127–52.

Brown, D. 1997, 'Pots from Houses', *Medieval Ceramics* 21, 83–94.

Brown, D. 1998, 'Documentary Sources as Evidence for the Exchange and Consumption of Pottery in 15th Century Southampton', Actas das 2. *As Jornadas de Ceramica Medieval e Pos-Medieval – metos e resultados para o seu estudo*, 429–38.

Brown, D. 1999, 'Class and Rubbish', in P. Funari, M. Hall and S. Jones (eds), *Historical Archaeology, Back from the Edge*, Routledge, 150–63.

Brown, D. 2002, *Pottery in Medieval Southampton*, CBA Research Report 137.

Brown, D. 2003. 'Bound by Tradition: A Study of Pottery in Anglo Saxon England', in D. Griffiths, A. Reynolds and S. Semple, (eds), *Anglo Saxon Studies in Archaeology and History* 12, Oxford University Press, 21–27.

Brown, D. 2005, 'Pottery and Manners', in M. Carroll, D. Hadley and H. Willmott, (eds), *Consuming Passions. Dining From Antiquity to the Eighteenth Century*, Tempus, 87–99.

Brown, D., Thomson, R., Vince, A. and Williams, D. 2006, 'The Pottery' in A. Saunders (ed), *Excavations at Launceston Castle, Cornwall*, Society for Medieval Archaeology Monograph, 24, 269–96.

Brown, M. 1988, 'The Behavioural Context of Probate Inventories: An Example from Plymouth Colony', in M. Beaudry (ed), *Documentary Archaeology in the New World*, Cambridge University Press, 79–82.

Brown, L. and Walker, W. 2008, 'Prologue: Archaeology, Animism and Non-Human Agents', *Journal of Archaeological Method and Theory* 15, 297–99.

Brück, J. 1999a, 'Houses, Lifecycles and Deposition on Middle Bronze Age Settlements in Southern England', *Proceedings of the Prehistoric Society* 65, 245–77.

Brück, J. 1999b, 'Ritual and Rationality: Some Problems of Interpretation in European Archaeology', *European Journal of Archaeology* 2(3), 313–44.

Brück, J. 2004, 'Response to Round Barrows and Dykes as Landscape Features by C. Tilley', *Cambridge Archaeological Journal* 14(2), 201.

Brück, J. 2006, 'Fragmentation, Personhood and the Social Construction of Technology in Middle and Late Bronze Age Britain', *Cambridge Archaeological Journal* 16(3), 297–315.

Brughmans, T. 2010, 'Connecting the Dots: Towards Archaeological Network Analysis', *Oxford Journal of Archaeology* 29(3), 277–303.

Bryant, V. 2012, 'The Mystery of the Missing Miskins. Rubbish Disposal and Dispersal in a Medieval Urban Context', *Medieval Ceramics* 32, 1–8.

Buteux, V. and Jackson, R. 2000, 'Rethinking the Rubbish Pit in Medieval Worcester', in S. Roskams (ed), *Interpreting Stratigraphy : Site Evaluation, Recording Procedures and Stratigraphic Analysis*, BAR Int. Ser. 910, 193–6.

Callon, M. 1999, 'Actor-network Theory – The Market Test', in J. Law and J. Hassard (eds), *Actor Network Theory and After*, Blackwell/The Sociological Review, 181–95.

Cañete, C. and Vives-Ferrándiz, J. 2011, 'Almost the Same: Dynamic Domination and Hybrid Contexts in Iron Age Lixus, Larache, Morroco', *World Archaeology* 43(1), 124–43.

Casella, E. and Croucher K. 2011, 'Beyond Human: The Materiality of Personhood', *Feminist Theory* 12, 209–17.

Chaffers, W. 1850, 'On Medieval Earthenware Vessels', *Journal of the British Archaeological Association* 5, 22–39.

Chapman, J. and Gaydarska, B. 2011, 'Can we Reconcile Individualisation with Relational Peronhood? A Case Study from the Early Neolithic', *Documenta Praehistorica* 38, 21–44.

Clarke, D. 1968, *Analytical Archaeology*, Methuen.

Cochrane, A. 2012, 'The Immanency of the Intangible Image. Thoughts with Neolithic Expression at Loughcrew', in I.M. Back Daniellson, F. Fahlander and Y. Sjostrand (eds), *Encountering Imagery. Materialities, Perceptions, Relations*, Stockholm Studies in Archaeology 57, 133–60.

Cohn, S. 2012, 'Renaissance Attachment to Things: Material Culture in Last Wills and Testaments', *The Economic History Review* 63(3), 984–1004.

Conneller, C. 2011, *An Archaeology of Materials. Substantial Transformations in Early Prehistoric Europe*, Routledge.

Conradson, D. 2005, 'Landscape, Care and the Relational Self: Therapeutic Encounters in Rural England', *Health and Place* 11, 337–48.

Corcos, N. 2001, 'Churches as Pre-Historic Ritual Monuments: A Phenomenological Perspective from Somerset', *Assemblage* 6, http://www.assemblage.group.shef.ac.uk/issue6/Corcos_web.html)

Cotter, J. 1997, *A Twelfth-Century Pottery Kiln at Pound Lane, Canterbury: Evidence for an Immigrant Potter in the late Norman Period*, Canterbury Archaeology Trust Occasional Paper 1.

Cotter, J. 2006, 'The Site and its Pottery Supply', in K. Parfitt, B. Corke and J. Cotter, *Townwall Street, Dover: Excavations 1996*, The Archaeology of Canterbury New Series 3, 407–16.

Courtney, P. 1997, 'Ceramics and the History of Consumption: Pitfalls and Prospects', *Medieval Ceramics* 21, 95–108.

Crane, B. 2000, 'Filth, Garbage and Rubbish: Refuse Disposal, Sanitary Reform and Nineteenth-Century Yard Deposits in Washington DC', *Historical Archaeology* 34(1), 20–38.

Creese, J. 2012, 'The Domestication of Personhood: A view from the Northern Iriquoian Longhouse', *Cambridge Archaeological Journal* 22(3), 365–86.

Creighton, O. and Liddiard, R. 2008, 'Fighting Yesterday's Battle: Beyond War and Status in Castle Studies', *Medieval Archaeology* 52, 85–93.

Crombie, L. 2011, 'Unity and Honour in the Feasts of the Archery and Crossbow Cofraternities of Bruges', 1445–1481, *Journal of Medieval History* 37(1), 102–13.

Croucher, S. 2010, 'Developing an Archaeology of African Consumers', *Archaeological Dialogues* 17(1), 33–7.

Cubbit, C. 2000, 'Monastic Memory and Identity in Early Anglo-Saxon England' in W. Frazer and A. Tyrrell (eds), *Social Identity in Early Medieval Britain*, Leicester University Press, 253–76.

Cumberpatch, C. 1997, 'Towards a Phenomenological Approach to the Study of Medieval Pottery', in P. Blinkhorn and C. Cumberpatch (eds), *Not So Much a Pot, More a Way of Life*, Oxbow, 125–51.

Cumberpatch, C. 2006, 'Face-to Face With Medieval Pottery: Some Observations on Medieval Anthropomorphic Pottery in North-east England', *Assemblage* 9, http://www.assemblage.group.shef. ac.uk/issue9/cumberpatch.html

Curta, F. 2007, 'Some Remarks on Ethnicity in Medieval Archaeology', *Early Medieval Europe* 15(2), 159–85.

Dalwood, H. and Bryant, V. 2004, 'Rubbish Disposal', in H. Dalwood and R. Edwards (eds), *Excavations at Deansway, Worcester, 1988–89: Romano-British Small Town to Late Medieval City*, CBA Research Report 139, 84–8.

Damen, M. 2007, 'Princely Entries and Gift Exchange in the Burgundian Low Countries: A Crucial Link in Late Medieval Political Culture', *Journal of Medieval History* 33(3), 233–49.

Davey, P. 1988, 'Theory and Practice in Medieval Ceramic Studies', *Medieval Ceramics* 12, 3–14.

Davey, P. 2000, 'Identity and Ethnicity: A Ceramic Case-Study from the Isle of Man', *Medieval Ceramics* 24, 31–9.

Davey, P. and Hodges, R. 1983, 'Ceramics and Trade: A Critique of the Archaeological Evidence', in P. Davey and R. Hodges (eds), *Ceramics and Trade*, Sheffield: University of Sheffield, 1–16.

DeBoer, W. and Lathrap, D. 1979, 'The Making and Breaking of Shipibo-Conibo Ceramics', in C. Kramer (ed), *Ethno-archaeology. Implications of Ethnography for Archaeology*, Columbia University Press, 102–38.

De Clerq, W., Dumolyn, J. and Haemers, J. 2007. "Vivre Noblement": Material Culture and Elite Identity in Late Medieval Flanders, *Journal of Interdisciplinary History* 38(1), 1–31.

Dellino-Musgrave, V. 2005, 'British Identities Through Pottery in Praxis: The Case Study of a Royal Navy Ship in the South Atlantic', *Journal of Material Culture* 10(3), 219–43.

Dewsbury, J. 2010. 'Language and Event: The Unthought of Appearing Worlds', in B. Anderson and P. Harrison (eds), *Taking Place: Non-Representational Theories and Geography*, Ashgate, 147–60.

Dewsbury, J., Harrison, P., Rose, M. and Wylie, J. 2002, 'Introduction: Enacting Geographies', *Geoforum* 33, 437–40.

Dolwick, J. 2008, 'In Search of the Social: Steamboats, Square Wheels, Reindeer and Other Things', *Journal of Maritime Archaeology* 3(1), 15–41.

Douglas, M, 1966, *Purity and Danger*, Routledge.

Douny, L. 2007, 'The Materiality of Domestic Waste. The Recycled Cosmology of the Dogon of Mali', *Journal of Material Culture* 12(3), 309–31.

Dowdell, G. 1990, 'Excavations at Sully Castle 1963–9', *The Bulletin Board of Celtic Studies* 37, 308–60.

Drell, J. 1999, 'Cultural Syncretism and Ethnic Identity: The Norman 'conquest' of Southern Italy and Sicily', *Journal of Medieval History* 25(3), 187–202.

Driscoll, S. 1984, 'The New Medieval Archaeology: Theory vs History', *Scottish Archaeological Review* 3, 104–9.

Driscoll, S. 1988, 'The Relationship Between History and Archaeology: Artefacts, Documents and Power', In S. Driscoll and M. Nieke (eds), *Power and Politics in Early Medieval Britain and Ireland*, Edinburgh University Press.

Duffy, E. 2006, 'Elite and Popular Religion: The Book of Hours and Lay Piety in The Later Middle Ages', in K. Cooper and J. Gregory (eds), *Elite and Popular Religion*, The Ecclesiastical History Society, 140–61.

Dunning, G. 1967, 'Late Medieval Jugs with Lettering', *Medieval Archaeology* 11, 233–41.

Dunning, G. 1968, 'The Trade in Medieval Pottery around the North Sea', *Rotterdam Papers: A Contribution to Medieval Archaeology*, 35–58.

Dunning, G. 1974, 'A Late Medieval Jug with Lettering from Canons Ashby, Northamptonshire', *Medieval Archaeology* 18, 160–3.

Dyer, C. 1983, 'English Diet in the Later Middle Ages', in T. Aston, P. Coss, C. Dyer and J. Thirsk (eds), *Social Relations and Ideas: Essays in Honour of RH Hilton*, Cambridge University Press, 191–216.

Dyer, C. 1994, 'Gardens and Orchards in Medieval England', in C. Dyer (ed), *Everyday Life in Medieval England*, 113–32, Hambledon Press.

Dyer, C. 1998, *Standards of Living in the Later Middle Ages*: Social Change in England c.1200–1520, Cambridge University Press.

Eckhardt, H. and Williams, H. 2003, 'Objects Without a Past? The Use of Roman Objects in Anglo-Saxon Graves', in H. Williams (ed), *Archaeologies of Remembrance: Death and Memory in Past Societies*, Kluwer/Plenum, 141–70.

Edensor, T. 2005, 'Waste Matter: The Debris of Industrial Ruins and the Disordering of the Material World', *Journal of Material Culture* 10(3), 311–32.

Edmonds, M. 1999, 'Inhabiting Neolithic Landscapes', *Quaternary Proceedings* 7, 485–92.

Effros, B. 2002, *Creating Community with Food and Drink in Merovingian Gaul*, Palgrave Macmillan.

Effros, B. 2003, 'The Ritual Significance of Vessels in the Formation of Merovingian and Christian Communities', in R. Corradini, M. Diesenberger and H. Reimitz (eds), *The Construction of Communities in the Early Middle Ages: Texts, Resources, Artefacts*, Brill, 213–27.

Effros, B. 2004, 'Dressing conservatively: Women's brooches as markers of ethnic identity?', in L. Brubaker and J. Smith (eds), *Gender in the early medieval world. East and west, 300–900*, Cambridge University Press, 165–84.

Egan, G. 2005, 'Urban and Rural Finds: Material Culture of Country and Town c.1050–1500', in C. Dyer and K. Giles (eds), *Town and Country in The Middle Ages. Contrasts, Contacts and Interconnections, 1100–1500*, Society for Medieval Archaeology Monograph 22, 197–210.

Egan, G. 2010, *The Medieval Household. Daily Living c.1150–c.1450. Medieval Finds from Excavations in London*, Boydell.

Ermarth, E. 1991, (1997), Extract from *Sequel to History: Postmodernism and the Crisis of Time*, in K. Jenkins (ed), *The Post-Modern History Reader*, Routledge, 47–64.

Evans, D. and Davison, A. 1985, 'Excavations at Botolph Street and St George's Street (Sites 170N, 281N and 284N), in M. Atkin, A. Carter and D. Evans (eds), *Excavations in Norwich 1971–1978 Part II*, 87–91, East Anglian Archaeology Report 26.

Fahlander, F. 2008, 'Same, Same, But Different? Making Sense of the Seemingly Similar', in K. Chilidis, J. Lund and C. Prescott (eds), *Facets of Archaeology. Essays in Honour of Lotte Hedeager*, 67–74, OAS.

Fahlander, F. 2012, 'Articulating Stone. The Material Practice of Petroglyphing', I.M. Back Daniellson, F. Fahlander and Y. Sjostrand (eds), *Encountering Imagery. Materialities, Perceptions, Relations*, Stockholm Studies in Archaeology 57, 97–116.

Farley, M. 1978, 'Saxon and Medieval Walton, Aylesbury: Excavations 1973–4', *Records of Buckinghamshire* 20, 153–290.

Faulkner, P. 1958, 'Domestic Planning from the Twelfth to the Fourteenth Centuries', *The Archaeological Journal* 115, 151–83.

Faulkner, P. 1975, 'The Surviving Medieval Buildings', in C. Platt and R. Coleman-Smith (eds), *Excavations in Medieval Southampton 1953–1969*, University of Leicester Press, 83–5.

Fennel, C. 2003, 'Group Identity, Individual Creativity, and Symbolic Generation in a BaKongo Diaspora', *International Journal of Historical Archaeology* 7(1), 1–31.

Field, R. 1965, 'Worcestershire Peasant Buildings, Household Goods and Farming Equipment in the Later Middle Ages', *Medieval Archaeology* 9, 105–45.

Finch, J. 2008, 'Three Men in a Boat: Biographies and Narrative in the Historic Landscape', *Landscape Research* 33(5), 511–30.

Flambard Héricher, A-M. 2004, 'Archaeology and the Bayeux Tapestry', in P. Bouet, B. Levy and F. Neveux (eds), The Bayeux Tapestry: Embroidering the Facts of History, University of Caen, 261–87.

Fleming, A. 2006, 'Post-processual Landscape Archaeology: A Critique', *Cambridge Archaeological Journal* 16(3), 267–80.

Fleming, R. 2007, 'Acquiring, Flaunting and Destroying Silk in Late Anglo-Saxon England', *Early Medieval Europe* 15(2), 127–58.

Fowler, C. 2001, 'Personhood and Social Relations in the British Neolithic With a Study from the Isle of Man', *Journal of Material Culture* 6(2), 137–63.

Frieman, C. 2010, 'Imitation, Identity and Communication: The Presence and Problems of Skeumorphs in the Metal Ages', in B.V. Eriksen (ed), *Lithic Technology in Metal Using Societies*, Jutland Archaeological Society, 33–44.

Gaimster, D. 2007, 'A Parallel History: The Archaeology of Hanseatic Urban Culture in the Baltic c.1200–1600', *World Archaeology*, 37(3), 408–23.

Gardiner, M. 2008, 'Buttery and Pantry and their Antecendents: Idea and Architecture in the English Medieval House', in M. Kowaleski and P. Goldberg (eds), *Medieval Domesticity. Home, Housing and Household in Medieval England*, Cambridge University Press, 37–65.

Gell, A. 1998, *Art and Agency: an Anthropological Theory*, Oxford University Press.

Gerrard, C. 1997, 'Mispaced Faith? Medieval Pottery and Fieldwalking', *Medieval Ceramics* 21, 61–72.

Gerrard, C. 1999, 'Opposing Identity: Muslims, Christians and the Military Orders in Rural Aragon', *Medieval Archaeology*, 43, 143–60.

Gerrard, C. 2003, *Medieval Archaeology: Understanding Traditions and Contemporary Approaches*, Routledge.

Gero, J. 1996, 'Amazing Grace: Once Lost, Now Found', *Cambridge Archaeological Journal* 6(1), 126–8.

Gibson, J. 1979, *The Ecological Approach to Visual Perception*, Houghton Mifflin.

Giddens, A. 1979/2002, 'Agency, Structure', in C. Calhoun, J. Gerteis, V. Indermoten, J. Moody and S. Pfaff (eds), *Contemporary Social Theory*, Blackwell, 232–43.

Gilchrist, R. 1994, *Gender and Material Culture: The Archaeology of Religious Women*, Routledge.

Gilchrist, R. 1999, *Gender and Archaeology: Contesting the Past*, Routledge.

Gilchrist, R. 2008, 'Magic for the Dead? The Archaeology of Magic in Later Medieval Burials', *Medieval Archaeology* 52, 119–59.

Gilchrist, R. 2009, 'Medieval Archaeology and Theory: A Disciplinary Leap of Faith', in R. Gilchrist and A. Reynolds (eds), *Reflections: 50 Years of Medieval Archaeology, 1957–2007*, Society for Medieval Archaeology Monograph 30, 385–408.

Giles, K. 2000, *An Archaeology of Social Identity: Guildhalls in York, c.1350–1630*, BAR Brit. Ser. 315.

Gleeson, P. 2012, 'Constructing Kingship in Early Medieval Ireland: Power, Place and Ideology', *Medieval Archaeology* 56, 1–33.

Goldberg, P. 2008, 'The Fashioning of Bourgeois Domesticity in Later Medieval England: A Material Culture Perspective', in M. Kowaleski and P. Goldberg (eds), *Medieval Domesticity. Home, Housing and Household in Medieval England*, Cambridge University Press, 124–44.

Golding, B. 1994, *Conquest and Colonisation. The Normans in Britain 1066–1100*, MacMillan.

Gosden, C. 1994, *Social Being and Time*, Blackwell.

Gosden, C. 2005, 'What Do Objects Want?', *Journal of Archaeological Method and Theory* 12(3), 193–211.

Gosden, C. and Marshall, Y. 1999, 'The Cultural Biography of Objects', *World Archaeology* 31(2), 169–78.

Gosselain, O. 2000, 'Materializing Identities: An African Perspective', *Journal of Archaeological Method and Theory* 7(3), 187–217.

Gowland, R. 2007, 'Beyond ethnicity: Symbols of Social Identity from the Fourth to Sixth Centuries in England' in H. Williams and S. Semple (eds), *Anglo-Saxon Studies in History and Archaeology* 14, 56–65.

Greenhough, B. 2010, 'Vitalist Geographies: Life and the More Than Human', in B. Anderson and P. Harrison (eds), *Taking Place: Non-Representational Theories and Geography*, Ashgate, 37–54.

Gregson, N. and Rose, G. 2001, 'Taking Butler Elsewhere: Performativities, Spatialities and Subjectives', *Environment and Planning D* 18, 433–52.

Grenville, J. 2008, 'Urban and Rural Houses and Households in the Late Middle Ages: A Case Study from Yorkshire', in M. Kowaleski and P. Goldberg (eds), *Medieval Domesticity. Home, Housing and Household in Medieval England*, Cambridge University Press, 92–123.

Groleau, A. 2009, 'Special Finds: Locating Animism in the Archaeological Record', *Cambridge Archaeological Journal* 19(3), 398–406.

Gutierrez, A, 2000, *Mediterranean Pottery in Wessex Households (13th–17th Centuries)*, BAR Brit. Ser. 306.

Hadley, D. 2002, 'Viking and Native: Re-thinking Identity in the Danelaw', *Early Medieval Europe* 11(1), 45–70.

Hadley, D. 2004. 'Negotiating Gender, Family and Status in Anglo-Saxon Burial Practices., *c.*600–950', in L. Brubaker and J. Smith (eds), *Gender in the Early MedievalWworld. East and West, 300–900*, Cambridge University Press, 301–23.

Halfacree, K. and Rivera, M.J. 2012, 'Moving to the Countryside… and Staying: Lives Beyond Representations', *Sociologia Ruralis* 52(1), 92–114.

Hall, M. 2006, 'Identity, Memory and Countermemory: The Archaeology of Urban Landscape', *Journal or Material Culture* 11(1/2), 189–209.

Hall, M. 2011, The Cult of Saints in Medieval Perth: Everyday Ritual and the Materiality of Belief, *Journal of Material Culture* 16(1), 80–104.

Hall, M. 2012, 'Money Isn't Everything: The Cultural Life of Coins in the Medieval Burgh of Perth, Scotland', *Journal of Social Archaeology* 12(1), 72–91.

Hall, M., Henderson, I. and Scott, I. 2005, 'The Early Medieval Sculptures of Murthly, Perth and Kinross: An Interdisciplinary Look at People, Politics and Monumental Art', in S. Foster and M. Cross (eds), *Able Minds and Practised Hands. Scotland's Early Medieval Sculpture in the 21st Century*, Society for Medieval Archaeology Monograph 23, 293–314.

Halsall, G. 1996, 'Female Status and Power in Early Merovingian Central Austrasia: The Burial Evidence', *Early Medieval Europe* 5(1), 1–24.

Halsall, G. 2004, 'Gender and the End of Empire', *Journal of Medieval and Early Modern Studies*, 34(1), 17–39.

Hamerow, H. 1993, *Excavations at Mucking Volume 2: The Anglo-Saxon Settlement*, English Heritage.

Hamerow, H., Hollevoet, Y. and Vince, A. 1993, 'Migration Period Settlement and 'Anglo-Saxon' Pottery from Flanders', *Medieval Archaeology* 38, 1–18.

Hamerow, H. 2006, "Special Deposits' in Anglo-Saxon Settlements', *Medieval Archaeology* 50, 1–30.

Härke, H. 1990, 'Warrior graves? The Background of the Early Anglo-Saxon Weapon Burial Rite', *Past and Present* 126, 22–43.

Harrison, R. 2003, ''The Magical Virtue of These Sharp Things'. Colonialism, Mimesis and Knapped Bottle Glass Artefacts in Austrialia', *Journal of Material Culture* 8(3), 311–336.

Harvey, P. 1983, 'English Archaeology After the Conquest: A Historian's View', in D. Hinton (ed), *25 Years of Medieval Archaeology*, University of Sheffield/Society for Medieval Archaeology, 74–82.

Harvey, D. 2002, 'Constructed Landscapes and Social Memory; Tales of St Samson in Early Medieval Cornwall', *Environment and Planning D* 20(2), 231–48.

Hawkes, J. 2003, 'Reading Stone', in C. Karkov and F. Orton (eds), *Theorizing Anglo-Saxon Stone Sculpture*, West Virginia University Press, 5–30.

Hayden, B. and Cannon, A. 1982, 'Where the Garbage Goes: Refuse Disposal in the Maya Highlands', *Journal of Anthropological Archaeology* 2, 117–63.

Henderson, I. 1987, 'The Book of Kells and the Snake-Boss Motif on Pictish Cross-Slabs and the Iona Crosses', in M. Ryan (ed), *Ireland and Insular Art A.D. 500–1200*, Royal Irish Academy, 56–65.

Henrickson, E. and McDonald, M. 1983, 'Ceramic Form and Function: An Ethnographic Search and an Archaeological Application', *American Anthropologist* 85, 630–43.

Herva, V.P. 2009, 'Living (With) Things: Relational Ontology and Material Culture in Early Modern Northern Finland', *Cambridge Archaeological Journal* 19(3), 388–97.

Herva, V.P. and Nermi, R. 2009, 'Beyond Consumption: Functionality, Artifact Biography, and Early Modernity in a European Periphery', *International Journal of Historical Archaeology* 13, 158–82.

Herva V.P. Nermi, R. and Symonds, J. 2012, 'Engaging With Money in a Northern Periphery of Early Modern Europe', *Journal of Social Archaeology* 12(3), 287–309.

Hicks, D. 2007, '"Places for Thinking' from Annapolis to Bristol: Situations and Symmetries in 'World Historical Archaeologies"', *World Archaeology* 37(3), 373–91.

Hicks, L. 2009, 'Magnificent Entrances and Undignified Exits: Chronicling the Symbolism of Castle Space in Normandy', *Journal of Medieval History* 35(1), 52–69.

Hill, J.D. 1995, *Ritual and Rubbish in the Iron Age of Wessex: A Study on the Formation of a Specific Archaeological Record*, BAR Brit. Ser. 242.

Hinchliffe, S. 2010, 'Working with Multiples: A Non-Representational Approach to Environmental Issues', in B. Anderson and P. Harrison (eds), *Taking Place: Non-representational Theories and Geography*, Ashgate, 303–20.

Hinton, D. 2009, 'Medieval Identity Issues', in R. Gilchrist and A. Reynolds (eds), *Reflections: 50 Years of Medieval Archaeology, 1957–2007*, Society for Medieval Archaeology Monograph 30, 453–64.

Hodder, I. 1979, 'Economic Stress and Material Culture Patterning', *American Antiquity* 44(3), 446–54.

Hodder, I. 1982, 'Sequences of Structural Change in the Dutch Neolithic', in I. Hodder (ed), *Symbolic and Structural Archaeology*, Cambridge University Press, 162–77.

Hodder, I. 1994, 'The Interpretation of Documents and Material Culture', in N. Denzin and S. Lincoln, *Handbook of Qualitative Research*, Sage, 393–402.

Hodge, C. 2006, '"Articles too Tedious to Enumerate": The Appreciation of Ceramics in mid-18th Century Newport, Rhode Island', *Northeast Historical Archaeology* 35(1), 1–14.

Hodges, R. 1982, *Dark Age Economics*, Duckworth.

Hodges, R. 1983, 'New Approaches to Medieval Archaeology, Part 2', in D. Hinton (ed), *25 Years of Medieval Archaeology*, University of Sheffield/Society for Medieval Archaeology, 24–37.

Holdsworth, P. 1980, *Excavations at Melbourne Street, Southampton, 1971–1976*, CBA Research Report 33.

Holten, L. 1997, 'Interpretation of Material Culture', *Acta Archaeologica* 68, 183–8.

Horning, A. 2010, 'Small Trenches. Archaeology and the Postcolonial Gaze', *Archaeological Dialogues* 17(1), 27–30.

Howey, M. 2011, 'Colonial Encounters, European Kettles and the Magic of Mimesis in the Late Sixteenth and Early Seventeenth Century Indigenous Northeast and Great Lakes', *International Journal of Historical Archaeology* 15, 329–57.

Hurcombe, L. 2008, 'Organics from Inorganics: Using Experimental Archaeology as a Tool for Studying Perishable Material Culture', *World Archaeology* 40(1), 83–115.

Hurst J. 1969, 'Red-Painted and Glazed Pottery in Western Europe from the Eighth to the Twelfth Century', *Medieval Archaeology* 13, 93–147.

Hurst, J. 1974, 'Sixteenth- and Seventieth-Century Imported Pottery from the Saintonge', in V. Evison, J. Hurst and H. Hodges (eds), *Medieval Pottery from Excavations: Studies Presented to Gerald Clough Dunning*, John Baker, 221–55.

Hurst, J, 1976, 'The Pottery' in D. Wilson (ed), *The Archaeology of Anglo-Saxon England*, Cambridge University Press, 238–348.

Hurst, J. 1978, 'Spanish Pottery Imported into Medieval Britain', *Medieval Archaeology* 11, 68–105.

Hurst, J. 1981, 'Medieval Pottery Imports in Sussex', *Sussex Archaeological Collections* 118, 125–8.

Hurst, J. 1991a, 'Antiquarian Finds of Medieval and Later Pottery', in E. Lewis (ed), *Custom and Ceramics. Essays Presented to Kenneth Barton*, APE, 7–24.

Hurst, J. 1991b, 'Italian Pottery imported into Britain and Ireland', in T. Wilson (ed), *Italian Renaissance Pottery: Papers Written in Association with a Colloquium at the British Museum*, British Museum Press, 212–31.

Impey, E. 2000, 'The Seigneurial Residence in Normandy, 1125–1225: An Anglo-Norman Tradition?', *Medieval Archaeology* 43, 45–73.

Ingold, T. 1993, 'The Temporality of Lanscape', *World Archaeology* 25(2), 152–74.

Ingold, T. 2007, 'Materials against Materiality', *Archaeological Dialogues* 14(1), 1–16.

Irving, A. 2011, *A Research Framework for Post-Roman Ceramic Studies in Britain*, Medieval Pottery Research Group Occasional Paper 6.

Jenkins, R. 1996, *Social Identity*, Routledge.

Jennings , S. 1981, *Eighteen Centuries of Pottery from Norwich*, East Anglian Archaeology Report 13.

Jennings, S. 2002, 'The Pottery', in M. Atkins and D. Evans, 'Excavations in Westwick', in M. Atkins and D. Evans, (eds), *Excavations in Norwich 1971–1978 Part III*,. Norwich, East Anglian Archaeology Report 100, 134–45.

Jervis, B. 2008, 'Pottery and Identity in Late Saxon Sussex', *Medieval Ceramics* 29, 1–8.

Jervis, B. 2009a, 'Pottery from Late Saxon Chichester: A Reassessment of the Evidence', *Sussex Archaeological Collections* 147, 61–76.

Jervis, B. 2009b, 'For Richer, For Poorer. A Synthesis and Discussion of Medieval Pottery from Eastern Southampton in the Context of the High and Late Medieval Towns', *Medieval Ceramics* 30, 73–94.

Jervis, B. 2011, 'A Patchwork of People, Pots and Places: Material Engagements and the Construction of 'the Social' in Hamwic (Anglo-Saxon Southampton), UK', *Journal of Social Archaeology* 11(3), 239–65.

Jervis, B. 2012. 'Making-do or Making the World? Tempering choices in early-mid Anglo-Saxon pottery manufacture' in B. Jervis and A. Kyle (eds), *Make-do and Mend: Archaeologies of Compromise, Re-use and Repair*, British Archaeological Reports International Series 2408, 67–80.

Jervis, B. 2013a. 'Cuisine and Urban Identities in Medieval England. Objects, Foodstuffs and Urban Life in 13th–14th Century Hampshire', *The Archaeological Journal* 169, 453–79.

Jervis, B. 2013b. 'Objects as Agents of Social Change: A case-study from Anglo-Norman Southampton' in A. Jones, J. Pollard and B. Alberti (eds), *Archaeology After Interpretation. Returning Materials to Archaeological Theory*, Left Coast Press, 219–34.

Jervis, B. 2013c, 'Ceramics, Conquest, Continuity and Change. Beyond Representational Approaches to Continuity and Change in Early Medieval England. A Case-Study from Anglo Norman Southampton', *Early Medieval Europe* 21(4), 455–87.

Jervis, B. 2013d, 'Rubbish and the Creation of Urban Landscape' in Bintliff, J. and Carcoscio, M. (eds), Pottery and Social Dynamics in the Mediterranean and Beyond in Medieval and Post-medieval Times, BAR Int. Ser., 57–72.

Jervis, B. In Prep. 'Changing Places: Home-making in mid-Saxon Hamwic and late Saxon Southampton' in L. Broderick, I. Grau. and B. Jervis (eds), *Urban Life in Medieval Europe: Artefact and Environmental Based Approaches,* Brepols.

Jervis, B. In press a. 'Organic Residues and Medieval Pottery: Progress and Potential', in J. Edwards and S. Paynter (eds), *Recent Research on Ceramics and Glass. Studies in Honour of Sarah Jennings*, Medieval Pottery Research Group Occasional Paper.

Jervis, B. In press b. 'A Picture Says a Thousand Words: Re-thinking the Decoration of Medieval Pottery' in S. Coxon, B. Jervis and E. Sibbesson (eds), *Insights Through Innovation: Studies in Honour of David Peacock*, University of Southampton Series in Archaeology.

Jiminéz, A. 2011, 'Pure Hybridism: Late Iron Age Sculpture in Southern Iberia', *World Archaeology* 43(1), 102–123.

Johnson, E. 2004. 'Normandy and Norman Identity in Southern Italian Chronicles', *Anglo-Norman Studies* 27, 85–100.

Johnson, E. 2006, 'Origin Myths and the Construction of Medieval Identities: Norman Chronicles

1000–1100', in R. Corradini, R. Meens, C. Possel and P. Shaw (eds), *Texts and Identities in the Middle Ages*, Verlag Osterreichische Akademie, 153–64.

Johnson, M. 1988, 'Late Medieval Houses in Western Suffolk: New Directions in the Study of Vernacular Architecture', *Scottish Archaeological Review* 5, 114–20.

Johnson, M. 1993, *Housing Culture: Traditional Architecture in an English Landscape*, Routledge.

Johnson, M. 2006, *Ideas of Landscape*, Blackwell.

Johnson, M. 2010, *Archaeological Theory: An Introduction*, Blackwell.

Jolly, K. 2002, 'Medieval Magic: Definitions, Beliefs, Practices', in B. Ankarloo and S. Clark (eds), *Witchcraft and Magic in Europe. The Middle Ages*, University of Pennsylvania Press, 1–72.

Jones, A. 2002, *Archaeological Theory and Scientific Practice*, Cambridge University Press.

Jones, A. 2005, 'Lives in Fragments? Personhood and the European Neolithic', *Journal of Social Archaeology* 5(2), 193–224.

Jones, A. 2007, *Memory and Material Culture*, Cambridge University Press.

Jones, A. 2009, 'Into the Future', in B. Cunliffe, C. Gosden and R. Joyce (eds), *The Oxford Handbook of Archaeology*, Oxford University Press, 89–114.

Jones, A. and Boivin, N. 2011, 'The Malice of Inanimate Objects: Material Agency', in D. Hicks and M. Beaudry (eds), *The Oxford Handbook of Material Culture Studies*, Oxford University Press, 333–51.

Jones, R. 2005, 'Signatures in the Soil: The Use of Pottery in Manure Scatters in the Identification of Medieval Farming Regimes', *The Archaeological Journal* 161, 159–88.

Jones, R. 2011, 'Elemental Theory in Everyday Practice: Food Disposal in the Later Medieval English Countryside' in J. Klápště and P. Sommer (eds), *Processing, Storage, Distribution of Food. Food in the Medieval Rural Environment*, Ruralia VIII, Brepols, 145–54.

Jones, S. 1997, *The Archaeology of Ethnicity*, Routledge.

Jones, S. 2004, *Early Medieval Sculpture and the Production of Meaning, Value and Place: The Case of Hilton Cadboll*, Historic Scotland.

Jones, S. 2011, 'Geography, Memory and Non-Representational Geographies', *Geography Compass* 5(12), 1–11.

Jope, E. 1947, 'Medieval Pottery in Berkshire', *Berkshire Archaeological Journal* 50, 49–76.

Jope, E. 1964, 'The Saxon Building-Stone Industry in Southern and Midland England, *Medieval Archaeology* 8, 91–118.

Jordanova, L. 2000, *History in Practice*, Arnold.

Joy, J. 2010, *Iron Age Mirrors. A Biographical Approach*. BAR Brit. Ser. 518.

Kamerick, K. 2008, 'Shaping Superstition in Late Medieval England', *Magic, Ritual and Witchcraft* 3(1), 29–53.

Kavanagh, H. Unpublished. *SOU 175 Site Archive Report*. Southampton City Museum.

Kieckhefer, R. 1990, *Magic in the Middle Ages*, Cambridge University Press.

King, C. 2007, 'The Interpretation of Urban Buildings: Power, Memory and Appropriation in Norwich Merchants' Houses, c.1400–1660', *World Archaeology* 41(3), 471–88.

Kirk, T. 2006, 'Materiality, Personhood and Monumentality in Early Neolithic Britain', *Cambridge Archaeological Journal* 16(3), 333–47.

Klaasen, F. 2012, 'Subjective Experience and the Practice of Medieval Ritual Magic', *Magic, Ritual and Witchcraft* 7(1), 19–51

Knapp, B. and Van Dommelen, P. 2008, 'Past Practices: Re-thinking individuals and agents in archaeology', *Cambridge Archaeological Journal* 18(1), 15–34.

Knappett, C. 2002, 'Photographs, Skeuomorphs and Marionettes. Some Thoughts on Mind, Agency and Object', *Journal of Material Culture* 7(1), 97–117.

Knappett, C. 2005, *Thinking Through Material Culture*, University of Pennsylvania Press.

Knappett, C. 2008, 'The Neglected Networks of Material Agency: Artefacts, Pictures and Texts', in C. Knappett and L. Malafouris (eds), *Material Agency. Towards a Non-Anthropocentric Approach*, Springer, 139–56.

Knappett, C. 2011, A*n Archaeology of Interaction. Network Perspectives on Material Culture and Society*, Oxford University Press.

Kopytoff, I. 1986, 'The Cultural Biography of Things: Commodization as Process', in A. Appadurai (ed), *The Social Life of Things*, Cambridge University Press, 64–91.

Kyle, A. 2012, 'More Than Just a Quick Fix? Repair Holes on Early Medieval Souterrain Ware' in B. Jervis and A. Kyle (eds), *Make Do and Mend: Archaeologies of Compromise, Repair and Reuse*, BAR Int. Ser. 2408, 91–96

Law, J. 1992, *Notes on the Theory of the Actor Network: Ordering, Strategy and Heterogeneity*, http://comp.lancs.ac.uk/sociology/soc054jl.html.

Law, J. 2004, *After Method: Mess in Social Science Research*, Routledge.

Law, J. and Hassard, J. (eds) 1999, *Actor Network Theory and After*, Blackwell/The Sociological Review.

Law, J. and Mol, A. 1995, 'Notes on Materiality and Sociality', *The Sociological Review* 43(2), 274–94.

Latour, B. 1993, *We Have Never Been Modern*, Harvard University Press.

Latour, B. 1999, 'On Recalling ANT', in J. Law and J. Hassard, (eds), *Actor Network Theory and After*, Blackwell/The Sociological Review, 15–25.

Latour, B. 2005, *Reassembling the Social. An Introduction to Actor Network Theory*, Oxford University Press.

Latour, B. 2010, *The Making of Law. An Ethnography of the Conseil D'État*, Polity.

Le Patourel, J. 1969, 'Documentary Evidence and the Medieval Pottery Industry', *Medieval Archaeology* 12, 101–26.

Leone, M. 1988, 'The Relationship Between Archaeological Data and the Documentary Record: 18th Century Gardens in Annapolis, Maryland', *Historical Archaeology* 22, 29–35.

Lewis, C. 1994, 'The French in England Before the Norman Conquest', *Anglo-Norman Studies* 17, 123–144.

Lewis, M. 2005. *The Archaeological Authority of the Bayeux Tapestry*. BAR Brit. Ser. 404.

Lilley, K. 2004, 'Cities of God? Medieval Urban Forms and Their Christian Symbolism', *Transactions of the Institute of British Geographers (New Series)* 29(3), 296–313.

Lilley, K. 2009, *City and Cosmos. The Medieval World in Urban Form*, Reaktion Books.

Livitt, P. 1990, 'The Origin of Villages Study and Gazetteer', in A. Down and M. Welch (eds), *Chichester Excavations 7: Apple Down and the Mardens*. Chichester District Council, 1–8.

Lorrimer, H. 2005, 'Cultural Geography: The Busyness of Being 'More-Than-Representational'', *Human Geography* 29, 83–94.

Loud, G. 1981, 'The 'Gens Normannorum' – Myth or Reality?', *Anglo-Norman Studies* 4, 104–16.

Loveluck, C. and Evans, D. (eds) 2009, *Life and Economy at Early Medieval Flixborough c.AD600–1000*, Oxbow, 166–86.

Loveluck, C. and Tys, D. 2006, 'Coastal Societies, Exchange and Identity Along the Channel and Southern North Sea Shores', *Journal of Maritime Archaeology* 1, 140–69.

Malafouris, L. 2004, 'The Cognitive Basis of Material Engagement: Where Brain, Body and Culture Conflate', in E. DeMarrais, C. Gosden and C. Renfrew (eds), *Rethinking Materiality: The Engagement of Mind with the Material World*, McDonald Institute Monograph, 53–62.

Malafouris, L. 2008, 'At the Potter's Wheel: An Argument for Material Agency' in C. Knappett and L. Malafouris (eds), *Material Agency. Towards a Non-Anthropocentric Approach*, Springer, 19–36.

Margesson, S. 1993, *Norwich Households. Medieval and Post-Medieval Finds from Norwich Survey Excavations 1971–78*, East Anglian Archaeology Report 58.

Martin, A. 1989, 'The Role of Pewter as a Missing Artifact: Consumer Attitudes Toward Tablewares in Late 18th Century Virginia', *Historical Archaeology* 23, 1–27.

Martin, T. 2012, 'Riveting Biographies: The Theoretical Implications of Early Anglo-Saxon Brooch Repair, Customisation and Use-Adaptation', In B. Jervis and A. Kyle (eds), *Make-do and Mend: Archaeologies of Compromise, Repair and Reuse*, BAR Int. Ser. 2408, 53–66.

Massey, D. 2006, 'Landscape as a Provocation. Reflections on moving mountains', *Journal of Material Culture* 11(1–2), 33–48.

Matthew, D. 2005, *Britain and the Continent 1000–1300*, Hodder Arnold.

Matthews, C. and Chadwick Hawkes, S. 1985, 'Early Saxon Settlements and Burials on Puddlehill, Near Dunstable, Bedfordshire', *Anglo-Saxon Studies in Archaeology and History* 4, 59–115.

McEwan, J. 2005, 'Horses, Horsemen, and Hunting: Leading Londoners and Equestrian Seals in the late Twelfth and Early Thirteenth Centuries', *Essays in Medieval Studies* 22, 77–93.

McClain, A. 2012, 'Theory, Disciplinary Perspectives and the Archaeology of Later Medieval England', *Medieval Archaeology* 56, 131–70.

McCormack, D. 2010, 'Thinking in Transition: The Affirmative Restraints of the Experience/Experiment', in B. Anderson and P. Harrison (eds), *Taking Place: Non-representational Theories and Geography*, Ashgate, 201–20.

McHardy, A. 2006, 'Superior Spirituality versus Popular Piety in Late-Medieval England', in K. Cooper and J. Gregory (eds), *Elite and Popular Religion*, The Ecclesiastical History Society, 89–98.

Mellor, M. 2004, 'Changing Rooms: Fixtures, Fittings and Movable Goods in European Lifestyles', *Medieval Ceramics* 28, 125–38.

Merrifield, R. 1987, *The Archaeology of Ritual and Magic*. Guild Publishing.

Miller, D. 1985, *Artefacts as Categories: A Study of Ceramic Variability in Central India*, Cambridge University Press.

Miller, D. 2005, 'Materiality: An Introduction', in D. Miller (ed), *Materiality*, Duke Press, 1–50.

Moorhouse, S. 1978, 'Documentary Evidence for the Uses of Medieval Pottery: An Interim Statement', *Medieval Ceramics* 2, 3–22.

Moorhouse, S. 1983, 'Documentary Evidence and its Potential for Understanding the Inland Movement of Medieval Pottery', *Medieval Ceramics* 7, 45–87.

Moorhouse, S. 1986, 'Non-Dating Uses of Medieval Pottery', *Medieval Ceramics* 10, 85–124.

Moreland, J. 2000, 'Ethnicity, power and the English", in B. Frazer and A. Tyrell (eds), Social Identity in Early Medieval Britain and Ireland, Leicester University Press, 23–51.

Moreland, J. 2006, 'Archaeology and Texts: Subservience or Enlightenment', *Annual Review of Anthropology* 35, 135–151.

Morris, J. 2011, *Investigating Animal Burials: Ritual, Mundane and Beyond*, BAR Brit. Ser. 535.

Morris, J. and Jervis, B. 2011, 'What's So Special? A Reinterpretation of Anglo-Saxon 'Special Deposits", *Medieval Archaeology* 55, 66–81.

Murray Jones, P. 2007, 'Amulets: Prescriptions and Surviving Objects from Late Medieval England', in S. Blick (ed), *Beyond Pilgrim Souvenirs and Secular Badges. Essays in Honour of Brian Spencer*, Oxbow, 92–107.

Musgrave, E. 1998, 'Pottery Production and Proto-Industrialisation: Continuity and Change in the Rural Ceramics Industries of the Saintonge Region, France, 1250 to 1800', *Rural History* 9, 1–18.

Myres, JNL, 1969, *Anglo-Saxon Pottery and the Settlement of England*, Oxford University Press.

Myres, JNL. 1977, *A Corpus of Anglo-Saxon Pottery of the Pagan Period*, Cambridge University Press.

Mytum, H. 2010, 'Ways of Writing in Post-Medieval and Historical Archaeology: Introducing Biography', *Post Medieval Archaeology* 44(2), 237–54.

Naum, M. 2010, 'Re-Emerging Frontiers: Postcolonial Theory and Historical Archaeology in the Borderlands', *Journal of Archaeological Method and Theory* 17, 101–31.

Naum, M. 2011, 'Ambiguous pots: Everyday practice, migration and materiality. The Case of Medieval Baltic Ware on the Island of Bornholm (Denmark)', *Journal of Social Archaeology* 12(1), 92–119.

Needham, S. and Spence, T. 1997, 'Refuse and the Formation of Middens', *Antiquity* 71, 77–30.

Neuport, M. 2000, 'Clays of Contention: An Ethnoarchaeological Study of Factionalism and Clay Composition', *Journal of Archaeological Method and Theory* 7(3), 249–72.

Nieves Zedeno, M. 2009, 'Animating by Association: Index Objects and Relational Ontologies', *Cambridge Archaeological Journal* 19(3), 407–17.

Ó Carragáin, T. 2007, 'Skeuomorphs and Spolia: The Presence of the Past in Irish pre-Romanesque Architecture', in R. Moss (ed), *Making and Meaning in Insular Art*, Four Courts Press, 95–109.

Olsan, L. 1992, 'Latin Charms of Medieval England: Verbal Healing in a Christian Oral Tradition', *Oral Tradition* 7(1), 116–42.

Olsen, B. 2007, 'Keeping Things at Arm's Length, a Genealogy of Asymmetry', *World Archaeology* 39(4), 579–88.

Olsen, B. 2010, *In Defense of Things. Archaeology and the Ontology of Objects*, Altamira Press.

Orton, C. 1985, 'Infusion or Impedance – Obstacles to Innovation in Medieval Ceramics', *Medieval Ceramics* 921–34.

Orton, C., Tyers, P. and Vince, A. 1993, *Pottery in Archaeology*, Cambridge University Press.

Pantin, W. 1963, 'Medieval English Town-House Plans', *Medieval Archaeology* 6–7, 202–39.

Pearce, J., Vince, A. and Jenner, A. 1985, *Medieval Pottery: London Type Ware*, London and Middlesex Archaeological Society Special Paper 6.

Pearce, J. and Vince, A. 1988, *A Dated Type-Series of London Medieval Pottery. Part 4: Surrey Whitewares*, HMSO.

Pearson, S. 2005, 'Rural and Urban Houses 1100–1500', in K. Giles and C. Dyer (eds), *Town and Country in The Middle Ages. Contrasts, Contacts and Interconnections, 1100–1500*, Society for Medieval Archaeology Monograph 22, 40–60.

Peters, E. 2002, 'The Medieval Church and State on Superstition, Magic and Witchcraft: From Augustine to the Sixteenth Century', in B. Ankarloo and S. Clark (eds), *Witchcraft and Magic in Europe. The Middle Ages*, University of Pennsylvania Press 173–245.

Perry, G. Forthcoming. 'All Form One and One Form All: The Relationship Between Pre-Burial Function and the Form of Early Anglo-Saxon Cremation Urns', in P. Blinkhorn and C. Cumberpatch (eds), *The Chiming of Crack'd Bells: Current Approaches to Artefacts in Archaeology*, BAR Brit. Ser.

Phillips, K. 2005, 'The Invisible Man: Body and Ritual in a Fifteenth-Century Noble Household' *Journal of Medieval History* 31, 143–62.

Pitt-Rivers, A. 1890, *King John's House, Tollard Royal, Wilts*, Privately Printed.

Pitts, M. 2007, The Emperor's New Clothes? The Utility of Identity in Roman Archaeology, *American Journal of Archaeology* 111(4), 693–713.

Platt, C. 1973, *Medieval Southampton: The Port and Trading Community, AD 1000–1600*, Routledge.

Platt, C. 2007, 'Revisionism in Castle Studies – A Caution', *Medieval Archaeology* 51, 83–102.

Platt, C. and Coleman-Smith, R. 1975, *Excavations in Medieval Southampton 1953–69, Volume 2: The Finds*, University of Leicester Press.

Pluskowski, A. 2007, 'Communicating Through Skin and Bone: Appropriating Animal Bodies in Medieval Western European Seigniorial Culture', in A. Pluskowski (ed), *Breaking and Shaping Beastly Bodies. Animals as Material Culture in the Middle Ages*, Oxbow, 32–51.

Price, N. 1995, 'House and Home in Viking Age Iceland: Cultural Expression in Scandinavian Colonial Architecture', in D. Benjamin and D. Stea (eds), *The Home: Worlds, Interpretations, Meanings and Environments*, Ashgate, 109–30.

Pollard, J. 2001, 'The Aesthetics of Depositional Practice', *World Archaeology* 33(2), 315–33.

Preucel, R. 2008, *Archaeological Semiotics*, Wiley.

Rahtz, P. 1979, *The Saxon and Medieval Palaces at Cheddar: Excavations 1960–62*, BAR Brit. Ser. 65.

Rahtz, P. 1983, 'New Approaches to Medieval Archaeology Part 1', in D. Hinton (ed), *25 Years of Medieval Archaeology*, University of Sheffield/Society for Medieval Archaeology, 12–23.

Rahtz, P. 1984, 'The Neur Medieval Archaeology: Theory vs History – Comment on Driscoll', *Scottish Archaeological Review* 3, 109–112.

Randsborg, K. 1980, *The Viking Age in Denmark*, Duckworth.

Read, D. 2007, *Artifact Classification: A Conceptual and Methodological Approach*, Left Coast Press.

Rees-Jones, S. 2008, 'Building Domesticity in the City: English Urban Housing Before the Black Death', in M. Kowaleski and P. Goldberg (eds), *Medieval Domesticity. Home, Housing and Household in Medieval England*, Cambridge University Press, 66–91.

Reno, J. 2009, 'Your Trash is Someone's Treasure. The Politics of Value at a Michigan Landfill', *Journal of Material Culture* 14(1), 29–46.

Richards, J. 1987, *The Significance of the Form and Decoration of Anglo-Saxon Cremation Urns*, BAR Brit. Ser. 166.

Roberts, E. and Parker, K. 1992, *Southampton Probate Inventories 1447–1575. Volume 1*, Southampton Record Series XXXIV.

Rose, M. 2002, 'Landscape and Labyrinths', *Geoforum* 33, 455–67.

Rose, M. and Wiley, J. 2006, 'Animating Landscape', *Environment and Planning D* 24, 475–9.

Russel, A. 2010, 'Medieval Pottery', in M. Smith, 'Features Associated with Southampton Franciscian Friary from Ocean Boulevard, Ocean Place, Southampton', *Hampshire Studies* 65, 146–9 (124–66).

Rye, O. 1977, *Pottery Technology: Principles and Reconstruction*, Taraxacum.

Rynne, E. 1998, 'Ireland's Earliest 'Celtic' High Crosses: The Ossory and Related Crosses', in M. Monk and J. Sheenan (eds), *Early Medieval Munster. Archaeology, History and Society*, Cork University Press, 125–37.

Saldenha, A. 2010, 'Politics and Difference', in B. Anderson and P. Harrison (eds), *Taking Place: Non-Representational Theories and Geography*, Ashgate, 283–302.

Salzmann, L. 1953, *A History of the Count of Sussex: Volume 4, The Rape of Chichester*: http://www.british-history.ac.uk/source.asp?pubid=287

Saunders, A. 2006, *Excavations at Launceston Castle, Cornwall*, Society for Medieval Archaeology Monograph 24.

Saunders, T. 1990, 'The Feudal Construction of Space: Power and Domination in the Nucleated Village', in R. Samson (ed), *The Social Archaeology of Houses*, Edinburgh University Press, 181–96.

Saunders, T. 2000. 'Class, Space and 'Feudal' Identities in Early Medieval England', in W. Frazer and A. Tyrrell (eds),. *Social Identity in Early Medieval Britain*, Leicester University Press, 209–32.

Saussure, F. 1972, (trans. 1983), *Course in General Linguistics*, Duckworth.

Sawyer, P. 1983, 'English Archaeology Before the Conquest: A Historian's View', in D. Hinton (ed), *25 Years of Medieval Archaeology*, University of Sheffield/Society for Medieval Archaeology, 44–7.

Schiffer, M. 1987, 'Formation Processes of the Archaeological Record', University of New Mexico Press.

Schiffer, M. 1999, *The Material Life of Human Beings*, Routledge.

Schofield, J. 1994, 'Social Perceptions of Space in Medieval and Tudor London Houses', in M. Locock (ed), *Meaningful Architecture: Social Interpretations of Buildings*, Avebury, 188–206.

Shanks, M. 2007, 'Symmetrical Archaeology', *World Archaeology* 39(4), 589–96.

Shanks, M. and Tilley, C. 1992, *Re-Constructing Archaeology. Theory and Practice (2nd Edition)*, Routledge.

Shoesmith, R. 1985, *Hereford City Excavations Volume 3: The Finds*. Council for British Archaeology Research Report 56.

Sindbæk, S. 2007, 'Networks and Nodal Points: The Emergence of Towns in Early Viking Age Scandinavia', *Antiquity* 81, 119–132.

Sjostrand, Y. 2012, 'A Quest of Questions. On the Paradigm of Identification Within Rockart Research' in I.M. Back Daniellson, F. Fahlander and Y. Sjostrand (eds), *Encountering Imagery. Materialities, Perceptions, Relations*, Stockholm Studies in Archaeology 57, 161–76.

Skibo, J. 2013, *Understanding Pottery Function*, Springer.

Skibo, J., Schiffer, B. and Reid, K. 1989, 'Organic-tempered Pottery: An Experimental Study', *American Antiquity* 54(1), 122–46.

Smith, S. 2009a, 'Materializing Resistant Identities Among the English Peasantry. An Examination of Dress Accessories from English Rural Settlement Sites', *Journal of Material Culture* 14(3), 309–332.

Smith, S. 2009b, 'Towards a Social Archaeology of the Late Medieval English Peasantry: Power and Resistance at Wharram Percy', *Journal of Social Archaeology* 9(3), 391–416.

Sofaer, J. 2006, 'Pots, Houses and Metal: Technological Relations at the Bronze Age Tell at Szazhalombatta, Hugary', *Oxford Journal of Archaeology* 25(2), 127–47.

Soulat, J., Boucquet-Liénard, A., Savary, X. and Hincker, V. 2012, 'Hand-made Pottery Along the Channel Coast and Parallels with the Scheldt Valley', in R. Annaert, T. Jacobs, I. Ven and S. Coppens (eds) *ACE Conference Brussels: The Very Beginning of Europe? Early-Medieval Migration and Colonisation*, Flanders Heritage Agency, 215–224.

Spavold, J. 2010, 'Faith Made Manifest: An Interpretation of the Decoration on Cistercian Ware', *Medieval Ceramics* 31, 33–48.

Sterner, J. 1989, 'Who is Signalling Whom? Ceramic Style, Ethnicity and Taphonomy Among the Sirak Bulahay', *Antiquity* 63, 451–9.

Stoodley, N. 2000, 'From the Cradle to the Grave: Age Organization and the Early Anglo-Saxon Burial Rite', *World Archaeology* 31(3), 456–72.

Stoodley, N. 2012, 'New Light on the Southern Edge of Hamwic: Excavations at the Deanery by Southampton City Council Archaeological Unit and Wessex Archaeology', *Hampshire Studies* 67(2), 420–2.

Strathern, M. 1988, *The Gender of the Gift: Problems with Women and Problems with Society in Melenesia*, University of California Press.

Streeton, A. 1981, 'Potters, Kilns and Markets in Medieval Sussex: A Preliminary Study', *Sussex Archaeological Collections* 118, 105–18.

Sutton, D. 2001, *Remembrance of Repasts. An Anthropology of Food and Memory*, Berg.

Swanson, R. 2006, 'Prayer and Participation in Late Medieval England', in K. Cooper and J. Gregory (eds), *Elite and Popular Religion*, The Ecclesiastical History Society, 130–39.

Sykes, N. 2007, *The Norman Conquest: A Zooarchaeological Perspective*, BAR Int. Ser. 1656.

Tabaczynski, S. 1993, 'The Relationship Between History and Archaeology: Elements of the Present Debate', *Medieval Archaeology* 37, 1–14.

Tarlow, S. 2003, 'Reformation and Transformation: What Happened to Catholic Things in a Protestant World?', in D. Gaimster and R. Gilchrist (eds), *The Archaeology of Reformation 1480–1580*, Maney, 108–21.

Theuws, F. 2009, 'Grave Goods, Ethninicity, and the Rhetoric of Burial Rites in Late Antique Northern Gaul', in T. Derks and N. Roymans (eds), *Ethnic Constructs in Antiquity. The Role of Power and Tradition*, Amsterdam University Press 283–320.

Thomas, G. 2012, 'Carolingian Culture in the North Sea World: Rethinking the Cultural Dynamics of Personal Adornment in Viking-Age England', *European Journal of Archaeology* 15(3), 486–518.

Thomas, H. 2003, *The English and the Normans. Ethnic Hostility, Assimilation and Identity*, Oxford University Press.

Thomas, J. 1991, *Rethinking the Neolithic*, Cambridge University Press.

Thomas, R. 2006, 'Food and the Maintenance of Social Boundaries in Medieval England', in K. Twiss (ed), *The Archaeology of Food and Identity*, Center for Archaeological Investigations (Southern Illinois University) Occasional Paper 34, 130–51.

Thrift, N. 1999, 'Steps to an Ecology of Place', in D. Massey, J. Allen and P. Sarre (eds), *Human Geography Today*, Polity Press, 295–322.

Thrift, N. 2008, *Non-Representational Theory. Space, Politics, Affect*, Routledge.

Thrupp, S. 1948, *The Merchant Class of Medieval London*, University of Chicago Press.

Tilley, C. 1994, *A Phenomenology of Landscape: Places, Paths and Monuments*, Berg.

Tilley, C. 1999, *Metaphor and Material Culture*, Blackwell.

Tilley, C. 2004, 'Round Barrows and Dykes as Landscape Metaphors', *Cambridge Archaeological Journal* 14(2), 185–199.

Tischler, F., Myres, J., Hurst, J. and Dunning, G. 1959, *Anglo-Saxon Pottery: A Symposium*, CBA Research Report 3.

Tyson, R. 2000, *Medieval Glass Vessels Found in England c.AD1200–1500*, CBA Research Report 121.

Underwood, C. 1997, 'Pottery', in J. Hawkes and P. Fasham (eds), *Excavations on Reading Waterfront Sites, 1979–1988*, Wessex Archaeology Monograph 5, 142–61.

Underwood-Keevil, C. 1997, 'Pottery', in A. Hardy, 'Archaeological Excavations at 54–55 St. Thomas's Street, Oxford', *Oxoniensia* 61, 225–73.

Urry, J. 2000, 'Mobile Sociology', *British Journal of Sociology* 51(1), 185–203.

Van Dommelen, P. 2011, 'Postcolonial Archaeologies Between Discourse and Practice', *World Archaeology* 43(1), 1–6.

Van Houts, E. 1999, *Memory and Gender in Medieval Europe, 900–1200*, Palgrave MacMillan.

Van Oyen, A. 2013, 'Towards a Post-Colonial Artefact Analysis', *Archaeological Dialogues* 20(1), 81–107.

Verhaege, F. 1983, 'Medieval Pottery Production in Coastal Flanders', in P. Davey and R. Hodges (eds), *Ceramics and Trade*, University of Sheffield 63–94.

Villelli, M.B. 2011, 'Colonality in Patagonia. Historical Archaeology and Postcolonial Critique in Latin America', *World Archaeology* 43(1), 86–101.

Vince, A. 1977, 'The Medieval and Post-Medieval Ceramic Industry of the Malvern Region: The Study of a Ware and its Distribution', in D. Peacock (ed), *Pottery and Commerce: Characterization and Trade in Roman and Later Ceramics*, Academic Press, 257–305.

Vince, A. 1985, 'Saxon and Medieval Pottery in London: A Review', *Medieval Archaeology* 29, 25–93.

Vince, A. 1994, 'Approaches to Residuality in Urban Archaeology' in L. Shepherd (ed), Interpreting Stratigraphy 5, http://www.york.ac.uk/archaeology/strat/pastpub/95nor.htm, 9–14.

Vince, A. 2005, 'Ceramic Petrology and the Study of Anglo-Saxon and Later Medieval Ceramics', *Medieval Archaeology* 49, 219–45.

Voutsaki, S. 2010, 'Agency and Personhood at the Onset of the Mycenean Period', *Archaeological Dialogues* 17(1), 65–92.

Vroom, J. 2011, 'The Morea and its Links with Southern Italy after AD1204: Ceramics and Identity', *Archeologia Medievale* 38, 409–30.

Walsh, K. 2008, 'Mediterranean Landscape Archaeology: Marginality and the Culture-Nature Divide', *Landscape Research* 33(5), 547–64.

Webmoor, T. 2007, 'What About 'One More Turn After the Social' in Archaeological Reasoning? Taking Things Seriously', *World Archaeology* 39(4), 563–78.

Whatmore, S. 1999, 'Hybrid Geographies: Rethinking the 'Human' in Human Geography', in D. Massey, J. Allen and P. Sarre (eds), *Human Geography Today*, Polity Press, 22–39.

Whyte, W. 2006, 'How do Buildings Mean? Some Issues of Interpretation in the History of Architecture', *History and Theory* 45, 153–77.

Wicker, N. 1999, 'Archaeology and Art History: Common Ground for the New Millennium', *Medieval Archaeology* 43, 161–71.

Williams, H. 2003, 'Material Culture as Memory: Combs and Cremation in Early Medieval Britain', *Early Medieval Europe* 12(2), 89–128.

Williams, H. 2006, *Death & Memory in Early Medieval Britain,* Cambridge University Press.

Williams, H. 2011, 'The Sense of Being Seen: Occular Effects at Sutton Hoo', *Journal of Social Archaeology* 11(1), 99–121.

Williams, H. and Nugent, R. 2012, 'Sighted Surfaces. Ocular Agency in Early Anglo-Saxon Cremation Burials' in I.M. Back Daniellson, F. Fahlander and Y. Sjostrand (eds), *Encountering Imagery. Materialities, Perceptions, Relations*, Stockholm Studies in Archaeology 57187–208.

Willmott, H. 2005, 'Tudor Dining: Object and Image at the Table', in M. Carroll, D. Hadley and H. Willmott (eds), *Consuming Passions. Dining From Antiquity to the Eighteenth Century,* Tempus, 121–42.

Witmore, C. 2007, 'Symmetrical Archaeology: Excerpts of a Manifesto', *World Archaeology* 39(4), 546–62.

Woolgar, C. 2007, *The Senses in Late Medieval England,* Yale University Press.

Young, J. and Vince, A. 2005, *A Corpus of Anglo-Saxon and Medieval Pottery from Lincoln,* Oxbow (Lincoln Archaeological Studies 7).